D1345804

SCHOOL OF ORIENTAL
University of London

Please return this book on or before the last date shown

Long loans and One Week loans may be renewed up to 10 times
Short loans & CDs cannot be renewed
Fines are charged on all overdue items

Online: http://lib.soas.ac.uk/patroninfo
Phone: 020-7898 4197 (answerphone)

16 OCT 2007

African
Broadcast Cultures

African
Broadcast Cultures

Radio in Transition
Edited by
RICHARD FARDON & GRAHAM FURNISS

JAMES CURREY

Oxford

BAOBAB

Harare

DAVID PHILIP

Cape Town

PRAEGER

Westport, Connecticut

James Currey
73 Botley Road
Oxford OX2 0BS

Baobab
PO Box 1559
Harare

David Philip Publishers (Pty) Ltd
208 Werdmuller Centre
Claremont 7708
Cape Town

Published in the United States and Canada by
Praeger Publishers
88 Post Road West
Westport, CT 06881
An imprint of Greenwood Publishing Group, Inc.

British Library Cataloguing in Publication Data
African broadcast cultures : radio in transition
1. Radio broadcasting – social aspects – Africa 2. Radio
broadcasting – political aspects – Africa 3. Popular culture
– Africa
I. Fardon, Richard   II. Furniss, Graham
384.5'4'096
    ISBN 0-85255-828-7 (James Currey paper)
    ISBN 0-85255-829-5 (James Currey cloth)

Library of Congress Cataloging in Publication Data
African broadcast cultures : radio in transition / edited by Richard
Fardon and Graham Furniss.
    p.cm.
Includes bibliographical references and index.
ISBN 0-275 97060-4
1. Radio broadcasting--Africa. 2. Radio--Africa. I. Fardon, Richard.
II. Furniss, Graham.
HE8699.A35 A33 2000
302.23'44'096--dc21   ५८५९   00-029813

Typeset in 10/11.6 pt Monotype Photina
by Long House Publishing Services, Cumbria, UK
Printed in the United Kingdom
by Villiers Publications, London N3

Contents

II
Local Radio, Local Radio Culture
& the Culture of Radios

III
Radio, Conflict
& Political Transition

List of Figures

Preface

Under the auspices of the Centre of African Studies of the University of London, in 1991 we had jointly convened a workshop on language policy that brought together practitioners, policy-makers and academics (Fardon & Furniss 1994). A shared interest in the media (ignored in that volume) led to a subsequent plan to do something similar on radio. To a degree even more marked than in the field of language planning in African countries, it struck us that the academic and diversely applied interests in radio in Africa were largely divorced from one another. As previously, our intention was to bring together a range of such interests; as we hoped, the workshop engendered lively and provocative discussion. Given that neither of us is a specialist in the field, we have relied heavily on the advice of our contributors, especially our earliest recruits: Richard Carver, Graham Mytton and Debra Spitulnik, as well as André-Jean Tudesq whose guidance we appreciated although he was unable to join us for the workshop. Johan Pottier furnished valuable advice on research methods. The meeting took place at the School of Oriental and African Studies of the University of London on 12–13 June 1997, attended by roughly equal numbers of paper-givers and invited audience.

With Anna Debska's support, Jackie Collis of the Centre of African Studies took the major administrative responsibility for this workshop, as she did for our last. The proceedings were tape-recorded in their entirety, and some of the papers (and discussions) derive from transcriptions drafted for us by Caroline Tingay. Caroline also drafted translations of the papers originally delivered in French. Alison Surry made the electronic versions of the papers consistent after we had edited them. Caroline and Alison's gratefully acknowledged assistance has allowed us to pass relatively quickly from the conference to the published papers despite the diverse types of materials that needed to be edited. Given how rapidly the medium of radio is changing in Sub-Saharan Africa, this was essential; that it was feasible is also due to the material support of the Research Committee of the School of Oriental and African Studies, as well as to the generosity of the A.G. Leventis Foundation.

The SOAS Research Committee made possible the attendance of some of our speakers. Others were supported by the British Council offices in Pretoria, South Africa, Dakar, Senegal, and the British embassy in Abidjan, Côte d'Ivoire. The travel costs of other overseas contributors were supported by their own institutions; we are grateful to all concerned.

Those who participated in the workshop as presenters either submitted papers or allowed us to publish transcripts of their verbal presentations. Special thanks are due to Paul Richards whose essay appears here although the happy circumstance of an addition to his family prevented him from attending the meeting. Most essays in this book were submitted in written form (in either English or French); all were redrafted after the workshop, some several times. Sections of Chapter 4 and the whole of Chapter 12 consist of transcripts, which have been approved and revised by those who presented them, along with summaries of the ensuing discussions.

This collection of papers is not meant as an exhaustive survey, even of the field of Sub-Saharan African radio: its regional coverage is heavily biased towards 'Francophone' West Africa and 'Anglophone' southern Africa, and it virtually excludes East Africa. Particularly glaring among several substantive omissions is the failure of our efforts to find contributors willing to cover broadcast music on African radio, which accounts for such a high percentage of airtime. Eventually, we decided an admission of inadequacy was preferable to an attempt at tokenism. The politics and culture of music broadcasting in Sub-Saharan Africa deserves its own collection. Nevertheless, we thank Lucy Durán and Wolfgang Bender for their attendance at, and contribution to, the workshop. Despite these, and other, deficiencies we feel this collection raises a cross-section of contemporary concerns in a lively way.

Richard Fardon & Graham Furniss
London

Contributors

Mansur Abdulkadir teaches in the Department of English at Ahmadu Bello University, Nigeria. His doctoral dissertation at the University of London examined the language of Hausa advertising.

Richard Carver is an independent writer and researcher and Research Associate of Queen Elizabeth House, University of Oxford. He was formerly Head of the Africa Programme at Article 19, the International Centre Against Censorship. He has worked as a journalist for African publications and for Amnesty International and Human Rights Watch. He is the author of a forthcoming history of post-independence Malawi.

Christine Nimaga Ceesay worked on the project, the 'Regionalization of Radio in Niger', between 1994 and 1996. Before that she was a Senior Producer with the African Service of the BBC World Service in London. She now moves between The Gambia, Germany and the UK and works as a journalist and media consultant in different African countries.

Jean-Pascal Daloz works at the Centre d'étude d'Afrique noire (CEAN) of the Institut d'études politiques in Bordeaux. As a Senior Researcher of the Centre nationale de la recherche scientifique, he specializes in studies of African elites and leadership. He has written or edited eight books on African politics. **Katherine Verrier-Frechette** is completing a doctorate at Toronto and has been attached to CEAN; she has worked on media and human rights issues with reference to Africa.

Richard Fardon and **Graham Furniss** served successively as chairmen of the University of London's Centre of African Studies between 1989 and 1997. They previously collaborated on the editing of *African Languages, Development and the State* (1994), which, like the present volume, derived from a workshop attended by practitioners, activists and academics.

Tilo Grätz carried out research in Tanguiéta during 1995–6 as part of his doctorate (completed July 1998) on political transformation in northern Atacora, Benin. He is attached to the Max-Planck-Institute of Ethnological Research in Halle, Germany, and is currently researching gold-mining in Burkina Faso and Benin.

Jean-Pierre Ilboudo is the Communications Officer, Department of Sustainable Development at the FAO in Rome. One of the prime movers in the establishment of rural radio in Burkina Faso, he taught for 10 years at the CIERRO (Centre inter-Africain d'études en radio rurale de Ouagadougou).

Wendy James is Professor of Anthropology in the Institute of Social and Cultural Anthropology of the University of Oxford. Her many years of research in Sudan have resulted in two monographs on the Uduk people as well as numerous journal articles, essays and edited books.

Jeanette Minnie is Regional Director of the Media Institute of Southern Africa (MISA) which promotes media freedom, independence, pluralism and diversity through national chapters of MISA in 10 countries of the sub-continent. She has a long history as a press freedom campaigner in South and southern Africa. Some of her former positions include: Southern African Coordinator of the International Federation of Journalists' Media for Democracy Programme, Executive Director of the Freedom of Expression Institute in South Africa, Convenor of the Open Democracy Forum in South Africa, Executive Member of the Campaign for Independent Broadcasting in South Africa and Municipal Correspondent and Acting Night News Editor of the *Rand Daily Mail* newspaper in South Africa.

Mary Myers has travelled widely as a consultant on community radio and development, especially in Francophone West Africa. She is the author of reports on radio in Senegal and Mali and is currently completing her doctoral thesis on education through radio in Eritrea.

Graham Mytton became head of audience research at the BBC World Service after working for 10 years in the BBC African service. His interest in the media in Africa is of 30 years' standing and began with fieldwork in Tanzania in the mid-1960s. He is the author of (1983) *Mass Communication in Africa*, and *Handbook on Radio and TV Audience Research* (1999), both founding texts in their fields.

Urbain Nombré is an active participant in the planning, coordination and operation of rural radio in Burkina Faso.

Roger Nouma is a journalist and programme-maker employed in the educational outreach department of Radio France Internationale which receives African broadcasters for in-service training.

Elizabeth Ohene is the voice of the BBC World Service for Africa's most popular daily current affairs programme, 'Focus on Africa'. She has a broad journalistic background including the editorship of a Ghanaian daily newspaper.

Aida Opoku-Mensah was regional director for the Panos Institute's Southern Africa office based in Lusaka, Zambia, until becoming Programme Officer for Media, Arts and Culture for the West African Region of the Ford Foundation, Lagos, Nigeria in 1998. A linguistics graduate from the University of Ghana, she subsequently studied for a post-graduate diploma in International Relations (University of London) and an MA in Communication Policy (City University). She has taught Radio and Press Policy at City University, and is additionally a journalist and broadcaster working for the BBC and Radio Nederlands.

Paul Richards is Professor in the Technology and Agrarian Development Group at Wageningen University and Research Centre in the Netherlands and a Professorial Research Associate of University College, London. Among his many publications on West Africa, *Fighting for the Rainforest* (1996) has offered a vivid account of contemporary political events in Sierra Leone.

Ibrahima Sané is the Director of Senegalese national radio. He worked for some years for the BBC in London as a journalist and programme-maker. He is a well-known and experienced commentator on the media.

Debra Spitulnik is an Assistant Professor in the Department of Anthropology at Emory University. Her research interests include: media culture, sociolinguistics, nationalism and the experiences of modernity in Africa. She is currently completing a book on her long-term research in Zambia.

Abbreviations

ACCT	Agence de coopération culturelle et technique (French Government)
ADEMA	Alliance pour la démocratie au Mali
AM	Amplitude Modulation
AMARC Africa	Africa Office for the World Association for Community Broadcasters
ANC	African National Congress
ANSSP	Appui Néderlandais aux soins de santé primaire
APC	All Party Congress (Sierra Leone)
AZAPO	Azanian Peoples Organization
BBC	British Broadcasting Corporation
BCNN	Broadcasting Corporation of Northern Nigeria
CA	Communications Authority (Zambia)
CAO	*Centre Afrika Obota* (Benin)
CB	Citizen's Band
CD	Compact Disk
CDF	Civil Defence Force (Sierra Leone)
CFA	Communauté financière africaine
CIB	Campaign for Independent Broadcasting
CIDA	Canadian International Development Agency
CIERRO	Centre inter-Africain d'études en radio rurale de Ouagadougou
CIRTEF	Conseil international des radios et télévisions française (Brussels)
CLCAM	Caisse locale de crédit agricole mutuel (Benin)
CLG	Comité local de gestion
CNN	Cable News Network
COM	Campaign for Open Media
COMNESA	Community Media Network for East and Southern Africa
COSATU	Congress of South African Trade Unions
CPU	Commonwealth Press Union
CSI	Conseil supérieur de l'information (Burkina Faso)
DAB	Digital Audio Broadcasting

DFG	Deutsche Forschungsgemeinschaft
DTR	Development Through Radio
ECOMOG	Economic Community of West African States Monitoring Group (West African peace-keeping force)
EPLF	Eritrean People's Liberation Front
FAMWZ	Federation of African Media Women (Zimbabwe)
FAO	Food and Agriculture Organization (UN)
FGD	Focus Group Discussion
FINNATCOM	UNICEF project
FM	Frequency Modulation
FRCN	Federal Radio Corporation of Nigeria
FRR	Fédération des radios rurales (Benin)
FXI	Freedom of Expression Institute
GBC	Ghana Broadcasting Corporation
GTZ	Deutsche Gesellschaft für Technische Zusammenarbeit (German Development Agency)
HAAC	Haute autorité d'audiovisuel et de la communication (Benin)
HDTV	High Definition Television
IBA	Independent Broadcasting Authority
IBAR	International Broadcasting Audience Research (BBC)
ICCPR	International Covenant on Civil and Political Rights
IEC	Information/Education/Communication
IPS	Inter Press Service
ITU	International Telecommunications Union
KAP	Knowledge–Attitude–Practice
KCOMMNET	Kenya Community Media Network
KSMC	Kaduna State Media Corporation
LGA	Local Government Area
MARP	Méthode accélérée de recherche participative
MBC	Malawi Broadcasting Corporation
MCC	Ministère de la culture et des communications
MI5	Military Intelligence 5 (British Internal Security Service)
MISA	Media Institute for Southern Africa
MMD	Movement for Multi-Party Democracy (Zambia)
MMDS	Microwave Multipoint Distribution System
MNDD	Mouvement national pour la démocratie et le développement (Benin)
NACTU	National Council of Trade Unions
NAERLS/ABU	National Agricultural Extension and Research Liaison Service/Ahmadu Bello University, Zaria
NANGOF	National Union of Namibian Workers
NBC	Nigeria Broadcasting Corporation
NCC	Namibia Communications Commission
NDA	National Democratic Alliance (Sudan)
NEF	Near East Foundation
NGO	Non-Governmental Organization
NIF	National Islamic Front (Sudan)
NPC	Northern People's Congress (Nigeria)
NPRC	National Provisional Ruling Council (Sierra Leone)
OB	Outside broadcasting
OLF	Oromo Liberation Front
ORTB	Office de la radio et télévision du Bénin

ORTN	Office de la radiodiffusion et télévision du Niger
OXFAM	Oxford Committee for Famine Relief
PANA	Pan African News Agency
PBS	Public Broadcasting Service
PLAN	Foster Parents' Plan for Children
PRA	Participatory Rural Appraisal
PSI	Population Services International
RBAE	Radio Broadcasting for Adult Education
RDA	Rassemblement démocratique Africaine (Burkina Faso)
RFI	Radio France Internationale
RLG	Radio Listening Group
RPF	Rwanda Patriotic Front
RRA	Rapid Rural Appraisal
RRL	Radio rurale locale
RSLMF	Republic of Sierra Leone Military Force
RTK	Radio Television Kaduna
RTLM	Radio-télévision libre des mille collines (Rwanda)
RTS	Société nationale de radiodiffusion télévision Sénégalaise
RUF/SL	Revolutionary United Front (Sierra Leone)
SABC	South African Broadcasting Corporation
SADI	Solidarité africaine pour la démocratie et l'indépendance (Mali 1997)
SAP	Structural Adjustment Programme
SATRA	South African Telecommunications Regulative Authority
SLBS	Sierra Leone Broadcasting Service
SLPP	Sierra Leone People's Party
SPLA	Sudan People's Liberation Army
SPLM	Sudan People's Liberation Movement
SW	Shortwave
SWAPO	South West African People's Organisation (Namibia)
ULIMO	United Movement for Liberian Democracy
UN	United Nations
UNDP	United Nations Development Programme
UNESCO	United Nations Educational, Scientific and Cultural Organization
UNHCR	United Nations High Commission for Refugees
UNICEF	United Nations Children's Fund
URA	Upper Region Area (Ghana)
URTEL	Union des radios et télévisions libres (Mali)
URTNA	Union des radiodiffusions et télévisions nationales d'Afrique
USAID	United States Aid
USPP	Union souspréfectorale des producteurs
VCR	Video Cassette Recorder
VHF	Very High Frequency
VOA	Voice of America
VON	Voice of Nigeria
WHO	World Health Organization (UN)
ZAMWA	Zambia Media Women's Association
ZBC	Zimbabwe Broadcasting Corporation
ZNBC	Zambian National Broadcasting Corporation
ZUJ	Zambia Union of Journalists

1
African
Broadcast Cultures

RICHARD FARDON & GRAHAM FURNISS

By the mid-twentieth century there were estimated to be something over a million radio sets in Sub-Saharan Africa; at the end of the century this figure may well have reached 100 million. Over the same period, the real cost of the cheapest radio set probably dropped to about one-thirtieth of what it had been at the outset. That the sheer numbers of people with access to broadcast culture in African countries rose spectacularly in the second half of the twentieth century is beyond dispute. What do they listen to? Fifteen years ago, the audience's listening staples were provided by national and international broadcasters. Then, there were only three or four independent broadcasters based in Sub-Saharan Africa; now these must be numbered in hundreds, and they are highly varied (see Mytton, Chapter 2 and Ilboudo, Chapter 3). The growth in African broadcast culture on radio has been spectacular by whatever quantitative or qualitative criteria we choose to measure it. Via radio, African cultures are broadcast, both widely and narrowly, and influenced by the broadcasts of other cultures. At the end of the twentieth century, the media involved in this activity (both internationally and nationally) are in transition as, indeed, is much of the African political framework which is their context.

What are the key features of radio in Africa during the current transition? Two personal anecdotes may offer a starting point. A couple of days after Fardon's first arrival in Cameroon in 1984, a coup was attempted against the (then rather new) government of Paul Biya (see 'The "nightmare weekend"', in Whiteman 1993: 185–6). Something seemed badly amiss when he came down to find the radio broadcasting military music to a very muted audience of customers breakfasting in the restaurant of the downtown hotel where he had lodged on arrival. Although the radio had been on the previous day, it had been no more intrusive than muzak. The day of the coup, no one wanted to risk voicing an opinion about current developments in such a public place; so only the radio spoke, occasionally interrupting the turgid music to address its audience as 'Camerounais, Camerounaises, citoyens, citoyennes'. Upstairs, in the hotel bedrooms, the scene was quite different: a frantic searching through the shortwave bands of transistor radios to catch RFI, BBC and other international broadcasters who might be able to tell Cameroonians what was afoot in their own country. Little by little, people pieced together a picture from the resources of street gossip – not for nothing analogized as *radio trottoir* – and the different broadcasters. No newspapers were to be had. In situations of crisis, radio comes to the fore as an informational medium; but interpreting its statements and silences, knowing how to combine different radio accounts with street knowledge and background expectations to triangulate some – at least for a moment – credible account of what may be happening only a short distance away, belongs with all those other local capacities that outsiders have to learn by participation.

In some respects, Furniss's anecdote is the obverse of this. After a particularly arduous journey, he found himself in what any film producer would recognize as remote Africa: a mountainous region, isolated, rugged, in the Nigeria–Cameroon borderlands. He entered into conversation in Hausa with an aged, barefoot, *montagnard* farmer anticipating some discussion of the prospects for the harvest, the state of the weather or such-like; however, his interlocutor brought the conversation around to the politics of Pakistan, on which he discoursed knowledgeably covering a range of topics that made it clear that he had been following Pakistani politics since before the time of his hero, the late Zulfikar Ali Bhutto. The Swahili, Hausa or Somali services of Deutsche Welle, the Voice of America or the BBC's World Service may allow supposedly local, isolated, rural people of 'under-developed' parts of Africa to be better informed about the international scene than some of their counterparts in the supposedly information-rich US or EU. Though what they learn about may be surprisingly diverse: traffic jams on the M25 London orbital motorway or the Parisian *périphérique*, and the strengths and weaknesses of the Manchester United or Marseille midfield formations, as well as global politics. Cameroonians living in the capital, Yaoundé, may have to turn to the international broadcasters to learn what is happening – literally – across the road from them; but, by the same means, inhabitants of apparently remote regions may connect with the most current elements of global politics. In its pervasiveness and variety, radio thoroughly disrupts any neat association between the local and global as geographical referents. Assumptions of a profound local knowledge existing within the confines of a limited geographical area, and a more attenuated access to wider knowledge of the 'outside' world, are confounded by the complexity of current patterns of access to local and global information.

Differing patterns of access to information also provide evidence of the contrarieties of globalization processes. The growth of multinational media empires implies a potential homogenization of the world's media, and it threatens a concentration of control over decisions about programming and editorial control. Some international broadcasters – CNN, Sky or the BBC in television, or VOA, BBC or RFI in radio – have expanded their broadcast range, not only with stronger and more effective transmitters, but also, in the case of radio, through using local independent FM stations as subsidiary outlets relaying hours of their coverage. Yet to characterize the situation in Africa, on these grounds, as being one of straightforward media imperialism and homogenization would be to misrepresent the effects of the many changes under way. One of the effects of globalization has been the diversification of radio away from the single, state-monopoly broadcaster, creating a wide array of local and community radio stations which emphasize local issues and employ local languages, discourses increasingly embedded in the local rather than the global.

The communications revolution is normally conceived in terms of the potentially revolutionary effects of digital communication. Digital television, e-mail, the internet, computers – these are what dominate current discussion. Yet it is radio, and the technological changes that have taken place, and are taking place, within it that are of crucial significance in Africa. In Chapter 2 Mytton outlines the impact of the introduction of transistors, and the potential importance of satellite broadcasting for those who can gain access to it. Technological change provides both the spur to the further expansion of international broadcasting and also enables simplification and cost reduction for local broadcasters and for the listeners themselves. One by-product of the technological advance that has created simpler equipment for local broadcasters has been a blurring of the lines between public and private broadcasting. The conventions of public broadcasting traditionally differ from private radio communications: the CB radio operator, the mission radio, the radio doctor, the company radio, and indeed the radio communications of the police and the military. Regulation, editorial conventions of balance, of factual narrative and of journalistic integrity in public speech are not a part of the world of private radio communication and may not provide the frameworks within which local radio operates – as chat show, as music station, as listeners' letters or as voice of the liberation front. Combined with the use of cellphones, faxes and e-mails, political actors, be they rebellious soldiers or government spokesmen, have seen access to radio as an instrument of mobilization, and control of a radio station as a symbolic as well as practical mark of success in reaching their political or military objectives. The notorious use of a public radio station to signal force deployments in the pursuit of genocide in Rwanda is discussed by Carver in Chapter 14. While making the point that the station should have been closed under a responsible regulatory framework, Carver still suggests that encouraging a plurality of voices on the air is a more appropriate response to this disaster than suppression of free speech.

Diversification of radio broadcasting in Africa is very recent; even the pioneering efforts date from the 1980s and most initiatives are the product of the 1990s. It is much too soon to make any real judgement of its impact in specific cases, let alone on the continent as a whole. Since diversification in radio is closely tied to processes of political and economic liberalization, many developments in local, community and commercial radio will hinge crucially on the broader direction of changes on which particular countries are set – Zambia, South Africa and Burkina Faso provide hopeful examples in these pages; current expectations (January 1999) of Zimbabwe or Congo are less sanguine.

A key issue for radio stations has always been that of language. Whether at local level or for the international broadcasters (with the exception of Francophone Africa) the choice of languages in which to broadcast has always been delicate. Nothing so readily places a voice on the national sound stage as its language of address. That language may already connote a particular group, or else an alliance of forces may coalesce to identify it as its proprietary badge. To broadcast in one language is to fail to broadcast in another, and that is always taken as a message. Because the message of language choice may be divisive, a particular array of languages used on air may function as a symbolic mark of inclusion into a state, region or nation. For Niger State radio in Nigeria to broadcast in Nupe, Gwari and Hausa was to acknowledge the main political forces that made up the state, day after day in regularly repeated practice. From the point of view of the broadcaster, of course, there are manifest inefficiencies in the multilanguage broadcast: the 10-minute broadcast in three languages takes 30 minutes and requires extra paid employees translating scripts. For the listener too who knows he is hearing the same thing three times, whether he understands all three versions or not, the process can be more than a little irksome. More common is the separate language service with its own programming. The establishment of a separate regular audience for a particular language broadcast has been achieved with spectacular success by the African language sections of the BBC, Deutsche Welle, VOA and Radio Moscow, among others. The BBC African language services (Swahili, Hausa and Somali), for example, have been in existence for some 50 years and have regular audiences numbering many millions. The longstanding use of some African languages in international broadcasting has had a profound influence upon the spread of the language and its standardization and modernization. The choice of a particular dialect of Hausa for the standard form, for example, was a colonial measure, but one which meant that the engine of innovation very quickly focused upon that dialect (Furniss 1991). Each day in the newsroom in Bush House, Hausa journalists working for the BBC had to create, and most significantly standardize among themselves, terms for molecular biology, nuclear fission, guerrilla warfare, or humanitarian aid, for instance, so the new standards based on Kano dialect would be relayed and explained to Hausa speakers from Kaolack to Khartoum (for Swahili see the discussion in Blommaert 1994). For many African listeners, however, the sources of radio news have always been varied: in English, in African languages, in French and other languages, from international broadcasters; in local languages from local or national stations. The multilingual world of many Africans, both urban and rural, facilitates cross-tuning to a variety of sources since many stations tend to broadcast for short periods two or three times a day.

The most significant component of broadcast material on radio in Africa is, as elsewhere, music. A primary function of radio is to provide entertainment and pleasure, drawing upon the many and varied styles, forms, fashions and traditions of music, both from Africa and worldwide. This volume makes no attempt to cover this vast topic, as we indicated in our preface, and yet we are acutely conscious of the importance of the issue. We have ourselves often enjoyed parts of the kaleidoscope of musical styles across the continent – Hilife, Congo music, Afro-Cuban, hip hop and many others. We leave music to another volume and other editors (hopefully a volume with accompanying CDs). Nevertheless, to at least provide a feel for the salience of music in the world of African radio, we set out an extract from a magazine distributed by AVIS rental cars intended to introduce the visitor to driving, and therefore to radio, in South Africa (December 1998). The prominence of music is clear from the descriptions of contemporary radio stations, although the focus of this article may overly highlight the world of contemporary Western pop music as compared with African popular musical forms that figure more prominently in music broadcasting in other parts of the continent. We think this also gives a flavour of the developing picture of broadcasting in the new South Africa to set against Jeanette Minnie's discussion in Chapter 12 of the struggle to wrest control of broadcasting from the monopolistic tentacles of the old SABC, which, though broadcasting in a variety of African languages in addition to English and Afrikaans, maintained complete control over the airwaves.

Whether on business or on holiday, when you're driving around South Africa in your rented Avis car, don't get stuck on one station – take the opportunity to sample the delights of regional radio. You'll find a wide variety of styles to choose from.

Radio is still more popular than TV and if you want the low down on each region, tune into the popular regional stations for input on local affairs and opinions. For even more localised news and specialised formatting search for some of the campus and community radio stations in your area. Community Radio is a new development in this country with a total of 82 having been granted temporary licences cutting across cultural, religious, ethnic and political interests. These are non-profit stations with no compulsory play lists. As a result they allow for a more varied and innovative formatting, despite their skeleton, voluntary staff complement.

Unless you're in the Western Cape, FM reception is better. In the Cape MW frequency is an advantage because its flexibility enables it to curve over mountains. Its generally weak reception makes it more suitable for talk than for music radio and the talk stations have cottoned on to this fact. They've opted for MW in the knowledge that listeners won't have to hunt their frequency as they go around hospital bend or head over Kloof Nek.

Regional Stations

Eastern Cape
Radio Alagoa (94–94 FM) and *BRFM* (94–97 FM) have a combined footprint which extends from Plettenberg Bay in the South to East London in the North of the Eastern Cape. It is an Adult Contemporary music station where you'll hear the latest mainstream hits by artists like Bryan Adams, Phil Collins, Elton John, Celine Dion and Coleske. Programming is in both Afrikaans and English.

KwaZulu Natal
East Coast Radio's (94.95 FM) success lies in its Adult Contemporary mainstream formatting with a Rock and R&B edge. It is an up-beat station aimed at those between 24–34 years of age.

Lotus (FM 87.7 MHz and parts of Johannesburg on 106.8 MHz) aims to cater for the needs of South African citizens of Indian descent. It covers the five major linguistic groups, namely, Hindi, Tamil, Telugu, Urdu and Gujarati. All music played is in these five languages. The emphasis is on entertainment with a minor mix of information and education. There are women's magazine programmes which investigate fashion and social issues alike, sports programmes and twice-daily talk shows. Current affairs are woven into the up-beat morning and evening drive slots.

Gauteng
Highveld (94.7 FM). *Highveld*'s footprint covers primarily central and southern Gauteng. It targets the 25–49 age group with an emphasis on music and entertainment. The format is driven by mainstream adult contemporary music, or 'all-hit radio' as it is known, comprising the favourite songs of the past 25 years.

Jacaranda (94.2 FM). This is the only bi-lingual station in Gauteng, and its local music component includes Afrikaans music. The slogan of this station, which is 'more music, more stars' reflects its adult contemporary mainstream formatting. You won't hear any radical new hits but you will hear music with a familiar sound. Music is punctuated by news and traffic reports and informative lifestyle features from book news to food and wine to movies and even travel.

Gauteng and North West Province
YFM (99.2 FM) is a recently-launched youth music station which has proved to be a huge success. According to Marietjie van Rensburg of Radmark Independent Media Brokers, its success lies in the fact that it caters for a market never before catered for: 'a music and lifestyle station, for the young at heart rather than the young'. It is hit driven, concentrating on R&B formatting and a high percentage of local music, pumping out Kwaito, Hip Hop and rap to all of those who are between 16–24 and going on 40.

Kaya-FM (95.9 FM) is aimed at a modern, urban black audience who want to hear adult contemporary music with an African Soul. Although the footprint is the same as YFM, its listeners are older. The combination of music and information is consistently stimulating for both the heart and the mind.

Classic FM (102.7 FM). As the name implies, this station caters for classical music lovers with a dash of choral music thrown in.

Western Cape
Good Hope FM (94–97 FM). This is an urban, commercially-driven Public Broadcast Service. Primarily a music station it is aimed at people in the greater metropolitan area of Cape Town between the age groups 16–34 years. It's also a good way to keep up with Cape Town's populist pulse. This format follows international hit music trends blended with news and information, traffic reports, information about local sports and community oriented activities, as well as fund-raising campaigns.

KFM (94.5 FM). KFM broadcasts in both English and Afrikaans. With its slight bias to Afrikaans-speaking listeners, it is wholly reflective of the population of the Western Cape. It has contemporary mainstream formatting, targeted at adults. This means mainly music and current hits over the past few decades. It also boasts its own 'trafficopter' and trained on-board paramedics to ensure up-to-the-minute traffic reports and care in the event of car accidents.

P4 Radio (104.9 FM). This adult contemporary Jazz station is based in the Jazz capital, Cape Town. It emphasizes smooth jazz, so you're more likely to hear George Benson, Jonathon Butler, Grover Washington Jr and Jimmy Dlu Dlu than the fidgety likes of Coltrane or Gillespie.

Free State
OFM (*Radio Oranje*) (94–97 FM). OFM is one of the fastest growing commercial stations in the country and has gone through some vigorous changes. Broadcasting from Bloemfontein, it has put central South Africa firmly in the ears of its bilingual listeners. You'll find Bryan Adams in a mellow mood or Tina Turner musing about whether love has anything to do with it or not. Firmly in the Adult Contemporary mainstream stable, you'll also find Golden Oldie and Easy FM sounds.

Talk Radio

Cape Talk (567 MW) This is the station of identity for metropolitan Cape Town in the same way that 702 is synonymous with Gauteng. You'll recognise Cape Talk by its provocative hosts who stimulate talk on many issues, both serious and trivial. It has become Cape Town's information provider and talk entertainer. Not only does it have one of the best news services, but it is an essential source of all information – news, traffic, surf, sport, fishing, whale watching and even 'jolling'. Appealing to an informed audience that is 25 and older, it is Capetonian to the core. Well-known personalities such as Barry Ronge, Rod Suskin, Tim Noakes and Jani Allen have regular slots.

702 (702 MW). Transmitting from Gauteng, 702 was historically a music-based station transmitting from the former homeland of Bophutatswana. Although it now

has less music, having moved over to a commercial topical talk format covering many contentious issues, it has retained its former independent image. It punts itself as a platform for all in '702land' to have their say on issues that affect them, following an 'infotainment' format. Linked to Cape Talk, there are many overlapping programmes, including lifestyle, business, sports, film, quizzes and even a property show.

National

5FM (Jhb 98 FM, CT 89 FM) is aimed at the fashionable, metropolitan youth market between the ages of 16 and 34. There is continuous provision of music entertainment in the Contemporary 'Hit' radio (CHR) format in a humorous, sometimes irreverent style with many competitions and promotions. It strives to deliver a Rock-based music foundation that considers crossover musical genres.

RSG (FM 100–104; SW 3320 KHz for N. Cape and Namibia). RSG has been going for 60 years but has seen many name changes: Afrikaans Diens, Afrikaans Stereo, Radio SA. Following the IBA regulations that radio stations are not allowed to reflect ethnic divisions, its focus has shifted to being a full-spectrum Afrikaans program that is relevant and accessible to the total Afrikaans population. The hallmark of this station is its variety. It encompasses commercial and PBS formatting, appealing to both toddlers and the aged.

Metro (567 KHz MW). Radio Metro is a contemporary music station aimed at urban, sophisticated listeners between 16 and 34 years of age. There is an emphasis on R&B, Disco, Kwaito, and Hip Hop with a consistent delivery of local music, from Jazz to Mbaqanga. The music tempo and mood varies according to the days of the week and channels of the day. Talk shows are featured once daily and there are many current, topical issues pertaining to socio-political and economic matters. News is both international and local.

SAfm (104–107 FM). *SAfm* is the English National Public Service broadcaster. It provides news and current affairs programming covering local, national and international topics, including S. A. Live – a co-production between *SAfm* and the *BBC World Service*. Although it is primarily a news station with an emphasis on economic and business information, there are also specialist magazine programmes, talk shows, documentaries and dramas. The music shows are presented by specialists and feature classical music, rock, R&B, jazz and popular 'adult-sophisticated' repertoire. There are sport programmes seven days a week.

The report, fascinating as it is in its use of language, goes on to list, undescribed, the African language stations that are presumed to be less accessible to AVIS's regular customers:

African Language Stations

Ligwalagwala
(Nelspruit 92.5 MHz, Pretoria 89.3 MHz)
Munghana Lonene
(Jhb 103.2 FM, Pretoria 95.6 FM)
Phala Phala (Northern Province)
(99.1–101.7 FM)
Thobela (Northern)
(100 FM)
Ukhozi (KwaZulu Natal, Gauteng)
(90.8 FM)
Umhlobo Wenene (Eastern, Western, Northern Cape, Gauteng)
(91.3–92.4 FM)
(*AVIS magazine*, Cape Town, December 1998; capitalization etc. original; quoted by permission of Destinations Media, South Africa)

Writing on radio

Despite the arresting evidence of growing importance and crucial transition, mainstream academic attention to radio has been scanty (see Bourgault 1995, Chapter 4, for a useful overview). As Michael Traber writes, 'Studies on radio and television are an underdeveloped field of African scholarship' (Traber 1997: 56; but see also Head 1974, Wedell 1986). Many of the major academic Africanist journals have not carried an article on radio in the past decade (although other journals have, for example *New Scientist* 1995, *New African* 1995, *West Africa*, Barrett 1996); even television, a far less inclusive medium, seems to have grabbed more attention (Wedell and Tudesq 1996). The print media are also better served by the academic community; but then reading is what academics do. Video recordings of television programmes, as well as newspapers and magazines, are lugged to academic archives for close inspection. However, there is little evidence that radio transcripts, or off-air audiotapes, receive similar attention. Perhaps there is something too pervasive, transient and self-evident about the way that broadcast cultures pervade the African ether. Until something striking occurs, the buzz of the radio is simply there.

Returning to academic coverage, there is a literature on radio in Africa, but it tends to emanate predominantly from practitioners, lobbies and interest groups rather than from, say, anthropologists or political scientists. Interest groups write about radio in terms of its impingement on their interests; as, indeed, do lobbyists on behalf of human rights or development issues. Because radio is so pervasive, it is virtually impossible to study it per se in all its ramifications. Perhaps it deserves to remain the prerogative of diverse interests, relying upon occasions of dialogue to make the connections between these interests.

So what kinds of literature are there on radio? Of course, there is a professional literature: on training broadcast professionals, producing programmes, running radio stations and so forth (see Mytton, Chapter 2 and Nouma, Chapter 4). Such professionals have at their disposal more or less information, of greater or lesser accuracy, gathered by the arms of their organizations concerned with audience reaction. Or, if there is none, then unsolicited feedback and general familiarity with the audience must suffice. There is also the technical literature on the radio, and on the implications of the changing technologies (such as digital radio) which promise to revolutionize the numbers of frequencies available for broadcasting and the strength of reception over wide areas.

Another body of literature is particularly concerned with the regulatory frameworks within which broadcasters operate (for southern Africa see Carver, Chapter 14, Opoku-Mensah, Chapter 11 and Minnie, Chapter 12, Article 19, *et al.* 1996–7; for West Africa see Panos & CREDILA 1996). Who decides which stations are licensed, and who licenses the licensers? How is broadcasting made accountable, if it is, and to whom are broadcasters accountable? How open is access to the airwaves for different shades of opinion and sectors of the population? How are national governments to be prevented from making attacks against peaceful internal dissent (Senghor 1995, Article 19 & Index on Censorship 1997a/b)? These are questions about the control of the medium and its message in both formal, statutory, terms, and in terms of the way such frameworks are interpreted and implemented practically (for surveys see Article 19 & Index on Censorship 1995 on freedom of speech, and Panos Institute 1993 on radio pluralism, particularly community radio).

Graham Mytton, tongue-in-cheek (or perhaps not), referred to the model of broadcasting bequeathed by ex-French and British African colonies as the Stalinist model. The British and French colonial states monopolized the broadcasting of information both at home and in their colonies and since the colonial versions of domestic European services were even more closely tied to government than their originals, these providers readily became servants of the immediate, post-colonial successors to colonially defined states: states which worked upon a colonial inheritance of administrative means which they made even more centrist. When localization, liberalization and commercialization hit the European airwaves (later than in the US, see Pease & Dennis 1995), from the pirate stations of the 1960s onwards, African providers were taking a quite contrary route towards intensified monopoly.

Another literature comes upon radio from the perspective of local development. Rural radio and community radio (not quite the same thing, as we discuss below) are intended to bring broadcast voices closer to the concerns of their audience, ideally merging broadcasters and listenership. Radio is seen as a technology capable of empowering local communities in relation to some, or all, of their social, economic or political concerns. Local radio, in local languages, may address development issues (whether agricultural or health-related), encourage political debate (from the detail of national politics to more pervasive questions surrounding differences of age or gender), or simply entertain and stimulate. The London *Guardian* (4 January 1999) reported the effectiveness of a radio soap in Tanzania, 'Geuza Mwendo', depicting the AIDS-related illness of a truck driver, known as Mashaka. Four such dramas were at that time playing on Radio Tanzania addressing such issues as family planning and drugs. The *Guardian* report from Tanzania indicated that 'in a recent survey, 75 per cent of respondents said they had been made aware of AIDS, and its prevention, through radio programmes'. We use the term local radio as a more general term encompassing rural and community radio, to contrast with national or international radio. Local radio can be an offshoot of national radio or an independent/ commercial station. Rural radio, sponsored either by donors or the state, relates to specific initiatives to address rural as against urban populations regardless of whether the programme-makers are based in capital city, regional town or village. Community radio is used by our contributors to focus upon the situatedness of the station and its programme-makers within a particular community, however that is perceived.

If the state broadcaster loses its erstwhile monopoly role, then clearly it has to adjust its position within a more pluralized broadcasting system. The degree to which it is able to do so will be influenced by two factors: whether it will be funded to maintain a national coverage, and whether it will be distanced sufficiently from governmental control to exercise any moral authority in its remaining listening public.

The more ethnographic literature on radio has to surmount the problem of defining its object of study. If radio is in the ether, how do you study the ether? If so much of people's lives is impinged upon by radio, where is the line drawn for purposes of study? In practice, radio can be studied in its production or its consumption, or both. The problems of studying the two ends of the process are slightly different.

If the number of radio providers increases exponentially, it becomes increasingly difficult, and eventually impossible, to study the production of programmes and programming schedules in all of them ethnographically. Either a particular station must be studied in depth to identify exemplary issues (Grätz, Chapter 8), or stations must be surveyed less intensively (Myers, Chapter 6). In either case, we need to know about the power relations within the station which affect the cultures of programming and programme production. Who decides what will be broadcast, when and how (Spitulnik 1992, 1994)? What goes without saying in the culture of the radio station, and what becomes subjected to intensive discussion and, possibly, fraught contestation?

Reception studies are even more complex. Broad-based surveys may seek to establish who listens to what stations, what programmes, and so forth. But they have difficulty assessing how people listen, and what (if any) effects their listening habits have upon them. The most closely focused reception study in this volume (Spitulnik, Chapter 10 and 1993) stresses the situated and material characteristics of radio listenerships: when the radio is on (even if people's concentration is off), how radio sets circulate, how the expense of batteries curtails usage, and so forth. Between this approach and that of audience research dealing with national entities, clearly a chasm yawns. Qualitative methodologies of rural appraisal, such as PRA or RRA, discussed by Ilboudo in Chapter 3, seek to bridge this gap (also Kivikuru 1990 for Tanzania); but Ilboudo reveals at length just how poor our knowledge of the impact of radio is – even when we might most expect there to be surveys: in NGO-funded, radio-for-development projects, that need to credentialize their success in terms of their sponsors' goals.

The chapters in this volume are avowedly neither exhaustive nor even representative. The field is too vast, and the ramifications of radio as a broadcast medium too pervasive, to permit even the impression of exhaustive coverage. In order for the chapters to be representative, we would need to decide what they should be representative of. And, again, the field is too diverse to be readily straitjacketed by clear criteria. The chapters do, however, provide a sampling of the constituencies and interests invested in African radio broadcasting today. So, we shall take the opportunity of this introduction to foreground the perspectives from which our very varied contributors write or speak, for this is, we believe, the principal strength of the volume (cf. Fardon & Furniss 1994) and was the reason for our wishing to involve participants across the different divides of academic and practitioner, national and international broadcaster, lobby groups and radio journalists, professional audience researchers and ethnographic enquirers. The chapters are grouped in three parts.

Part I: Sub-Saharan Surveys

Following this Introduction, Part I includes a chapter by a senior practitioner in the field of radio audience research in Africa. Graham Mytton wrote one of the earliest academic works on radio based upon first-hand, intensive research in

Africa as well as a foundational book on the mass media in Africa (1983, contemporary with its French counterpart, Tudesq 1983). For almost a decade and a half he headed audience research for the BBC World Service, co-authoring the manuals (such as Scarlett Epstein *et al.* 1991) on which the BBC's local researchers draw for their methodology. His considered overview of trends in broadcasting is important both for setting the widest parameters of our subject, and for its indication of the way in which an international broadcaster like the BBC seeks to inform itself about its audience.

During the 1970s, Jean-Pierre Ilboudo was, as Urbain Nombré puts it, among the founding fathers of rural radio in Burkina Faso, the country which pioneered many aspects of local and community radio. He taught at CIERRO during the 1980s, where the in-course training of radio technicians and journalists in West African local radio was undertaken. His chapter reflects his current promotion of rural radio as a development tool on behalf of FAO, as well as his past experience. Ilboudo begins by contrasting the high emancipatory ambitions and development objectives of community and rural radio with a country-by-country survey revealing the very poor research basis that exists on the impact of rural radio initiatives (predominantly on Francophone Africa, but with Anglophone examples). For 30 years, radio broadcasters and journalists continued to produce programmes with little, or only superficial, knowledge of their audiences. Ilboudo indicates how qualitative research approaches (including the widely promoted technique of PRA) were adapted by CIERRO in order to train those who produce radio programmes to research into what their audience requires from its radio, and how the audience reacts to broadcasts (for the history of PRA see Chambers 1983 and especially 1992). Since the results of PRA are applied immediately to the creation of rural radio programmes in the field, the division between research and practice dissolves, and rural radio itself becomes one of the tools of social enquiry and development. Ilboudo sees PRA as an important corrective to the tendency of rural radio to be employed by the centre for campaigns at rural people, rather than being treated as a possession of rural people (see Myers, Chapter 6).

The fourth chapter brings together commentaries by senior practitioners in international broadcasting, along with transcripts of discussion that focused upon the role of international broadcasting in the development of radio in Africa. Ibrahima Sané left the BBC World Service to become the head of Senegalese radio and television. He passionately maintains that radio pluralism involves a vital role for an impartial, independent, properly funded and high-quality national broadcaster capable of 'holding the ring' between the contending voices unleashed on the airwaves. His advocacy of national broadcasters is not directed against the proponents of media pluralism, but he asks that they see the evolution towards democratic maturity of national broadcasters as another element of the transformation of the airwaves they seek to achieve. At present, national broadcasters like his own are hampered financially from discharging their role: their resources are greatly inferior to those of the international broadcasters, and this gap is growing.

Roger Nouma is responsible for in-service training of African radio professionals by the Direction des études on behalf of Radio France Internationale, the French external broadcasting service. He argues strongly for the complementarities between international and local broadcasters: in news services, programme provision and in-service training.

Elizabeth Ohene is the instantly recognizable voice of BBC World Service for Africa's 'Network Africa' news and current affairs programme. She cut her teeth as a journalist in Ghana before moving into radio. Her lively discussion of the changing situation of the current affairs presenter centred on the impact of technological change on news coverage (compare Richards, Chapter 16). The satellite telephone is now part of the basic equipment of insurgent movements, meaning that presenters have to react on air to being cold-called by people involved in the very events they are covering.

Part II: Local radio, local radio culture and the culture of radios

Part II presents a series of four case studies of small radio stations, for which Myers (Chapter 6) borrows the felicitous term 'microcasters', in Francophone West Africa (for a Liberian case study, see Bourgault 1995: 92–9). These are followed by a consideration of the way in which a local culture has adapted to exploit the radio medium, and a study of the culture of radio usage and ownership.

Urbain Nombré is among Jean-Pierre Ilboudo's successors in Burkina Faso. His chapter summarizes the evolution of devolution in that country's broadcasting policies. Following its return to multi-party democracy in 1991, Burkina Faso (already among the more innovative radio users) saw an explosion of commercial local radio, under a liberalization decree that set a regulatory framework for independent radio. Local offshoots of the national broadcaster were complemented by private and community radio stations across the country (for an earlier, extensive survey of the broadcast media in Burkina Faso see the chapter by René Lake in Panos Institute 1993 and on Haute Volta/Burkina Faso, pre-Sankara, see Tudesq 1983). The state as sponsor of radio has now been joined by donor agencies, churches and private businessmen, and some of these new initiatives have survived and some have gone under for lack of finance, staff and community participation.

Mary Myers has worked widely as a consultant on rural radio. Her chapter reports on research that she has carried out on the impact of a few of the hundred or so community radio projects begun in Mali and Burkina Faso in the 1990s, as well as in Senegal. This rapid growth is largely explicable in terms of donors' willingness to support development from below in the context of the antipathy to the state typical of the period of structural adjustment policy. Rural radios, run from the major urban centres, have been largely supplanted by community radio stations, situated within the communities they serve. Myers is cautiously optimistic about the prospects for local-level *animation* which has replaced top-down *vulgarisation* as the ascendant orthodoxy in the Francophone development world. However, she questions how much it is reasonable to anticipate of community radio in material 'development' terms, given the shoestring resources on which it must be run. There may be particular sorts of subjects to which radio is well suited, such as AIDS awareness and some environmental issues.

Christine Nimaga Ceesay moved from the BBC to coordinate the development of local radio in Niger under German sponsorship in the decade 1988–99. Like Myers, she recognizes the advantages these local stations enjoy from their proximity to the concerns of their listeners; and, from the evidence of research into changing patterns of radio use, she expects that the Niger national broadcaster (ORTN) will be squeezed inexorably between the local attractions of the microcasters and the authoritative role in news dissemination of the international broadcasters. Like Myers also, Ceesay recognizes a tension between a genuinely local basis to the ownership of a broadcasting culture and the aspirations that a higher level of regional or national administration may still harbour to use it is a means of top-down propaganda or direction.

Tilo Grätz, an anthropologist, is more circumspect about the local embeddedness of microcasters, as well as their relations with higher tiers of administration. His chapter derives from a recently completed doctoral project on the politics of establishing a new rural radio station in northern Benin. Grätz takes us to the heart of local politics involving struggles for control over the siting, staffing, funding and direction of the station, and over its language policy. Radio Tanguiéta itself became one of the stakes that local political interests contested; and in the context of the post-1990 democratic renewal in Benin, Grätz cautions that small radio stations can easily become the tools of local or ethnically-based political interests.

The Nigerian academic, Mansur Abdulkadir, introduces us to the world of commercial radio, appropriately through an analysis of the Hausa culture of advertising mediated through one its most skilful exponents (for other West African examples, see Ugboajah 1985). Northern Nigerian radio is no microcaster, since it reaches as many as 40 million listeners. Abdulkadir demonstrates both the continuities and innovations that the veteran journalist, Bashir Isma'ila Ahmed, has wrought on Hausa oral genres and that have made his advertisements cult listening in northern Nigeria. His pair of stock characters, as recognizable as Laurel and Hardy, have their own following regardless of the product they are used to advertise – the airline, political party, bank or insurance company whose qualities they enumerate. The commercialization and localization of radio provide the opportunity for the emergence of forms of cultural discourse unanticipated by the bureaucracies and political elites that seek to keep them on message. Abdulkadir's account demonstrates again that there is no necessary contradiction in a vehicle of commercialism also innovating within the terms of a local cultural discourse, a point that might not require mention if claims to cultural authenticity were not so often made for rural and community forms of radio (as if commercial stations were devoid of authentic cultural interest).

As an anthropologist and media specialist, Debra Spitulnik is concerned to question any illusions we may entertain about the transparency of why, how and when people listen to the radio. She urges our attention to the relation between the materiality of media technology and the social contexts in which media are received. Her chapter follows a radio set in its odyssey around a Zambian village, before detailing the unexpected disruptions a radio cassette player visited upon a rural Zambian wedding. In its ethnographic specificity, the methodology she urges on us occupies one end (the sociocentric) of a methodological spectrum, the other pole of which would be the large-scale surveys into individual listening habits which make up part of the methodology used by Mytton's teams of enquirers. Somewhere in the middle of the spectrum may be the position in which to place Ilboudo's advocacy of the techniques of PRA. As Spitulnik notes, different kinds of ethnographies of media audiences are produced depending on the types of reception in which the investigator is interested. This leaves the audience's reactions either sphinx-like in their inscrutability (to borrow the image de Certeau used of consumers) or, what comes down to much the same thing, theoretically underdetermined and thus prone to a high degree of malleability in their representation. In short, quite what is supposed to be going on among an entity called the audience is a matter of great consequence (often financial consequence) for those who depend on representing themselves to their sponsors in terms of their impact on that audience, but it is in principle both difficult to know how any audience reacts and all too easy to speak or write as if one did.

Part III: Radio, conflict and political transition

Part III turns to the most widely reported recent role of radio: its relation to the political transitions occurring so widely and diversely in Sub-Saharan Africa in the closing years of the twentieth century.

Chapters 11 and 13 consider relatively peaceful political transition in southern Africa, with especial reference to Zambia: one of the 'success stories' of democratization (on another of the 'success stories', Ghana, see Karikari 1994). At the time of our workshop Aida Opoku-Mensah headed the office of the southern African branch of the Panos Institute, based in Lusaka, Zambia. The Panos Institute has been one of the most persistent and persuasive campaigners on behalf of media pluralism (see Panos 1993 and their bulletin *Radio-Actions*, 1994–present). In restating some of the grounds propitious to the expansion of community radio stations (ideally owned and managed in some form by the community), Opoku-Mensah's chapter returns us to the subject of microcasting that was addressed with reference to Francophone West Africa in Part II. She particularly emphasizes two aspects crucial to the functioning of community radios: the regulatory framework under which they are licensed and operate, and the financial underpinnings of the operation (beginning with ownership). On both grounds, southern African countries are diverse, with different mixes of national, commercial and community broadcasting stations. Of particular interest is Opoku-Mensah's account of a 1997 forum held in Zambia to propose guidelines for the regulation, licensing and operation of, in particular, community or grassroots radio stations (see Panos 1997). Opoku-Mensah and Panos more generally see the establishment of viable legal and financial frameworks for community radio as essential if this is not, to quote her, to be 'yet another fashionable concept that will soon die a natural death'.

Jeanette Minnie's chapter draws a dramatic picture of the reform of public broadcasting in Africa. Through her roles as an activist in the Campaign for Open Media and Campaign for Independent Broadcasting, Minnie was closely involved with a crucial phase in the evolution of South African broadcasting policy up to and during the transition to post-apartheid democracy. Her personal testimony of the negotiations involved in the run-up to the elections shows how persistent the advocates of an open media environment needed to be in order to ensure that the elections could be contested fairly (in a system which attempted to treat even the broadcasting of music on apartheid lines, see Hamm 1991). Fundamentally, the grip of the National Party on the South African Broadcasting Corporation had to be released before an information environment conducive to the democratic process could evolve. Her accounts of the evolution of SABC, and of the attempts to establish an Independent Broadcasting Authority, are particularly crucial because, as noted above and despite whatever shortcomings Minnie outlined, the South African experience was seized upon by several of our discussants in that session as a precedent for developments elsewhere in Africa. But, as Minnie reiterated in discussion, the concessions wrought from the South African government were not won without concerted, politically inclusive and protracted agitation; and such democratic achievements may easily be lost in the face of apathy or the abuse of privilege.

Zambia recurs as the subject of the chapter by Jean-Pascal Daloz and Katherine Verrier-Frechette, respectively political scientist and media specialist, whose argument, like Carver's, is couched in terms of the current political transition involving the democratization process. They note that the power of radio is manifest in the way that political regimes seem happier to countenance a pluralism of opinion in the print rather than the broadcast media. Wondering just how deep the transition in Zambia has gone, they take the example of the recently established Radio Phoenix, which according to Opoku-Mensah presents itself as a community radio. The ZNBC, like so many other monopoly state broadcasters in the immediately post-colonial period, was fundamentally a propaganda organ on behalf of the presidency. Radio Phoenix has set out its stall to provide a more impartial news service, but the authors question how politically independent it is able to be, given that it needs to operate in an environment of clientelism and that its future depends upon commercial and political sponsorship.

At the time of the meeting Richard Carver was the head of the Africa Section of the freedom of information and anti-censorship lobby group named after Article 19 of the ICCPR. He drew upon his own longstanding experience, as well as the insightful analysis of his colleague Linda Kirschke, to revisit the carnage of Rwanda, the role of the notorious Radio-télévision libre des milles collines in ethnocide, and the general implications to be drawn from this human disaster. Carver disputes the complete atypicality of Rwanda; its unique features are not in question, but Rwanda shared in the situation of economically and politically coerced transition to 'democracy' that has been so common in Sub-Saharan countries since the structural adjustment of the 1980s. What was unique about Rwanda was the preconceived plan to subvert the democratic process. RTLM was clearly complicit in this plan, but it did not instigate it. Rwanda, more realistically, suffered from a deficit of broadcasting pluralism, since Hutu extremists controlled both the national broadcaster and the even more rightwing RTLM. Other voices on the airwaves might at least have contested the ethnic hatred being broadcast by RTLM, and while they would not have prevented ethnocide, they could have given better warning of it. The moral – that RTLM should have been shut down for its incitement to ethnic hatred and violence – is unaffected, but the implication – that the precedent of RTLM has a general, and negative, bearing upon the promotion of radio pluralism and freedom of speech – is, as effectively, disputed.

As an ethnographer of Sudan and Ethiopia, Wendy James was close to the civil war in the Sudan before the outbreak of its second phase in 1983. Drawing upon the underutilized resource of the BBC *Summary of World Broadcasts*, she demonstrates how the contending voices in the Sudanese airspace have gradually shifted away from addressing local participants in the conflict until they speak predominantly to one another and to an international constituency. As the war has escalated, so has the rhetoric and intransigence of broadcasting. Radio broadcasts appear more of an obstacle to peace than one of the means of bringing it about.

Paul Richards, with a similarly longstanding and close involvement in Sierra Leone, stresses the obverse potential of radio. Richards expands his previous analysis of Sierra Leonean civil strife in terms of the disaffection with the corruption of the post-colonial state on the part of elements of Sierra Leonean youth who see no future for themselves within it. These groups, enclaved in the forests and supported by the mineral and human resources found there, have embarked on a process of cultural and social schismogenesis, reinforced by ideologies of opposition to the state and practically reinforced by violence calculated to polarize their relation to the national civic society after the fashion of sectarian organizations. Radio, Richards proposes, in its combination of social and cultural intimacy at physical distance, is one of the few means to build upon such social and cultural relations as still exist between the centre and its enclaved peripheries so as to rebuild a common civic culture from the wreckage of conflict.

The differences between these last three accounts strike us as deriving less from disagreements between the writers than from the diverse forms of civil strife in the countries they report upon. This seems worth mentioning if only because political commentators on Africa sometimes refer to a rising tide of violence sweeping the continent, as if to imply that the condition from which Africa suffers is in some way unitary. The Sudanese civil war is more than four decades old and reflects regional, ethnic and religious cleavages at the very heart of the state-building project. The Sierra Leonean disorder is far less clearcut, being not regional, ethnic or religious in any neat sense. Its precedents are to be sought, as Richards has demonstrated, in the (interrelated) corruption of the post-colonial state and the poverty of the country which together led to disaffection of the youth elements, and to the promotion of new techniques for the destabilization of state regimes. Rwanda's genocide – whatever its historical conditions – has immediate origins, on Carver's argument, in coerced and incomplete democratization. Being embedded in such different contexts, it would be unrealistic to expect radio to play a similar role in each case.

African radio in transition: policies and practices

The variety of these contributions adds weight to our introductory comments on the scope of our topic: radio in contemporary Africa impinges on every aspect of the current changes in the sub-continent, reflecting and affecting social, cultural, political and economic processes. For all that its ramifications are so wide, the medium of radio does offer a privileged vantage point from which to survey the changes. Radio is relatively cheap, efficient, immediate and undemanding as a technology (at least to use in a basic fashion). In principle its broadcasts are unaffected by the parlous state of the roads or the variation of the seasons. Literacy poses no barrier; though language does. Its range and impact is immensely greater than either television or even the printed word. African public cultures at a national level are – not only still but increasingly – radio-driven cultures. This is why such vital interests come into play in the ownership, control and design of what goes out over the airwaves.

Fundamentally, the African broadcasting scene now consists of three elements: international, national and local broadcasters, among which the last is extremely diverse. The relations between the three are a recurrent concern. Until recently, the major distinction was between national and international broadcasters, a situation to which listeners reacted by judiciously combining their sources of information. The emergence of local radio has begun to change patterns of listening, and perhaps also listeners' orientations to the media. The arguments for media pluralism in principle are many and persuasive: whether approached via politics, economic development, health education, cultural promotion, or the more general sense of immediacy between local listeners and local programme-makers. However, all these positive arguments, while accepted in principle, are open to cautious questioning in practical implementation.

National broadcasters may have been hijacked for sectional interests at the centre, but it is questionable whether, and how far, the local broadcasters redress this situation. Under what regulatory framework do they operate? This affects their independence, both formally and in terms of their informal, or self-imposed, censorship. Can licensing practices provide a covert counterpart to formal restriction? Daloz and Verrier-Frechette suggest they may. To what extent will local radios align themselves with sectional interests, whether regional, ethnic or religious, and promote these without a sense of responsibility to the national society? Richards, Carver and James give compelling examples of this possibility. How commercially viable will the new local broadcasters transpire to be? Their ownership and sponsorship are highly varied: there are nationally owned and supported stations, stations sponsored by religious interests, stations dependent on overseas NGO-funding, and also commercial ventures in the strict sense. Most, as Ilboudo noted, seem unable to support audience research. Each is constrained by its need to react to the agenda of those who hold its purse-strings and impose their conditions on funding to a greater or lesser extent. Ibrahima Sané wondered out loud how many of the current crop of stations would survive a decade or more. Tilo Grätz adds to these cautions a compelling account of the extent to which local radio itself becomes a focus of contention in the local political field.

Advocacy of local radio has frequently sought justification in developmental or educational arguments, and this does provide one of the grounds appealed to by several of our contributors (for an early argument, see McAnany 1975; see also Chapters 3, 5, 6, and 7). However, this is not to argue that all local radio stations fulfil this mission well. André-Jean Tudesq writes that educational radio seems to have more of a past than a future in Francophone Africa (1994: 126). Much depends upon the abilities of often under-trained and under-equipped tyro-journalists to produce programmes that are absorbing, relevant, inclusive and unpatronizing. Where these criteria are reasonably satisfied, as Mytton notes, local broadcasters are demonstrably preferred by listeners to their international counterparts. The issues of cultural promotion and local immediacy clearly belong with the same set of issues. Ilboudo's advocacy of PRA for rural radio producers precisely addresses the potential gap between broadcasters and their listeners even at local level.

The growth of local broadcasting, in all its diversity, has complicated the relations between the three grossly distinguished forms of broadcasting. Ibrahima

Sané sees state radio holding the ring among the contesting voices, ideally keeping them honest and maintaining their standards. This is much the same argument to which national broadcasters like the BBC appeal in order to justify their public funding. As an ideal it is attractive; however, the (short) colonial and (longer) post-colonial track-records of African national broadcasters are not encouraging in this respect. The growth of local broadcasters has unleashed many voices that are not committed to the idea of balance, but have a prior commitment to the promotion of particular interests.

Various two-way links continue to operate between international broadcasters and both state and local broadcasters: through training which leads to the reproduction of conventions about programming, in the recirculation of programmes and in the process of news-gathering. Not only have the BBC, RFI and other international stations including the now much reduced Radio Moscow provided opportunities for African journalists to work abroad, training has been an important part of these stations' functions in relation to African broadcasting (for instance in Deutsche Welle's support for CIERRO, Tudesq 1983: 184–5). Training has been both technical and editorial, producing expectations of standards in broadcasting that then become the norm in local and state radio. Many conventions become best practice within the media community: for example, those that operate to suggest that news items should be presented, at least initially, without an interpretative gloss; that journalistic comment should be identifiable to the listener by being contained within commentary sections of a broadcast; that balance is necessary and so if one speaker is interviewed to present one side of a case then the voice of an opposing position should be included within the framework of the item. The difficulty of ascertaining what is reliable information and the incessant problem of resisting political pressure is the constant headache for the broadcaster. Training has also produced a consensus on the structure of programming: that news headlines, typically on the hour, are followed by fuller reports combining reportage with studio news-readings; that commentary follows before a switch to a series of less time-bound programmes in the form of features (farming programmes, health programmes, listeners' letters, humorous programmes, etc). Such standard packages are, however, expensive and time-consuming to make. There has to be a sophisticated news-gathering infrastructure with links to the international press agencies, an editorial and news-writing team, a studio production and technical team, and a staff of announcers and commentators.

The expense of maintaining such a level of resourcing has meant that state radio has often needed to recirculate programmes and information taken from the international broadcasters. RFI, for example, was providing in 1997 three news bulletins a day to 48 French-speaking radio stations in Africa. Local radio has moved into a completely different field of broadcasting, the much cheaper, and often more cheerful, talk show, listeners' hour or taped music. This latter form is often beset by technical problems and operates with a flavour of *bricolage* both technically and editorially. The recirculation of broadcasts occurs both through the allocation of station time to a 'feeder' broadcaster and through the rebroadcasting of tapes acquired from other broadcasters. This process extends occasionally beyond the oral medium into print. Certain Nigerian newspapers have, for example, taken the scripts of radio broadcasts and printed them in their pages.

The third area in which there are close cross-cutting links is in the area of news-gathering. Local correspondents will work for a number of different news agencies and broadcasters, reworking material where necessary. A particularly significant part of the news-gathering process is the role of monitoring. International broadcasters are able to have speedy access to the information being transmitted on a wide variety of local stations, in such a way that they can feed that information into their own editorial processes, using conventions on cross-checking with a number of independent sources before making decisions about whether the information is reliable. In recent years the speeding up of the processes of communication and the spread of technology has meant that rule-of-thumb conventions, such as that which operates at the BBC requiring two independent corroborative reports or one single report from a BBC correspondent before broadcast, have been circumvented by the sudden and often unexpected 'appearance' of the actors whose doings are being reported live on air from a cellphone in a clearing in the bush. The role of broadcasting in making real that which was rumoured is one of the issues addressed in this volume in the chapters by Richards (Chapter 16), and Sané, Nouma and Ohene (Chapter 4).

Shadowing discussion of all these issues are the great difficulties, both epistemologically and practically, of reception studies. It may be reasonably straightforward to enquire how many people switch their radios to which stations, and how often they do this. But problems arise in relation to: what, if any, impact their listening has upon them; how, and whether, they are changed by it; and how their cultural and social milieux change as a result. Here there is a role for detailed ethnographic study, since the complexities of these problems are most similar, in principle, to those confronted by anthropologists in their role as writers of ethnography.

Whether the academic study of radio in Africa per se will be a growth area, we cannot foretell, but it does strike us as seriously under-researched. Radio impinges so widely on African public life, and is doing so in such rapidly changing ways, that it does seem safe to predict that research on virtually any aspect of contemporary Africa that neglects radio will be missing a large part of the big sound stage.

References

Article 19 & Index on Censorship (1995) *Who Rules the Airwaves: Broadcasting in Africa*, London: Article 19.

—— (1997a) *Unshackling the Nigerian Media: an Agenda for Reform*, London: Article 19 & Media Rights Agenda.

—— (1997b) *Cameroon: a Transition in Crisis*, London: Article 19.

Article 19, Freedom of Expression Institute, Media Institute of Southern Africa (1996–7) *Media Law and Practice in Southern Africa*, Vols 1–6, London, Johannesburg & Windhoek.

Barrett, Lindsay (1996) 'Power of Radio', and 'Broadcasting in Ghana: an unrecorded interview with Hon Totobie Quakye, Minister of Education and Culture', *West Africa* 24–30 June: 984–85.

Blommaert, Jan (1994) 'The metaphors of development and modernization in Tanzanian language policy and research', in Richard Fardon & Graham Furniss (eds) *African Languages, Development and the State*, pp. 213–26. London: Routledge.

Bourgault, Louise M. (1995) *Mass Media in Sub-Saharan Africa*, Bloomington: Indiana University Press.

Chambers, Robert (1983) *Rural Development: Putting the Last First*, Harlow: Longman.

—— (1992) *Rural Appraisal: Rapid, Relaxed and Participatory*, Institute of Development Studies, Sussex, Discussion Paper 311.

Fardon, Richard & Furniss, Graham (eds) (1994) *African Languages, Development and the State*, London:

Routledge.

Furniss, Graham (1991) 'Standards in speech, spelling and style – the Hausa case', in N. Cyffer, K. Schubert & H.-I. Weier (eds) *Language Standardization in Africa*, pp. 97–110, Hamburg: Helmut Buske.

Hamm, Charles (1991) '"The constant companion of man": separate development, Radio Bantu and music', *Popular Music* 10 (2): 147–73.

Head, Sydney W. (ed.) (1974) *Broadcasting in Africa: A Continental Survey of Radio and Television*, Philadelphia: Temple University Press.

Karikari, Kwame (ed.) (1994) *Independent Broadcasting in Ghana*, Accra: Ghana Universities Press.

Kivikuru, Ullamaija (1990) *Tinned Novelties or Creative Culture? A Study on the Role of Mass Communication in Peripheral Nations*, Helsinki: University of Helsinki.

McAnany, Emile G. (1975) 'African rural development and communication: five radio-based projects', *Rural Africana* 27: 59–72.

Mytton, Graham (1983) *Mass Communication in Africa*, London: Edward Arnold.

New African (1995) 'Revolution on the air waves', July/August, 16–17.

New Scientist (1995) Special Issue *Africa South of the Sahara*, including features by Peter Coles on Mali 'Turn your radio on', 7 October: 38–9.

Panos Institute (1993) *Radio Pluralism in West Africa: A Survey Conducted by the Panos Institute Paris and l'Union de Journalistes d'Afrique de l'Ouest*, Vol. 3 (*Burkina Faso, The Gambia, Mali, Senegal, Sierra Leone, Nigeria, Ghana*), Paris: Institut Panos & L'Harmattan.

—— (1994–) *Radio-Actions: Bulletin for Radio Pluralism in West Africa*.

—— (1997) *Broadcasting and Society. Forum on Broadcasting in Zambia: National Seminar for Members of Parliament and NGOs*, Lusaka: Panos Institute for Public Policy and Policy Debate for Southern Africa.

Panos Institute and CREDILA (1996) *Breaking Monopolies: Legislation and Radio Pluralism in West Africa*, Lusaka: Panos.

Pease, Edward C. & Dennis, Everette E. (eds) (1995) *Radio the Forgotten Medium*, New Brunswick NJ: Transaction Publishers.

Scarlett Epstein, T., Gruber, Janet & Mytton, Graham (1991) *A Training Manual for Development Market Research (DMR) Investigators*, London: BBC World Service, IBAR; Hassocks: Innovative Development Research.

Senghor, Diana (1995) 'Safeguarding radio pluralism', *Radio-Actions, Bulletin for Radio Pluralism in West Africa* 3: 3–4.

Spitulnik, Debra (1992) 'Radio time sharing and the negotiation of linguistic pluralism in Zambia', *Pragmatics* 2 (3): 335–54.

—— 1993) 'Anthropology and mass media', *Annual Reviews in Anthropology* 22: 293–315.

—— (1994) 'Radio cycles and recyclings in Zambia: public words, popular critiques and national communities', *Passages* 8: 10, 12, 14–16.

Traber, Michael (1997) review of Gretchen Walsh *The Media in Africa and Africa in the Media*, *Media Development* XLIV (3): 55–6.

Tudesq, André-Jean (1983) *La radio en Afrique noire*, Paris: Pedone.

—— (1994) 'Radios et télévisions scolaires', *Afrique contemporaine*, Special Number *Crises de l'éducation en Afrique* 172: 126–33.

Ugboajah, Frank O. (ed.) (1985) *Mass Communication, Culture and Society in West Africa*, Munich: Hans Zell.

Wedell, George (ed.) (1986) *Making Broadcasting Useful: The African Experience*, Manchester: Manchester University Press for the European Institute for the Media.

Wedell, George and Tudesq, André-Jean (1996) *Television and Democracy in Africa: The Role of Television in the Democratisation of the Countries of Sub-Saharan Africa*, Report of a Study Undertaken for the Commission of the European Union (DG VIII).

Whiteman, Kay (ed.) (1993) *West Africa over 75 Years: Selections from the Raw Material of History*, London: West Africa Publishing.

I
Sub-Saharan Surveys

2
From Saucepan to Dish

Radio & TV in Africa
GRAHAM MYTTON

This chapter was written because I felt it was time to make available to those studying contemporary Africa some of the rich and varied data on contemporary media collected by the BBC World Service's audience research department IBAR (International Broadcasting Audience Research). I was in charge of this major research unit from 1982 to 1996. Previously I spent ten years or so working in the BBC African Service.

I was not new to audience and media research. My PhD thesis had been on the place of the mass media in political development in Tanzania (Mytton 1976). In 1967–8 I had conducted field research in Tanzania. My research showed how radio, which had arrived in Tanzania as a mass medium at about the time of that country's independence, had quickly become a major factor in daily life.

The rapid growth of radio access in Tanzania, made possible by the arrival of cheap, portable, battery-powered transistor radios, had provided a new means of political and cultural communication unlike anything that had preceded it. The impact of this new medium has largely been neglected in contemporary and later scholarship in Tanzania and elsewhere; see, however, Kivikuru (1990).

Later, in 1970–3, I did similar work at the Institute for African Studies at the University of Zambia. This involved, among other work, a comprehensive, national survey of media access and use, focusing especially on the contentious and complex question of language comprehension and media use. This work has been published in Mytton 1974 and 1983.

From 1982 to 1996 I was involved in global research. IBAR had a team of 14 professional research staff whose responsibility it was to measure audiences for the BBC and other international broadcasters throughout the world. It also conducted qualitative and quantitative research into the ways in which the media were used, the types of programmes listened to on the radio or watched on television, the image of various media and other related matters. Each year more than 100 separate research projects were conducted. A significant proportion of these were in Africa.

This chapter will concentrate entirely on Sub-Saharan Africa and on the measurement of media access and use in those countries from which data have been collected. The BBC has in the past few years commissioned or participated in measurement surveys in Angola, Benin, Burkina Faso, Burundi, Cameroon, Congo, Ethiopia, Gabon, Ghana, Guinea, Côte d'Ivoire, Kenya, Mali, Mauritania, Mozambique, Namibia, Niger, Nigeria, Senegal, Sierra Leone, Somalia, South Africa, Sudan, Tanzania, Uganda, Zaïre, Zambia and Zimbabwe. In some cases the surveys have been designed to be representative of the entire adult (15+) population. In others, such comprehensive coverage is not possible and surveys have been possible only in major towns or in limited areas of the country. In some cases, surveys have been carried out on a number of successive occasions, allowing us to plot changes in media use and access over time. Such is the case with Angola, Cameroon, Ghana, Côte d'Ivoire, Kenya, Mozambique, Nigeria, Senegal, South Africa, Tanzania, Uganda, Zambia and Zimbabwe. Sometimes the research has been conducted in close cooperation with other broadcasters. In a few cases, the research has been initiated by domestic broadcasters or media organizations and the BBC has been one among many clients. But in most cases the BBC World Service has been the sole organizer and initiator of the research. Some of our work has been pioneering. This has been the case where the first ever national or near-national media surveys have been carried out: in Sudan, Mozambique, Ghana, Côte d'Ivoire, Senegal and Ethiopia (Mytton 1993).

The primary purpose of IBAR has been to measure audiences of the BBC World Service in Africa, as elsewhere. The BBC broadcasts to Sub-Saharan Africa on shortwave, in English, French, Portuguese, Somali, Swahili and Hausa. The transmitters used are situated in Seychelles, South Africa, Cyprus, Ascension Island and the UK. The BBC has large audiences in a few countries, but the largest BBC audience anywhere in the world outside the UK, as a percentage of the adult population, is found in Africa. This has happened for a number of reasons. Listening to foreign radio stations anywhere in the world is negatively correlated with the availability of domestic media. Generally speaking, the fewer local sources there are to choose from, the greater the degree of state monopoly, the more likely it is that people will seek out alternative sources of information and entertainment coming from outside the country. Another important factor in the high levels of listening, although not a cause in itself, is the widespread use of shortwave for domestic broadcasting. Most African countries use shortwave radio transmission to provide services to their populations.

The UK and France bequeathed to their former colonies a state monopolistic system of broadcasting that has, for the most part, survived to this day. Moreover, broadcasting has mostly, until now, been national in coverage. It is only relatively recently that local and commercial, and for the most part city-based and urban-focused radio has emerged. When I wrote *Mass Communication in Africa* in 1983 there were only three or four non-governmental broadcasters in the whole of Africa. Now there are 300 or more and the number is growing quite rapidly. Changes in technology are also having an effect with the arrival of the VCR, satellite and MMDS (this is sometimes described as cable-less cable TV, and is transmitted over limited areas. It is found in Dakar, Abidjan and a few other places, and provides a multi-channel service to subscribers).

Technology

New technology in electronics has transformed communications in Africa, as elsewhere. I was reminded of this when, in 1991, I visited the late Harry Franklin, the pioneer of broadcasting in what was then Northern Rhodesia, at his retirement home in Hampshire, England. In 1941, 50 years earlier, the tiny radio station, established in Lusaka by the colonial authority's newly-established Information Department, began broadcasting programmes to indigenous people in their own languages. It was the first in Africa broadcasting in indigenous languages. A major impetus for this development was the need to broadcast news of the progress of the war, especially to the families of Africans serving in the Northern Rhodesia Regiment, then fighting in Somaliland.

The problem was that hardly any Africans had radio sets. In those early days, wireless sets required mains voltage electric current. The very few in African homes were mostly not portable and needed to be plugged in to a home electricity supply. This was because sets used valves (or in American English, 'tubes') which used a relatively large amount of electric current. Few houses of indigenous people at this time had mains electricity supply. What is more, wireless sets were expensive and this put them beyond the reach of most Africans.

During the war some chiefs in Northern Rhodesia were supplied with radio sets, powered by large batteries, but after the war Harry Franklin, who was the official in charge of broadcasting in the colony, set out determined to provide a cheap battery-driven set so that radio could be a much more widely used medium. It is difficult now to appreciate, perhaps, what a revolutionary – and unpopular – idea this was. He encountered a lot of hostility and opposition from the European settler population which could not see the reason for broadcasting to and for Africans.

Despite the technical problems, Franklin was sure that a low-cost small valve set requiring minimum electric power could in fact be portable and be powered by a battery and thus be suitable in African conditions. He was eventually successful in persuading the battery makers, Ever Ready, to manufacture and market a small battery set, the 'Saucepan Special'. It was so-called because the prototype was built in the shell of a metal saucepan and the eventual production line used the same design. Sets went on sale from 1949 at £5 each (US$14) and £1.25 (US$3.50) for the large dry battery required. They were an immediate success and spread rapidly in African townships and even rural areas (Franklin 1950; Fraenkel 1959). But the 'Saucepan' became obsolete when the transistor radio arrived about 10 years later.

Ironically, the transistor was invented at about the same time as the 'Saucepan' appeared. The discovery was made in 1948 by Bardeen and Brattain at the Bell Telephone Laboratories in the United States that an impure crystal could be used to amplify electric currents in the same way as a diode valve. Previously, crystals had been used mainly for the detection of radio signals (hence the crystal sets of the early days of wireless). Another scientist, Shockley, often properly associated with Bardeen and Brattain, developed their discovery and made it more reliable and ultimately manufacturable. The three were fittingly rewarded with the Nobel Prize for Physics in 1956. However, it is a curious fact that they are still largely unknown despite the development of a technology that transformed communications in the twentieth century. The fiftieth anniversary of this important development in 1998 deserved to be celebrated.

It was some years before reliable transistors were manufactured. These electronic semiconductors eventually replaced valves entirely, in radio sets, gramophones, tape recorders and televisions. They were also developed for use in radio and television studios. Transistors have a number of advantages. But the most important for the development of radio sets was that they used much less electric current than valves. This meant that a radio set could be run on small, inexpensive, low-voltage torch batteries. Radios suddenly became completely portable. You could take your radio anywhere – and people did, much to the annoyance of some. The transistor radio or 'tranny' was carried in the street, taken on outings, played at work or in the fields. No longer did you have to be near a mains electricity supply.

In the poorer areas of the world, the transistor brought an even greater change. It meant that radio was not only portable; for the first time it became available to almost everyone except those living entirely in the subsistence economy. The few thousand 'Saucepan Specials' and the few other wireless sets in the third world gave way to a flood of imports of cheap transistor radios which, although more expensive initially than, for example, the 'Saucepan', did not require expensive batteries. An early transistor radio in 1958 might cost £10 or £15 in Lagos or Nairobi (US$30 or US$45) but its batteries cost only a few pence to replace at that time, much less than the cost of the high-voltage batteries previously required for valve sets. (The price of transistor radio sets dropped very rapidly in real terms over the next few years. It is difficult to make comparisons, but the lowest priced radio set now costs about one-thirtieth of the price of the cheapest set nearly 40 years ago, if one makes comparisons allowing for the change in the value of money.)

The transistor meant that radio became dependent neither on mains electricity nor on cumbersome batteries. The market for transistor radio sets grew very rapidly. Accurate figures are very hard to establish but the situation in Tanganyika, now Tanzania, is illustrative of a general picture. In 1960 the Tanganyika Broadcasting Corporation in Dar es Salaam seemed to be happy at an estimate of 72,000 sets in African ownership. By then the transistor revolution had only just begun. As prices fell with mass production, sales rose rapidly. The 1960 estimate was based on independent market research, as was an estimate 14 years later which put the figure at over 1.7 million (Tanganyika Broadcasting Corporation 1960; Radio Tanzania 1974).

Tanzanian data are among the best we have, as they are based on similar sample surveys of the whole population. Similar rates of growth have been seen elsewhere. The following table shows contemporary estimates of the number of radio sets in Africa, south of the Sahara, excluding South Africa. There was a tenfold increase between 1955 and 1965 and a fourfold increase over the next decade. North and South Africa, the more developed parts of the continent, have also seen high rates of growth and these figures are included for comparison (IBAR annual since 1955).

Estimated number of radio sets in Africa, 1955–95 ('000)

	1955	1965	1975	1985	1995
Africa, South of Sahara, (excluding South Africa)	460	4,800	18,500	42,600	70,200
South Africa	775	2,600	4,800	10,000	13,000
North Africa	1,405	7,100	14,100	29,400	41,360

The growth over the past 10–15 years in some countries has been slower, mainly due to difficult economic circumstances which have restricted imports. Data on the growth of radio and television in Africa as a whole and in some individual countries are shown in the Appendices.

I began this section with the story of the 'Saucepan' and the transistor for two reasons. The first is that the importance of the transistor revolution in the third world is easily forgotten. The development of the transistor led to the production of radio sets which were ideally suited to modern African communication needs. Here was an example of a technological innovation developed in the West, meeting one kind of market demand there, being transferred very successfully to non-industrialized countries and becoming a very significant innovation there – making, perhaps, even more social, cultural and political impact than in the West from where it came. It should be noted also that its arrival in large quantities on the African market coincided almost exactly in most countries with the date when political independence from Europe was achieved. This new communications medium arrived independently of those political changes, but radio seemed certain to have a major role to play in the unfolding of events that followed. The coincidence of the arrival of transistor radios and political independence over much of Africa is examined and discussed in Mytton (1983).

The second reason I began with the remarkable story of the transistor in Africa is to point out that technology in broadcasting can have a very rapid effect and can make fundamental changes in the way communications occur. Within a very short time, the transistor made radio into a truly global mass medium, penetrating even some of the very poorest areas.

The transistor has been followed by other developments in technology whose impact has also been important. The further development of the transistor led to the tiny integrated circuits enabling the construction of computers only a fraction of their former size. These computers and their associated technology have made further developments in broadcasting possible. Miniaturization has made communications satellites economically practical because the complex control equipment required can now be made very small and light in weight.

There is a high risk in predicting the future. Thirty years ago there were no micro-computers. Computers were vast machines occupying large air-conditioned buildings and had to be operated by specialists. Portable electronic calculators were rare and expensive. Satellites were in operation but links were unreliable and very limited. Video-recorders existed only in television studios. The vinyl long-playing gramophone record was thought to have an indefinite future. Radio telephones were rare and very cumbersome.

Now, primary schools in Europe and America have computers, sometimes many in each classroom. Electronic calculators are cheaper than the paper log tables, and the wood and plastic slide-rules they replaced. There are millions of households with satellite dishes; international telecommunications traffic via satellite and fibre-optic cable has grown massively. Video-recorders are found in both cities and rural areas in most parts of the world. In the developed world the digital compact disc has replaced the vinyl record, while cellular radio telephones are now commonplace in the industrialized world and are appearing fast in less developed countries also.

At a 1989 broadcasting seminar in Ghana a government official, Kofi Totobi Quakyi, voiced the concerns of many about the rapid pace of technological change:

> Advances in broadcast technology and systems pose several challenges to developing countries. Most of these countries cannot afford to keep pace with these changes.

He continued that it was not really necessary always to acquire the latest technology, especially when the skills needed for maintenance were not available. It was more important for technical staff to master the ability to handle what they had. He also regretted that broadcasting organizations in Africa had not been able to design their own suitable equipment, for example, for the new local community FM radio stations:

> Unless we learn to build and assemble simple equipment we will always be repairers and not inventors. (BBC Monitoring Service 1989)

There is much more to the debate than this. The technology available to African broadcasters is developed in the industrialized world where the circumstances – economic, social, political, organizational and cultural – are different. Technology is not neutral. It reflects the circumstances within which it is created. Much studio equipment, to give just one example, is now designed to save labour in developed countries where costs, especially of skilled labour, are very high. The technology in radio and television studios has been designed to use the minimum number of people.

The manufacturers of studio, transmitting and receiving equipment have brought in many innovations over the past 40 years – stereo radio, colour television, video-recording, portable light-weight video cameras, digital recording and now high-definition television. They have been motivated by opportunities in rich countries' markets. Their businesses have prospered from innovative enterprise which has encouraged demand for new products and then met those demands.

Very little technological innovation in broadcasting has been introduced with the circumstances of developing countries in mind. There are still no mass-produced solar-powered or solar-charged television or radio sets. The only technological development I can think of in this field, designed with the needs of the poor in mind, is the BayGen clockwork radio, being manufactured in South

Africa. The problem with Quakyi's defiant statement about technology is that it is not possible to ignore all new inventions and say that Africa can do without them. The point is to understand new technology, to see its potential, to be able to choose wisely and if necessary adapt to local conditions and circumstances.

Technological innovations in broadcasting have not slowed down. Indeed, if anything, the process of change has speeded up. The silicon chip, and the miniaturized computers and associated functions now made possible by it, are leading to a bewildering array of new developments. It is difficult and risky to predict which of these will be of importance and value to African broadcasters. And we have to remember that success in technological development depends mainly on what happens elsewhere, in the large and rich markets. The large electronics firms Telefunken, Philips, Sony, Matsushita and others design equipment and plan their marketing strategies mainly for mass markets in the developed industrialized world.

What is likely to succeed and what technological development will be of importance for Africa and other parts of the third world? Does the new technology itself pose special problems? Zimbabwe's Minister of Information, Posts and Telecommunications suggested so at an International Telecommunications Union conference in 1989. Africa had not yet caught up with existing technology. Maintenance of what they had was difficult enough without new and different problems. Very often the biggest questions were not what kind of transmitter to build or what new telecommunications systems to invest in, but whether the roads and electricity supplies to make these things possible would be ready and available. Witness Mangwende's warnings and commonsense, down-to-earth realism were a very necessary reminder to those who get carried away with enthusiasm for every new technological possibility. He pointed out that innovation must be related to need and to the infrastructure necessary to make anything work properly. He did remind us of a particular problem of solid state micro-processor technology faced in tropical countries like Zimbabwe. They are more easily damaged by such common African problems as voltage fluctuations and electrical storms.

But was Mangwende correct when he developed his theme further?

> Although we are aware of other technological developments such as HDTV, fibre optics, etc. – and the possible immense advantages to be derived therefrom – these are of no immediate significance to the developing countries who are currently grappling with the problems of establishing basic electronic media infrastructures. (Mangwende 1989)

It is my argument here that some of the new technology is of immediate significance. Some innovations, adapted and modified for African conditions, could be of great value and relevance. Mangwende is right to warn about the basic infrastructural problems facing African broadcasters when deciding where to site a new radio transmitter to extend national coverage. But some of the possibilities in new transmission technology may make the building of so many relay transmitters unnecessary. Some of the technical innovations may, in fact, provide answers to some of the most difficult problems faced in extending communications services in the continent. DAB, satellite delivered, is one clear example of a new technology which provides exciting possibilities for Africa.

The immediate question is how DAB, a new transmission and reception system, developed in the industrialized world, with the selling point of near-CD quality reception, should be relevant and of value to much of the third world. It could be argued that Africa does not need high fidelity; the quality of the sound is not so important. Many people are still not adequately provided with the most basic necessities of life and to be discussing new rich-world luxuries might seem inappropriate. Certainly to discuss technological advances in the terms used in the developed world would be wrong. Africa's priorities have to be different.

At first glance, digital technology in radio seems to have little or no immediate relevance for Africa. But that may be because of the way it is usually discussed and promoted. The manufacturers are keen to sell their products. They therefore use the arguments which will attract customers in their targeted markets. Most of the sales of digital recording, transmission and reception services and equipment will be in the developed world. One of the biggest (but not the only) selling points is the greater fidelity of digital technology. In a competitive developed environment this is important. But there is more that the technology can offer, especially in the field of radio transmission. And it is in the other benefits of digital technology that we can see the potential for Africa.

Most broadcasting in Africa is still national in scope. All African countries have national radio stations belonging to the state, with the objective of reaching the whole country. The picture is a little more complex of course. In Nigeria, each of the states has separate broadcasting systems which seek to reach the populations in those states. There is some local private broadcasting in some countries and there has been a lot of growth in this area in the past 10 years. But generally speaking, African broadcasting is centralized, national and state dominated.

Since the beginning, a major problem has remained. How can a national broadcaster achieve national coverage? Many African countries are large with widely scattered populations. There were three strategies that could be followed. The best and the most expensive was the one adopted in South Africa by the SABC, and that is to provide a network of FM stations using VHF signals which could repeat the national service or services. But full and satisfactory coverage in any country using FM is very expensive and difficult to achieve. To achieve national coverage in the UK on FM, the BBC has some 150 transmitting stations and in-fill relays and claims now to cover 98 per cent of the population.

In the whole of Africa, apart from small island states, only South Africa has so far achieved near national coverage with FM. Ghana, Guinea, Zambia, Zimbabwe and others have plans to do so. But the two greatest constraints are finance and infrastructure. Transmitters need electrical power. If they have to cover large areas they need quite a lot of it. They need to be maintained and serviced. Roads, electricity supply and a trained pool of engineers, maintenance and security staff are essential; the shortage of any one can cause a national radio transmission system dependent on FM stations to break down.

The second alternative strategy is to build a network of mediumwave AM stations. Not so many are needed for national coverage. But the same constraints of finance and infrastructure apply. And even with an adequate number of transmitters, mediumwave is not an ideal solution from a technical angle. During daylight hours national coverage may not be achieved because mediumwave does not reach far beyond the horizon. At night, mediumwave can reach much further because of changes in ionospheric conditions, but then the problem is that other mediumwave transmitters on similar or adjacent frequencies from quite distant places can also be picked up and can often interfere with good reception.

The third strategy, adopted by virtually every national radio station in Africa, has been, initially at least, to use shortwave transmission to achieve national coverage. This was what the colonial governments did when broadcasting began 50 or more years ago. The special properties of shortwave were ideal for the purpose. The transmitters could be sited where there was electricity supply and where the engineers could be accommodated and broadcasting studios were sited. Transmitters were needed on only one site. National coverage could be achieved from one place using one facility. Shortwave signals reflect off the ionosphere and return to earth at some distant point beyond the horizon. They can alternatively or additionally be aimed in such a way as to achieve all-round coverage. Theoretically, any place, near or distant, can be reached by shortwave signals.

However, there are many problems associated with the technology. Solar storms can severely affect the behaviour of the ionosphere, sometimes blocking out all shortwave transmission on certain frequencies. The ionosphere is not stable. It moves and changes in density, reflecting the shortwave signals in an uneven way. Shortwave signals are reflected not only off the ionosphere, but also off the ground or off water. They then travel up to the ionosphere to be reflected down again. They can go on travelling like this over vast distances – right around the world in fact. On occasions this means that the signals received in one place can be interfered with by signals using the same frequency coming from another transmitter from a distant place in another country and directed at a different audience. The shortwave bands are very congested. But despite all these problems, shortwave is still an appropriate technology for poorer countries seeking to maintain national radio coverage. It is also the main means of international radio transmission.

DAB now makes possible new prospects for broadcasting in Africa: a fourth transmission strategy. DAB transmission by satellite – combined probably with some urban terrestrial delivery – really does provide exciting possibilities for Africa and other less-developed areas of the world. A system developed and designed to solve the problem of congestion and multi-path distortion and other perceived reception difficulties in the rich world also happens to have qualities which could make it ideal for the very different circumstances of Africa. It could be very much cheaper to instal and run a DAB service using satellite delivery for a country like Tanzania than to develop a full terrestrial FM network. One satellite transmitter could give full coverage of the country and be receivable everywhere. (Much depends on the system used, the degree of terrestrial in-fill necessary in some areas and some as yet unknown factors. I am aware that more research is needed into satellite-delivered DAB, and some is currently under way.) Moreover, because of the nature of digital technology, more than one service could be carried on each transmitter by multiplexing the services in one signal and leaving it for the receiver to decode. Furthermore, in areas where high-fidelity sound quality may be seen as of secondary importance, the capacity of this digital system can be used in another way. Sound quality can be exchanged for extra programme capacity, if required, on the same digital system. For example, the DAB capacity required for one high-quality stereo broadcast can be exchanged for the capacity to carry at least four separate medium-quality broadcasts which will still be substantially better than conventional AM, including shortwave, broadcasts. There are also exciting possibilities for interactive services and for the use of the technology to provide educational information for remote educational institutions. But this development is still in the future.

There is a new digital radio system now in Africa, provided by a US-based company, Worldspace, led by an Ethiopian-American, Noah Samara. It launched a satellite over Africa in 1998 which is now providing radio services to African countries, using a digital transmission system. The technology being used is quite different from the system now being used in Europe, Eureka 147. Independent experts seem to be agreed that the Worldspace system is technologically inferior, but this is chiefly because Eureka 147 was developed with the main objective of reception in moving vehicles. Samara's view is that it is too complex and expensive. His system is, he says, capable of providing excellent reception. If the latter is adopted it will mean, for the first time in radio, the existence of two incompatible radio delivery systems. However, the Worldspace system may well become much more widespread than Eureka, which may prove to be too sophisticated and costly. Following the launch of Worldspace's first satellite over Africa to provide radio services for the whole of Africa and the Middle East, a second satellite is to be launched over Asia by Worldspace shortly afterwards, providing services to an area extending from Pakistan to China. In 1999 a third satellite will provide services to Latin America and the Caribbean. Worldspace's choice of Africa for the first satellite radio service in the world is surely a unique example of a new technology arriving first in Africa. Technological developments happen sometimes at great speed and the problem for students of the media is to discern which of them could be important. One current development that could have major implications for Africa is the proposed development of digital shortwave. The major international radio broadcasters like the BBC are enthusiastically supporting this. Digital shortwave would provide enormous improvements in reception quality; the other great attraction is that it would enable old (analogue) and new (digital) systems to operate side by side, using the same transmission facilities during a transition period. Digital shortwave offers new technology with continuity, whereas satellite-delivered digital radio represents a much bigger break with the past and one that some broadcasters may find difficult to take.

Radio and television use and access today

All this is now beginning to happen. But at present, the broadcasting technology in use in Africa is identical to that in use in the rest of the world. In the following appendices I provide data on media access and use in selected African countries. The salience of radio is clear enough. Radio is still everywhere the most used medium. It might be thought that this is hardly worth comment – one would not expect television in poor countries to be ahead of radio. But recent research for the BBC in India has shown that in that country television now reaches more people than radio. Radio ownership and listening have actually declined in some countries while television ownership and viewing have continued to rise over recent years. An important factor in India is that while the state still maintains a monopoly of both radio and television terrestrial broadcasting, television is now de facto deregulated as far as satellite services are concerned. At very low cost, India's television owners can have access to many satellite TV services, provided on flourishing cable services. In Africa, by contrast, most private non-state broadcasting activity has been in radio. Only in Tanzania (ironically enough in a country which seemed more determined than most to maintain state control of electronic media) has private television become of prime importance. There is still little choice in African television, while radio is more varied and provides more choice. What satellite TV there is in Africa, provided mostly by South Africa's Multichoice, is very expensive to access. The only exception to this is in a few mainly Francophone cities where Microwave Multipoint Distribution System (MMDS) services are now being developed. The latest research shows MMDS as being available in 13 per cent of households in Dakar and 9 per cent in Abidjan.

Appendix I: Radio and TV set ownership in Africa, 1955–1995

The following charts and tables show the rate of growth of household ownership of radio and television sets over the 40 years 1955–95. I have separated the data into three categories – North Africa, South Africa, and Africa south of the Sahara. Data in these tables come from the annual *World Radio and TV Receivers*, a BBC World Service publication compiled from survey data and other reliable sources.

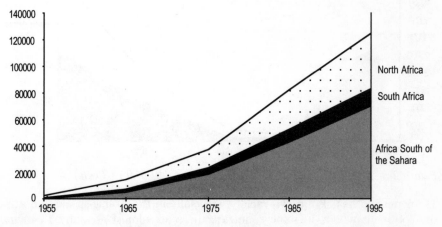

Figure 2.1 Estimated number of radio sets in Africa, 1955–95 ('000s)

As Figure 2.1 shows, the growth of radio set ownership was relatively unaffected by recession and the adverse terms of trade in Africa from 1975 to 1995. In some countries there was a levelling off of growth, but the overall African picture is one of sustained growth.

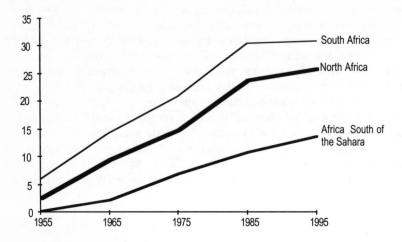

Figure 2.2 Radio sets per 100 population in Africa, 1955–95

In Figure 2.2 I have shown the growth rate in radio ownership against population growth. Here the rate continues to be an upward one, but the very high population increase has levelled the rate somewhat over the decade 1985–95.

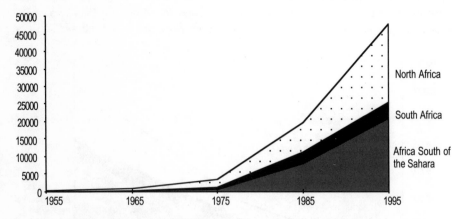

Figure 2.3 Estimated number of TV sets in Africa, 1955–95 ('000s)

TV ownership has also grown rapidly, especially in the Arabic-speaking north of the continent where, in some countries, there are almost as many TV-owning households as there are radio.

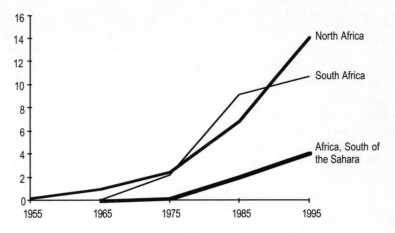

Figure 2.4 TV sets per 100 population in Africa, 1955–95

The rate of TV ownership relative to population growth has remained high except in South Africa during 1985–95.

Data on radio, TV, and VCR ownership in selected Sub-Saharan African countries (= data unavailable)*

A *(national data)*

Country, date	Radio (%)	TV (%)	VCR (%)
Ethiopia, 1995	68	9	3
Ghana, 1995	67	32	4
Côte d'Ivoire, 1992	68	39	5
Kenya, 1996	74	11	2
Namibia, 1994	71	23	10
Nigeria, 1996	62	31	13
Senegal, 1992	93	41	6
South Africa, 1995	91	76	34
Tanzania, 1995	76	4	2
Zambia, 1996	62	31	7
Zimbabwe, 1994	47	14	2

B *(partial coverage)*

Country, date	Radio (%)	TV (%)	VCR (%)
Mozambique – 4 Provinces, 1995	51	15	6
Sudan – North, 1995	52	30	7
Uganda – South, 1995	75	17	3

34   Sub-Saharan Surveys

C: *(Urban/Rural Comparisons)*

Country, date	Radio (%)	TV (%)	VCR (%)
Ghana – urban, 1995	75	52	9
Ghana – rural, 1995	63	22	2
Kenya – Nairobi, 1995	88	47	11
Kenya – rural, 1995	72	7	1
Mozambique – Maputo, 1995	88	60	25
Mozambique – Cabo Delgado, 1995	29	0	0
Sudan – Khartoum, 1995	77	67	20
Sudan – rural North, 1995	37	11	1
Namibia – urban, 1994	81	60	24
Namibia – rural, 1994	67	5	3
Tanzania – Dar es Salaam, 1995	90	27	10
Tanzania – rural, 1995	74	2	1
Zimbabwe – urban, 1994	76	54	11
Zimbabwe – rural, 1994	41	6	*

D *(urban areas where there is no rural data)*

Country, date	Radio (%)	TV (%)	VCR (%)
Mali – Bamako, 1993	96	58	18
Côte d'Ivoire – Abidjan, 1996	96	84	21
Sierra Leone – urban, 1992	74	9	3
Senegal – Dakar, 1995	97	75	24
Cameroon – Douala & Yaounde, 1996	91	63	25
Angola – Luanda & Huambo, 1966	74	57	23
Burkina Faso – urban areas, 1995	95	46	15

Appendix II: Recent survey data on media use

Data on the following pages are taken from surveys carried out in six different African countries showing trends over time. In every case, except in Senegal, the sample was designed to represent the population as a whole. These are probably the most reliable sets of data we have on household ownership of media equipment. Because it is a new and interesting phenomenon, I have also included VCR (video-cassette recorder) figures.

Each chart shows household ownership of television, radio and VCR sets in solid bars. It also shows weekly reach of radio and television among adults aged 15+.

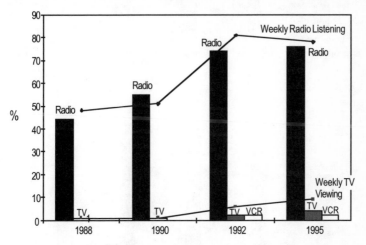

Figure 2.5   Tanzania: media trends, selected years 1988–95

The data show how important radio is in Africa. The great explosion of radio ownership in Africa happened between 1960 and 1970. Radio ownership is still growing, whereas television had a very slow and late start, having only recently arrived in Tanzania. And note here how important the VCR is, because television sets preceded transmitted television programmes. So if you had a television in Tanzania, in 1992, you had to have a VCR, otherwise you had nothing to watch, unless you were in Zanzibar, where there was a small television station.

Figure 2.6 shows the changes in Zambia: steady growth of radio over the years, continuing from 1972 to 1996.

The trends in weekly viewing and weekly listening are also shown in these charts. Both television and radio consumption have grown steadily, although recent results from some countries show a levelling off of radio and some decline in listening.

In Kenya, television growth has been very slow. This is unusual in comparison with some other countries in Africa. Kenya is a prosperous country compared with many others, but this prosperity has not translated into high levels of ownership of television. Radio ownership is much higher and continues to grow. But note how listening has levelled at about 80 per cent.

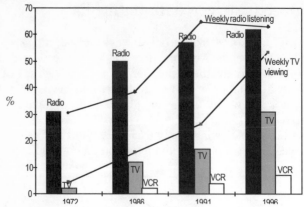

Figure 2.6 Zambia: media trends, selected years 1972–96

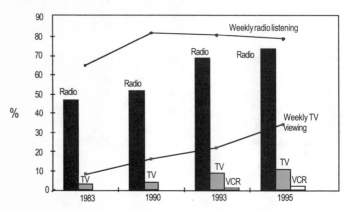

Figure 2.7 Kenya: media trends, selected years 1983–95

We have rather more limited data for West Africa, especially for Francophone countries. Most of the research in Francophone Africa has been confined to the cities only. It is only very recently that we have begun to get national data. The only countries in Francophone Africa for which we have national data are Senegal and Côte d'Ivoire. Unfortunately, for neither of them do we have trend data so we have to look at trends just in the cities.

In Senegal there is a very high penetration of radio in the city, meaning Greater Dakar and Pikine and the surrounding area. But there has been very rapid growth of television and of television viewing in Dakar in the period 1992–95.

In Ghana there has been a continual growth of radio. It levelled off in the 1980s and hardly changed at all, but then in the 1990s began to grow again, reflecting the regrowth of the Ghanaian economy in the early 1990s. We see television also lifting off there, reflecting greater economic prosperity, or relative prosperity, in Ghana.

As a last example of media equipment trends, we have some data from Nigeria, Africa's most populous country comprising 100 million people and more

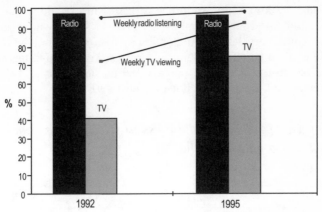

Figure 2.8   Senegal: Greater Dakar media trends, 1992 and 1995

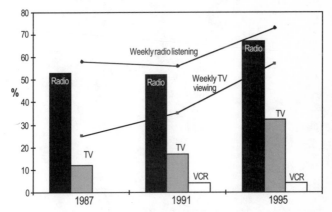

Figure 2.9   Ghana: media trends, selected years 1987–95

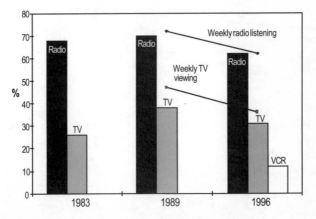

Figure 2.10   Nigeria: media trends, selected years 1983–96

television and radio stations than any other African country. But these are still heavily state-dominated. There is only one private station now in Lagos. Privatization has come very late to Anglophone Africa compared with Francophone. The radio is still a popular medium and has grown to a high level. But the recent economic downturn in Nigeria has affected media access and use. Radio and television access and use have declined in the 1990s.

Data on weekly use of radio, TV and press in selected Sub-Saharan African countries (* = data unavailable)

A (national data)

Country, date	Radio (%)	TV (%)	Newspapers (%)
Ethiopia, 1995	64	24	23
Ghana, 1995	73	57	*
Côte d'Ivoire, 1992	68	55	27
Kenya, 1996	79	33	*
Namibia, 1994	78	30	*
Nigeria, 1996	62	36	*
Senegal, 1992	95	69	*
South Africa, 1995	89	70	19
Tanzania, 1995	78	9	*
Zambia, 1996	57	36	25
Zimbabwe, 1994	57	31	36

B (partial coverage)

Country, date	Radio (%)	TV (%)	Newspapers (%)
Mozambique – 4 Provinces, 1995	48	21	17
Sudan – North, 1995	57	33	31
Uganda – South, 1995	79	16	*

C (urban/rural comparisons)

Country, date	Radio (%)	TV (%)	Newspapers (%)
Ghana – urban, 1995	76	72	*
Ghana – rural, 1995	72	50	*
Kenya – Nairobi, 1995	92	95	*
Kenya – rural, 1995	90	75	*
Mozambique – Maputo, 1995	85	74	55
Mozambique – Cabo Delgado, 1995	39	2	2
Sudan – Khartoum, 1995	75	65	61
Sudan – rural North, 1995	46	14	17
Namibia – urban, 1994	80	70	*
Namibia – rural, 1994	78	10	*

Tanzania – Dar es Salaam, 1995	92	67	*
Tanzania – rural, 1995	76	4	*
Zimbabwe – urban, 1994	86	74	71
Zimbabwe – rural, 1994	51	22	29

D *(urban areas where there are no rural data)*

Country, date	Radio (%)	TV (%)
Mali – Bamako, 1993	96	81
Ivory Coast – Abidjan, 1996	92	95
Sierra Leone – urban, 1992	73	15
Senegal – Dakar, 1995	99	93
Cameroon – Douala & Yaounde, 1996	95	87
Angola – Luanda & Huambo, 1966	69	65
Burkina Faso – urban areas, 1995	96	81

Note: Comparable data for newspaper readership is unfortunately available for only a few countries.

Charts showing media use in selected Sub-Saharan African countries

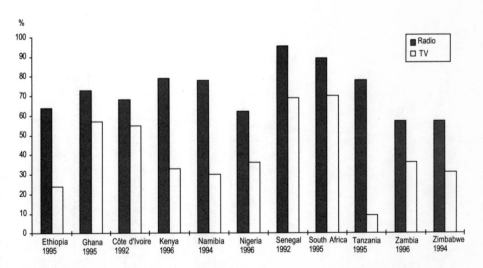

Figure 2.11 Weekly use of radio and TV in selected Sub-Saharan African countries (national data)

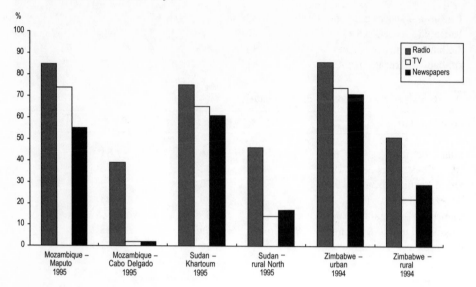

Figure 2.12 *Weekly use of radio, TV and press in Mozambique, Sudan and Zimbabwe with urban/rural comparisons*

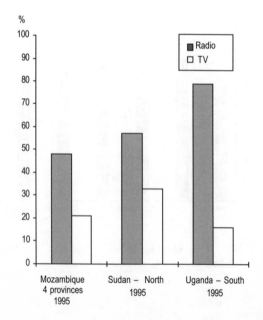

Figure 2.13 Weekly use of radio and TV in selected Sub-Saharan African countries (partial coverage)

References

BBC Monitoring Service (1989) *World Broadcast Information*, 20 October.

Fraenkel, Peter (1959) *Wayaleshi*, London: Weidenfeld and Nicolson.

Franklin, Harry (1950) *The Saucepan Special*, Lusaka: The Government Printer.

—— IBAR, BBC World Service (annual since 1955) *World Radio and Television Receivers*.

Kivikuru, Ullamaija (1990) *Tinned Novelties or Creative Culture? A Study on the role of Mass Communication in Peripheral Nations*, Helsinki: University of Helsinki.

Mangwende, Witness (1989) 'Electronic media development – how can developing countries benefit?' *Combroad*, December: 8–14.

Mytton, Graham (1974) *Listening, Looking and Learning*, Lusaka: Institute for African Studies.

—— (1976) 'The role of the mass media in nation building in Tanzania', PhD thesis, University of Manchester.

—— (1983) *Mass Communication in Africa*, London: Edward Arnold.

Mytton, Graham (ed.) (1993) *Global Audiences: Research for World-wide Broadcasting*, London: John Libbey.

Radio Tanzania (1974) *Audience Survey*.

Tanganyika Broadcasting Corporation (1960) *Audience Survey*.

3
Prospects for
Rural Radio in Africa

Strategies to Relate Audience Research
to the Participatory Production of Radio Programmes
JEAN-PIERRE ILBOUDO

The analysis I offer in this chapter largely derives from my own experience in the promotion of rural radio: first as a practitioner in Burkina Faso during the 1970s, then for a decade as a teacher in the same country at Centre inter-Africain d'etudes en radio rurale de Ouagadougou (CIERRO) (see Ilboudo 1992 for an analysis), and more recently as a communications officer for the Food and Agriculture Organization (FAO) in Rome. In all these roles, I have been challenged to find ways in which local people can be enabled to participate – far more than they do at present – in the production of radio programmes in Africa.

Currently, there are hundreds of millions of people, for whom it is difficult to establish democratic means of communication. Sometimes, particularly in developing countries, this can be explained by a lack of basic infrastructure, or by inadequate communication channels. But this is not the only cause. There are social and cultural minorities in industrialized countries which are disadvantaged by their exclusion from the democratic potential of communication technologies. The composition and extent of these groups varies from one country to another, as does the seriousness of their problems, but we find the communicationally deprived everywhere: the handicapped, the geographically isolated, those who are subjected to social, cultural or economic discrimination; ethnic, linguistic and religious minorities; women, children and the young. In some places, these groups are denied such fundamental rights as freedom of expression, or of opinion, or of congregation. Even larger numbers of people are disadvantaged by deep-rooted traditions and social attitudes; this is true above all for women, who represent more than half of the human population and who contribute as much as 80 per cent to the economy in African countries.

Recent years have seen an increasing number of initiatives to dismantle, or at least lower, the barriers to democratization which characterize the present situation of socio-political transition. As part of the process of democratization in Africa, the advent of community radio has enabled greater popular access to information systems, enhancing people's rights to respond to and criticize those who wield power. Diverse forms of feedback promote regular contacts between broadcasters and the public. All this might seem to respond to a need Bertolt Brecht identified as long ago as 1932,

> Radio must transform from being a means of diffusion to become a means of communication. Radio could become the most marvellous means of communication imaginable in public life, an immense conduit and it would be this if it were capable not only of broadcasting but also of receiving, of permitting listeners not just to listen, but also to speak; and not isolating them, but putting them in contact. (Brecht 1967 [1932]: 129)

Community radio does fulfil some of Brecht's ambitions. It has allowed non-professionals to take part in the production and broadcasting of programmes; and this has required them to use local sources of information actively; doing so has enabled the expression of their talents and, on occasions, their artistic creativity. Community radios create 'alternative means of communication', which are usually, but not invariably, local. Community radio enables those who use the media also to take part in management and decision-making; and such self-management is the most radical form of participation, since it involve numerous individuals, not just in making programmes and disseminating news, but actively taking part in the processes through which decisions about general policy are made.

However, these strengths of community radio in principle have often been its greatest weaknesses in practice. Indeed, programming would have been better had audience participation been greater; but many community radios hardly know their audiences and lack the methodological or material resources to get to know them. Rural radio has not in practice been as participatory as it is in principle and rhetoric, and this has prevented it fulfilling its true potential. In what follows, I shall survey the current state of audience research by rural radios, note its inadequacies, and then present an argument that the renewal of rural radio will depend on recognition of various similarities and compatibilities between the methodology of Participatory Rural Appraisal (PRA) and the use of rural radio as a tool of social enquiry. In short, both are designed to mediate between the village or rural area and its wider arena; and both are supposed to involve the former in representation to the latter. First, why has rural radio only partly fulfilled its initial promise? To answer this we need to look briefly at its history.

Two conferences important to the development of rural radio were held in 1966: one in Rwanda for Francophone Africa, the other in Tanzania for Anglophone Africa. Rural radio stations were established, sometimes on a shoestring, from 1968-9. Early programmes on agriculture were sponsored by UNESCO and FAO, but the stations concerned themselves additionally with health, family planning and a variety of cultural issues. Rural radio evolved rapidly, and produced programmes in the light of people's listening habits. Because each developed in relation to its listenership, these rural radio stations were more successful than, say, Radio Tribunale (which was introduced from Canada in 1941). In later years, the array of private, rural, community, religious and associative radio stations became increasingly and extraordinarily varied.

Such initiatives towards active participation were not restricted to Africa. There has been a tendency to decentralize the mass media in many industrialized countries: for instance by creating local radio stations, or increasing the numbers of programme production centres; and the introduction of cable television has accentuated this trend. As cultural instruments, the communication media promote or influence attitudes, motivate people and may favour the diffusion of models of behaviour which promote social integration. For millions of people, the communications media are the major channel through which they gain access to forms of creative, cultural expression. Faced by the 'synchronization of cultures' – via satellite transmissions and the other burgeoning pathways of cheap, commodified information – community radio needs to emphasize the values of local culture in the programmes it produces, and promote them as a counter-weight to external influence. This does not mean that community radios should be inward-looking; cultural development, whether local or national, cannot occur in isolation from other cultures. On the contrary, exchanges between community radios, and between different cultures and systems of values, are advantageous and may create a communication network both within and between communities.

Apart from globalization, numerous other challenges face community radio during the current period of socio-economic transition. These include their access to training, equipment and technology, as well as the legislative frameworks under which they operate. But I shall focus predominantly on a single challenge: community radios fundamentally have a single role, to serve the communities in which they are embedded. This means that, for their part, these communities will have to take responsibility for managing their radio stations and participating fully in the processes through which programmes are planned, drawn up, then produced and broadcast. Doing so, they need to draw upon forms of expression which belong to their community. This does not imply that they cannot learn from the experiences of other communities, or benefit from solidarity with all those associations, both regional and international, which work to promote the principles and practices of community radio. But the other side of this equation is the responsibility of those who run radio stations and produce programmes, to participate, come to know and identify with the communities they serve.

Knowing the audience

All this said, I must remark how much easier it is to sing the praises of radio as a means of communication and persuasion than to put these virtues into practice. As many African countries have recently learnt to their detriment, simply having educational radio is not enough to breathe new life into the development process and imbue it with an irreversible momentum. In so-called developing countries, the lack of all kinds of resources has meant that audience research has been undertaken infrequently; but such research is the broadcasters' only means to get to know the kinds of audiences they have, and to adapt their programmes to the aspirations and expectations of these listeners. In the absence of such research, broadcasters frequently address themselves to a potential public they imagine to share their own tastes and preoccupations; research often reveals that local preferences and concerns, however, do not correspond to those presumed by the people who run radio stations and make radio programmes.

Economic, linguistic and cultural factors all limit the accessibility of radio to its rural audiences. Notwithstanding the fact that we are currently witnessing an increasingly marked radio pluralism in Africa, the structures and systems of radio production, as well as the diffusion of information aimed at grassroots groups, largely remain in the hands of the African state. This state monopoly works against a democratization of media access which would allow programmes to be produced for and by grassroots groups. Instead, the state generates a unidirectional flow of educational and moralizing information based on a centralized model of communication, and it seldom involves those it addresses as participants. State broadcasting evolves as a function of public enlightenment programmes rather than in response to the preoccupations and aspirations of its grassroots listeners.

Centralized control of the communication media, combined with the economic crises that limit the resources that can be devoted to making and following up programmes, has meant that what appears in the media, especially on the radio, no longer even tries to identify and integrate the communicational and educational needs of its listeners. The fragility of some African states is unconducive to that decentralization or regionalization of radio which is a requirement of any process of participatory communication. Instead they restrict themselves to purely formal or highly regulated kinds of decentralization.

Who listens to rural radio? When, where and how do they listen? Which are the most popular programmes with different audiences? Has rural radio changed anything about the daily lives of its listeners? If rural radios cannot answer these questions, they will be unable to decide how radio programmes might evolve to take into account the needs expressed by their audience, and the contribution that the audience could, or might, want to make to this evolution. Audience studies carried out for rural radio in Africa are at best patchy. Yet they should be essential. As we shall see shortly, from the responses to three questions posed to 17 respondents, few rural radio stations have even a basic knowledge of their, audience, and so have no basis on which to encourage their participation.

The blame for this situation is not necessarily individual. People who work in radio have often been trained abroad in western schools, and the methods they have learned to survey audience participation simply cannot be applied in a rural context. More extensive audience researches in West African countries such as Benin, Mali, Senegal and Burkina Faso, have not been completed, and they are anyway insufficiently systematic or regular. The results of such surveys are often not used – even by those in charge of rural radio. Several UNICEF projects, especially those targeted at women and children, have carried out their own assessment of the impact of their programmes on developmental issues such as fishing and forestry. These narrow surveys, together with others conducted by NGOs, may not be wholly representative but do give some idea of the kind of popular participation that exists. However, being externally funded, such audience surveys take place irregularly, and may not even be available to rural radio stations. The fundamental fact is that because rural radio has not been organized on a self-sustaining financial basis, for the past 30 years radio journalists and broadcasters in Africa have simply not controlled the means of knowing their audiences.

As we have seen, when rural radio came to West Africa in the 1960s, it was funded by external aid. All the programmes were produced in French or English, regardless of the fact that most people in rural areas spoke neither language.

When the money stopped flowing, the programmes ceased to exist; and broadcasters, instead of going out to the field, would sit in their offices and create scripts which were without interest to their audience. In 1990, the World Bank began to heavily subsidize the educational, informational and foreign affairs sectors of African countries. Since few radio stations were able to get money from the state directly, they instead made proposals for programmes which could be funded under this pattern of sectoral support. But such programme funding did not usually include follow up surveys. There ensued a situation in which state radio might indeed broadcast programmes on matters to which it was committed, but it had no idea who listened to them.

The picture was slightly better in parts of Anglophone Africa – Tanzania, Zimbabwe, Zambia and The Gambia – where a number of audience studies were conducted under the auspices of the BBC. These employed various methods (including listeners' letters, phone-ins, survey fieldwork and group interviews). Only by knowing its audience can a radio station effectively focus the content of programmes targeted to particular listeners. Because broadcasting in rural areas is expensive, it really is worthwhile for rural radio teams to reflect upon their methods for matching programmes and listeners. As my colleague in audience research, Graham Mytton, has pointed out, commercial companies invariably undertake effective audience research as part of their market strategy for advertising. Radio people tend not to collaborate with advertisers, but, as Mytton succinctly put it, 'there is no reason why the devil should have the best tunes.'

Three questions were sent to respondents in 17 African countries to gain some indications of the state of audience research. What are the existing ways of finding out about the audience and what studies have been carried out in terms of them? What mechanisms exist for feedback to reach the rural radio? What methods and tools are used to measure the impact of programmes transmitted by the rural radio? The country-by-country results recorded in the appendix to this chapter make interesting and unsettling reading. I have indicated my questions where appropriate by number only, and acknowledged my respondent in each case. The picture that emerges is very patchy and generally unsatisfactory. Few rural radio stations can answer the most basic questions about their audiences. Where information is available, this is often by means of research carried out by partner organizations which used the facilities of radio as part of their development programme or campaign. The techniques used by the radio stations themselves – where these exist – are over-reliant on listeners' letters, telephone calls and somewhat random encounters with the public. Research methodology is largely absent, and what techniques there are hardly promote meaningful participation. These current inadequacies are one of the grounds for my urging the adoption of participatory strategies derived from PRA which could make good many of these deficiencies.

Rural radio as a tool for social enquiry

While it is far from exhaustive, the survey of audience research by African radio stations is enough to confirm the daunting task rural radios face in getting to know rural societies better. If radio communication is to be a tool for thought and for forging relations, it has to encourage profound mutual understanding. Radio broadcasters have to learn how to listen to their audience, get to know them and use their language. But this will require what is effectively an epistemological break with the present illusion of transparency which lends credibility to the idea of the fieldtrip as an occasion simply to collect information from the local population rather than to listen to them. Radio should be used as a tool of social enquiry that enables listeners to play a real part in the production of programmes.

The methodology of PRA has long remained unknown to rural radio communicators. In what follows, I want to compare some of the different stages and tools used in PRA with the techniques and methods employed in the production of rural radio broadcasts while out in the field. My point is that they are sufficiently similar to learn from one another and complement each other.

Partner organizations in rural development have conceded that the social surveys which often preceded big radio campaigns were unsatisfactory (as my appendix shows, they have been responsible for most in-depth surveys of audience reaction.) At best, even when these surveys were well done, their prospectuses were often written in only the official language (French or English) so that workers on the ground had to reconstrue them in local languages before they could be used for a specific radio campaign. At worst, radio interviews subsequently carried out in the languages spoken by people in their daily lives showed a complete mismatch between their expressed opinions and attitudes and those attributed to them by such sociological investigations.

However, preferable methodologies – such as those used by most rural radio stations in West Africa concerned with forest fires emphasized the way in which decentralized rural radio itself acted as a tool of social enquiry, as well as a way of listening attentively to the people among whom they lived. Thus, sociological enquiries and radio reports in rural areas ceased to be simply information raids and became genuine ways of listening to the people.

This is the approach I want to present, experiment with and deepen to see whether it is able to inspire a genuinely participant method of research. It goes without saying that this would be in the interests of radio, but it would also benefit all the other services and projects that take a genuine interest in what rural people think and want. It is up to broadcasters to get to know this participatory methodology, and to experiment with some of its techniques on the ground so as to develop a participative and interactive use of rural radio. Experience shows that some of the techniques of PRA are well adapted to rural radio, while others are more or less so depending on whether the scope of rural radio is central, regional or local.

Introduction to PRA applied to radio

It is useful to identify the similarities between the different stages and different techniques of PRA, on the one hand, and the methods of radio production on the ground, on the other, because I want to survey the various stages of both. In summary these stretch from the participatory formulation of villagers' ideas and needs, to the formulation of a plan of action and its execution, to the eventual follow-up research. Radio itself is at one and the same time both a tool which allows people to participate in the production of broadcasts, and a tool of social enquiry capable of investigating the rural milieu and evaluating development programmes. Identifying all the aspects and methodological tools that need to be taken into account to elaborate a participatory method for rural radio opens a whole new avenue of research; one which takes into account the problems of reliability in the information provided by the accounts of experts coming from abroad who may be less than fully aware of realities on the ground.

What are the aims of rural radio practitioners in the field? They should want:

- to create an instrument that will improve the quality of dialogue between farmers and technicians;
- to provide tools for democratization that will facilitate people's participation in development;
- to create a method for articulating better what radio offers with the concerns of different audiences;
- to find a way to restore a voice to the people;
- to find a method which allows people to play a part in evaluation.

These aims are enmeshed in particular problems:

- of involving people in debates which concern their future;
- of gathering information which is true and locally authored, and making sure that it is broadcast during peak listening times to those interested;
- of really discovering what rural people want;
- of approaching rural people and their lives in all of their diversity.

How do these aims mesh with a participatory approach? At the mention of the notion of participation, one thinks immediately of the *Méthode accélérée de recherche participative* (MARP) in French, or of Rapid Rural Appraisal (RRA) in English. The well-known names of Mamadou Bara Gueye or Robert Chambers, and other no less important points of reference, spring to mind. In West Africa, the participatory approach also goes back to the *Pédagogie diobass* formulated by Emmanuel Ndione, Hughes Dupriez and Pierre Jacolin; and there certainly exist other methodologies and pedagogies relevant to participation. PRA, which belongs to this family of methodologies, is a particularly powerful method for research in rural development. It is based on the work of an interdisciplinary team, which combines diverse techniques to gather and analyse information. These techniques require the team to hold extensive and informal dialogues with local people, taking into consideration local conditions and local customs; at the same time, the approach uses second-hand information, such as maps and administrative reports. PRA may take several days or months to carry out, depending on the objectives one wants to attain, the scale of the rural setting, the road conditions and means of transport employed. In a nutshell, one can define PRA as a sequence of interdisciplinary activities with the following characteristics:

- PRA is intensive and expedient, characterized by a process of rapid learning and work efficiency;
- it is based on small interdisciplinary teams, which enables the exploration of subjects that cannot be analysed from a single perspective;
- it uses methods that are specifically chosen, starting from a range of tools and techniques relevant to several disciplines;

- it is concerned with local knowledge, combining it with modern scientific expertise;
- it enables an exhaustive understanding, through a quick series of interactions in the field;
- it is pertinent and relatively low-cost from the point of view of time and money invested;
- it tests and verifies discoveries with special techniques of direct observation, trials and triangulation;
- it significantly reduces the process of planning, undertaking and analyzing research;
- it is scientific, practical and uses a friendly form of methodology.

Teams on the ground may apply a participatory approach in various ways, but in general its stages may be summarized as follows: information and familiarization (study of the milieu); sensitization or conscientization; identification of problems and solutions (hierarchization); programme formulation; organization; technical training; follow-up evaluation; self-evaluation. Villagers participating in the research are actively responsible for the ideas and actions that take place at every one of these stages.

Rural radio as a tool for social enquiry

As set out above, it is clear that the convergences between the aims of rural radio and PRA are numerous. However, until very recently, rural radio usually touched rural areas only as an agency that extended the range of rural mobilization or popularization (senses covered by the precise, yet difficult to translate, French *vulgarisation*). It was, not accidentally, during the 1980s that several researchers and practitioners in communication began to think about and draw attention to the participatory and interactive character of rural radio. This questioning of the use of radio coincided with the development of PRA, and the two developed in parallel, often drawing upon the same disciplinary sources and borrowing some techniques from one another. Rural radio is already used in several FAO projects which employ a participatory approach to communication. In these projects, rural radio has primarily contributed to two stages of project implementation: the initial stage of familiarization and study of context, and the final stage of evaluation of the activities and actions implemented. Through such techniques as public participation in broadcasts, community interviews and chat shows, rural radio has been a particularly effective instrument for gaining information and evaluating project impact, especially with respect to self-evaluation by project members. By giving voice to villagers in the most participatory forms of broadcasting, such as programmes in which members of the public have unrestrained licence to express themselves, rural radio enables a kind of triangulation to take place. When all the social categories of a village or rural community are involved in a public debate, opinions may be gathered on a particular theme that differ according to the age, sex, geographic location and social conditions of their proponents. Together with chat shows and interviews, this allows one to come to an evaluation or assessment of the impact of a policy and its implementation.

Such use of radio as a tool of social research requires that a certain number of conditions are satisfied beforehand. This leads me to a discussion of the way in which rural radio is used nowadays, from the point of fieldwork methodology. I am not going to dwell on the practical preparation of equipment used on field-trips. Taking this for granted, I want to stress the importance of the three or four days spent on familiarization. Few teams, perhaps even none, spend this much time. Too often fieldwork is organized on the lines of a raid, during which the producer alone plays a central role: he decides the programme themes, then makes highly directive programmes, may by chance stay a night in the village, and never evaluates what he has broadcast. Far from being participatory, using rural radio this way entirely debars it from being a tool of social enquiry.

A methodology for the participatory and interactive use of rural radio

Organizing fieldwork in rural radio involves both the collection of materials and the editing and broadcasting of them.

Preliminary fieldwork

First, as with all collections of material, the initial preparatory phase is funda-mental: gathering information and documentation on all aspects, domains and sectors of rural people and their lives. This is why the first methodological principle recommended is interdisciplinarity: the rural radio team has to under-stand and work with specialists from other sectors and domains of development interested in rural radio activities (agriculture, health, stock-breeding, water and afforestation, social affairs, etc).

Second, there is the time required for preparation: three or four weeks before going out, a smaller team visits the designated site for three or four days. There they collect secondary data on the village through the administrative structures, institutions of assistance and support, and by conversing with representatives of different social strata (customary chiefs, imams, village groups, etc) in order to gather as much information as possible so as to understand the people with whom they will produce a series of rural radio broadcasts. It is important that the team reconstructs the history of the village and identifies, along with various social groups, the themes that the villagers hope to discuss with rural radio and the problems that face them, as well as their aspirations. The team should make a tour of the village in order to understand its extent and its spatial layout. All this collected data will have to be collated and written up in a report; this will be used by the larger team, before going into the field, to distribute various tasks and to plan activities.

It is indispensable that, during this preliminary phase, a good initial relation-ship is established with the people and their main representatives: the village chief, the customary chief, the imam, the heads of village groups and of the groups with common economic interests, the heads of associations, the managers of decentralized technical services who intervene in village life, even if these services remain at the level of the *préfecture, sous-préfecture* or *département*.

Knowing whom to inform, with whom to negotiate and who decides is also essential. Precautions must be taken to specify the intended period (dates) of rural radio fieldwork and the duration of the team's stay (from a week to 10 days). This specification enables the planners to discuss any possible constraints that could arise during that time (important economic activities, ritual ceremonies, religious feasts, periods of heavy work), before reaching a collective decision which takes into consideration the availability of both parties. The problem of accommodation while out in the field, as well as the preparation of meals, will have to be discussed. In summary, the preparatory team will have to:

- gather secondary data ranging from place of residence to the institutional services provided on the ground;
- understand the history of the village working in conjunction with the person or people authorized to do this;
- use conversational techniques adapted to the situation in the field in order to verify, explore in more depth or understand a theme, problem, or situation.

Types of Interview Associated with Stages of Investigation

Types of investigation	Type of interview		
	Non-directed	Directed	Semi-directed
Exploratory	X		
Verification		X	X
Detailed		X	X

These interview techniques will be used in getting to understand the history of the village (non-directed), the geography of the area (the countryside, the rainfall), obtaining data on health, agriculture, plants, livestock breeding, cultural aspects (ethnic groups, family relations, customs, interests). They enable one simultaneously to understand the social achievements (schools, nursing homes, dispensaries), the infrastructure (dams, etc), and the various problems that villagers have to deal with (by directed interviews). The team will also need to tour the village to have an idea of the spatial and the geographical circumstances of the inhabitants and of the vegetation (gardens, woods, tree nurseries, dams, waterways).

Once back at the national or regional rural radio station, the team will have to put together all the data, organize the information and present it in the form of an accessible report which should cover the following:

1. The geographical features of the locality (the village) in relation to the radio station, the *préfecture, sous-préfecture* or *département*, and with respect to other regions, provinces, and neighbouring villages.
2. The history of the village (and significance of its name; toponymy in general), the name of its founder, its myth of foundation, other ethnic groups, customs,

prohibitions and important events (festivals, rituals).
3. The functions of administrative services and NGOs in the village.
4. The social and physical infrastructure.
5. Interesting achievements, past or future (communal development projects).
6. Problems and the solutions envisaged for them.
7. Themes suggested by villagers.
8. An analysis of all this information viewed from the angle of a fieldtrip by the rural radio.

Preparation for going into the field

Other than precautions taken to ensure the correct functioning of technical equipment (checking recording materials and testing all the technical equipment), the rural radio team will need: a meeting to discuss the division of tasks in the field; briefings with the sound technician, driver and rural radio producer; contacts with the agent or agents of technical services (agriculture or livestock, health, education, waterworks, social affairs), depending on the specific or particular features of the regions or themes to be dealt with. The meeting will need to define the themes or subjects to be dealt with based on the report of the exploratory team and analysis of the information they gathered.

The preliminary work session will also have to consider the techniques used for gathering data, the communication tools and radio genres to be used: public discussion broadcasts, oral traditions, local music, proverbial tales, chat shows, interviews, information programmes and what themes will be chosen for discussion. Finally, the team will decide upon prizes to award to the best participants in public broadcasts.

Going into the field: staying in the village

This may involve staying in one or several villages, and it is strongly recommended to choose neighbouring villages which have the same cultural (and linguistic) characteristics.

First day: the trip will begin quite early in the morning in order to have the time to conduct the usual formalities (courtesy visit to the *préfet, sous-préfet,* district chief) before arriving in the village around midday or at least before nightfall. Once in the village, the members of the team will go to greet all those in charge and then make their way to the huts or lodging provided to accommodate them.

Second day: the team begins to mix with the locals; they participate in events or activities going on at the time (baptisms, funerals, cultural events, agricultural work). All team members must take part in participatory observation in order to familiarize themselves with local faces and the environment and establish initial relationships. During the second night, the team may be able to organize a cultural evening, during which traditional music, tales and proverbs can be recorded; use of a public address system will allow the local populace to follow elements of oral tradition gathered, as well as creating a lively atmosphere.

Third day: the team begins to get to know their interlocutors in the village,

and to identify the themes and the subjects which could be used for the programmes they will produce (chat shows, public debates, interviews, informational
and/or thematic programmes and elements for micro-programmes). This third
day will be dedicated to visits and informal discussions, so as to prepare for the
production of transmissions. The team should begin to prepare discussion guidelines by the evening.

Fourth day: either the team continues the preparation for informal discussions
and the elaboration of interview guidelines, or they begin the first interviews
when they feel that some trust has been established with the people. It is only
then that recorders, microphones and cables should be brought out.

Fifth day: after gathering information through the use of different radio genres,
as many programmes as possible are made at the villagers' places of work.

Sixth day: the final full day sees all the material put together, using a variety
of radio genres; at the very least materials must be sufficient to create a mixed
programme of information on particular themes (involving interviews, music,
sound effects, testimonies, statements and proverbs). That afternoon or evening,
the team organizes a group discussion on the theme of rural radio, and listens to
criticisms made by villagers about the programmes, about the broadcasters,
listening hours, signal reception, listeners' thematic requirements, etc.

Seventh day: at the end of the stay, the rural radio team thanks all the key
people in the village, and the region. The team leaves all its remaining provisions
with the villagers. If the team decides to spend 10 days in the field, it will have
two extra days for work which will allow further consolidation.

This methodology which is valid for national (or centralized) rural radios and
for regional rural radios, but less so for local rural radios was developed by
CIERRO in Ouagadougou at the beginning of the 1980s. The centre used it to
train its students in rural radio. The same training also developed the idea of
'rural radio days' during which villagers conceived and produced rural radio programmes for themselves once the radio tools (microphones, wires and recorders)
had been demystified for them. This, a shining example of peasant participation
in radio, deserves to be encouraged.

Rural radio is currently in need of a second wind so that participatory and
interactive broadcasts become more real, numerous and systematic. This can be
achieved only by being rigorous in the preparation and execution of fieldwork,
and by using techniques for gathering information which are more lively and
interactive (public discussions, chat shows, semi-directed interviews). I have
argued that assessment of, and research on, rural radio as a tool for social
enquiry should draw upon participatory methods (such as RRA/MARP, PRA, or
Diobass) so as to enrich the interactive dimension of rural radio. Rural radio's
flexibility, energy, accessibility and spontaneity deal it a series of trump cards
that should ensure the physical, expressive and cognitive participation of rural
people. If this is not happening, then the fault lies not with rural radio itself, but
with the way it is used. I trust that the reader will already have recognized a
gulf between the survey of audience research I presented earlier and the
methodology now proposed. Next I want to consider how this methodology can
be refined further.

Extending the active methodology of participatory research

The characteristics of PRA

As already noted, the active methodology of participatory research, or PRA, used in rural areas is particularly appropriate for interdisciplinary teams. By using some of its methods and techniques of research, such teams are able to familiarize themselves quickly and effectively with situations and problems in the rural world. The most significant characteristic of PRA as a research methodology is that it gives priority to knowledge of and about local people; this knowledge accrues not only from local people's long experience but also from the investigators' scientific methodology. The practitioner of PRA seeks to draw the best result from the relation between these two types of knowledge. Before its arrival in Africa around the mid-1980s, precursors of PRA had appeared in the 1960s. Again the date is not accidental. This was a time when researchers recognized setbacks in the simple transference of technology to poor countries; by the 1970s and 1980s the new method was widely used in Asian countries. Fundamentally, PRA is a simple research method that can be used in the planning, study or evaluation of all development actions. We have seen how, over a few days, the PRA team collects information and establishes an inventory on an area. But, just as importantly, the team has to seek out those moments of interaction which allow them to evaluate their own activities and programmes and to set tasks for the following days. Before leaving the field, the team should present the results of their enquiries to the local people, inviting their corrections and improvements. It is through these reciprocal interactions, as much as by its more formal tools, that PRA achieves a better understanding of the realities of the rural world and of those who live there. It values the knowledge and experience they have accumulated, which is the foundation of local cultures and technologies, and gives it the respect it deserves by constituting traditional knowledge as one of the dominant subjects of research.

Four different types of PRA methodology may be distinguished:

1. Exploratory PRA consists of a ground-clearing or first stage of project planning in which preliminary hypotheses are defined that call for more intensive research.
2. Thematic PRA is used to answer a specific key question, or look more deeply into a problem.
3. Participatory PRA involves the rural population in all the stages of a development project from the identification of needs until the final project evaluation.
4. Follow-up PRA, as the term suggests, follows up actions previously undertaken.

PRA has several key concepts:

1. PRA is a process of *apprenticeship*. Its methodology involves the collection of facts on the ground so as to reinforce critical appraisal and deepen researchers' understanding of the phenomena they study.
2. It is interested in *traditional knowledge*. Researchers should not only trust their own knowledge but also respect and take into account the knowledge of the village community.

3. PRA is an *iterative* process which encourages researchers to revise their approach and hypotheses in the light of an improved knowledge of the problems under study.
4. PRA is *flexible*; while researchers need a clear vision of the types of information sought, they must also be prepared to adapt themselves flexibly to new situations.
5. PRA is open to *innovation* in the evolution of its tools and methods.
6. PRA is *interactive*, encouraging interaction both among researchers and between researchers and local people.
7. PRA is based on participation; researchers must not think of the people they question as objects of study but as fellow actors involved in the process of research.
8. PRA is *multidisciplinary* both in the range of problems it addresses and the researchers it involves.
9. PRA is a process of exploration; the best outcomes are the least anticipated. Curiosity is one of the chief virtues of PRA, and researchers should be prepared to discover that their focuses of interest can change over the course of a study.

The tools of PRA

The tools used to collect materials during PRA are numerous: direct observation, group interviews, diagrams, games and role-playing, anecdotes, proverbs, workshops and visual tools that vary with the type of information sought.

Three types of tool are used to investigate the temporal constitution of a village community. A historical profile is used to get to know the history of a village: the significance of its name, who founded it, what great events have marked its history. Recurrent temporal features are entered on a seasonal calendar, which records the activities of people during the year and gives a precise idea of the problems they face at different times, and how time is divided up locally. Finally, there is the historical matrix, especially relevant to the exploitation of natural resources, which allows a better understanding of any given opportunity in time.

To organize spatial materials, PRA makes maps to represent the village territory and to visualize the way space is filled, resources and activities localized, and the problems arising from this. Two types of map are generally used: maps of the village (with homes and infrastructure) and resource maps (showing soil types and land use). Maps also show information on topography, vegetation, agro-ecological zones, water resources, and so on. The transect is a tool used to synthesize information on an area; villagers who know the place well describe a topographical cross-section showing the principal zones of land usage.

Social and institutional data are systematized using Venn diagrams which simplify complex information into a condensed, visual form that make them easier to understand. Venn diagrams are especially useful for collecting information on people and organizations (both within and outside the village). Following an introductory talk, a Venn diagram should be made on the ground as follows: the boundaries of the village are represented by a circle; individuals, groupings, associations, institutions and so forth are represented, according to type, by cut-out figures, usually in four sizes. Everything inside the village is represented within the circle; everything outside the village is represented outside the circle. Intersections are represented by superimposed circles; the degree of superimposition indicates the closeness of collaboration between two or more related elements. Ideally, local people should carry out this task themselves, while the investigator notes criteria of differentiation from the placement of the figures; the intensity of relations can also be marked by arrows. Flow diagrams can also be used to show the relations between different entities, represent other localities with which the village maintains relations and indicate the intensity of those relations.

Socio-economic information can be systematized using matrices: preference matrices present the preferences of a local population by order of magnitude; matrices of wealth classify the social categories which exist in the village. The problem tree establishes relations of cause and effect among phenomena.

PRA and rural radio: application

Preparing for a fieldtrip by a rural radio requires that inventories of the tools both of PRA and of rural radio be drawn up. The two are similar in many respects: there is a counterpart in rural radio to virtually all the tools I have presented from PRA. Thus, the tools of rural radio can be used in PRA, and vice versa. Exploratory PRA is appropriate to central, regional or local types of rural radio; thematic PRA may be particularly helpful to regionally-based rural radios; a local radio station which knows its audience more closely will still benefit from follow-up PRA to gauge the impact of its programmes.

Here, it may be useful to mention briefly the conclusions of an experiment in participatory methodology carried out with the rural radio station of Kaolack, in Senegal, in 1996. This experience demonstrated that language is the single most important variable in the application of PRA. It also showed that it was difficult to both make a transect and carry out interviews at the same time. Having identified a particular zone or theme, it was very time-consuming (not to say arduous) to interrupt the transect walk in order to carry out interviews. By way of compensation, the work done during the transect proved to be a fertile source of themes that could later be explored in radio magazine programmes, and some of these provided programmes in their own right (on topography, soils, water, vegetation, land-holding, social problems). On these grounds, it is probably a good idea for the smaller team to make a transect during the preliminary investigations before the main fieldtrip.

The research did reinforce the general sense that rural radio has everything to gain by taking inspiration from PRA. Especially useful was the value PRA accords to traditional means of communication (griots, town criers, puppets), allowing radio to exploit the possibilities of these instead of being based entirely on exogenous genres. We found that the historical profile was imprecise, although to a tolerable degree, while the matrices were judged too complicated. Both direct observation and drawing up the seasonal calendar had the virtue of foregrounding the perceptions of peasants rather than those of fund-holders. With these reservations, the most valuable tools of PRA for enquiry in rural areas are: the resource map (apt for the introduction to a public debate), the historic profile, the transect, focus group discussion, direct observation, Venn diagrams and various interviews. The overall conclusion of the research reinforced the conviction that it is necessary to find a new way of using rural radio as a tool of social enquiry, and that PRA will be one, but only one, element of that initiative. However, this result is a far cry from the sense of some participants in the workshop that they were already seasoned users of PRA.

It is important to stress again how, in many of our African countries, rural radio is still used only to send out information at the beginning of campaigns, or assess impact at their end. Restricted to these roles, rural radio cannot fulfil its primary vocation which is to be the property of rural people. To redress this situation methods like PRA must be taught in schools of journalism and communication (as at CIERRO), and their use popularized at the various workshops and seminars where journalists and communicators gather. Training schools in communication should seek to renew and enhance the basic skills of those who presently run rural radio, so as to break with the sorts of routine that currently risk becoming entrenched in our radio stations. PRA offers a fresh dynamic to rural radio because it provides a new image of what makes for good programmes and how they should be produced. In this context, it is worth reiterating that rural radio and PRA have a shared commitment to the use of local languages.

PRA and rural radio: comparison

In the ways that they collect information both PRA and rural radio put familiarity with the rural world, and the knowledge of villagers, first. They share the thesis that peasants know their countryside better than experts coming from elsewhere. Of course, in order to achieve the best results, in both cases the researchers manage two bodies of knowledge: scientific, structured knowledge acquired through education, and the diffuse and unstructured knowledge familiar to peasants. The contingency of the second type of knowledge invites us to accept a margin of imprecision: not all the knowledge given by the peasant to the researcher is necessarily true. In any case, both systems seek to bring together the maximum information possible in a limited time. Both need a clear conception, in advance, of what they want to learn from the peasant. In both cases, accounts given by informants, as journalists know well, are not to be considered true unless they are verified from several sources; this is what PRA calls triangulation. Against this, one notes that the interaction and common efforts of the researcher and local population, envisaged by PRA as a way of regularly reviewing the information collected, is also shared by radio as a preoccupation with correcting errors. Both systems are aware of the factors which often constitute barriers or handicaps to the collection of good information: this is called 'bias' in PRA and applies equally to rural radio.

Against these similarities, it is worth underlining some differences. Programme-makers in rural radio, being generally known to their listeners, are more easily accepted and integrated. This is clearly an advantage in the collection of information. Moreover, rural radio enjoys a form of interaction with the people which is its own: the broadcast public debate. Throughout Africa, these encounters between rural radio and peasants are almost like popular festivals; this is where the researcher can collect rare information on the real concerns of the people in their liveliest form.

However, these public events should not be allowed to obscure the research objectives which will be met in different forms (maps, diagrams, calendars, matrices, figures, tables, etc). The fieldtrip to the village of Keur Ndiankou (described above) allowed us to conjoin some of the tools of PRA and rural radio. From this it transpired that the transect, little known or little used in rural radio, provided a good knowledge of the milieu in which investigations were being conducted; but more than this, being a random method of sampling it was also a precious and hardy tool, both useful in itself and a source from which to draw plenty of subjects for making other programmes, or planning a listener survey.

Inspired by some of the techniques of PRA, and using its own methods, rural radio has shown itself to be a vital tool, one capable of serving sponsors who want to avail themselves of serious enquiries, from the heart of the rural world, in the certainty that the results they will receive are close to the daily lived realities of their target population.

The way forward

To conclude, my experience in CIERRO and FAO suggests that rural radio can be used as part of development-related investigative processes in rural areas, providing the following points are explored to elaborate a participatory methodology.

First, rural radio teams in charge of a social enquiry project must themselves understand the objectives being pursued, so that they are able in turn to explain them to the people concerned. This preliminary work is done at the radio station itself.

Secondly, communal meetings with the populace, especially with leading members, are imperative and must occur even before the effective start of the survey, to ascertain the history of the village, the people's concerns, the projects already under way, and the political and social situation in the village. This is the moment for finding information for the elaboration of a village map, with its buildings, its activities, the characteristics of its populace, its living areas and its wealth. This is much more than a matter of simply finding one's way.

The third step is the heart of the enquiry – going out into the field for several days, familiarizing oneself with the place, its problems and its major opportunities – which is done by employing PRA tools, such as the transect with key informants and semi-structured local interviews. This is also the moment to discuss their problems with local people, and analyse them together, drawing up a real map of the area, and conducting interviews with resourceful people.

The fourth step is to analyse the strategies and main problems, category by category, notably through the medium of individual interviews which is a speciality of radio. This is the moment to bring out recording equipment, microphones and cables. PRA tools, such as Venn diagrams, are another precious aid for understanding the village institutions and their inter-relations.

Fifth, the rural radio teams may then get together in order to make initial analyses of opportunities for research and action. These participatory analyses should focus on the main problems suggested by the locals, their causes and their consequences. This step can be schematized in terms of the problem tree.

Sixth, the preceding step naturally leads to the analysis and hierarchization of possible solutions. In a participatory spirit, it is important to obtain the agreement of the people concerned on the activities to be pursued; their precise contribution to the resolution of their problems, and what will be asked for as assistance from outside. In the purist tradition of rural radio, this phase will take place during broadcast public discussions with prizes distributed to the winners.

The seventh and last step is a synthesis of everything on which people have made up their minds, arrived at in discussion with prominent members of the community or with people interviewed. This is followed by finalization of the field report by the researchers, and an internal evaluation of the work of the investigating team. One ought to conclude by making each person responsible for follow-up actions decided collectively.

I began by contrasting the high aspirations and potentialities of rural radio with its increasingly compromised practices. There are many marginalized communities in the world, and amelioration of their condition requires that they be enabled to participate in the media of communication that are in principle theirs. A participatory approach to rural radio, taking account of methods that derive from PRA, would go a long way towards mediating several divisions: between the information-rich and the information-poor, between developers and those they seek to affect, and between the high ideals and the less than ideal practices of community radio.

Appendix: A survey of audience research on rural radio in African countries

1) Existing audience research, 2) research feedback to radios, 3) how impact is measured (see p. 46 for details).

Benin (Jacques-Philippe da Matha)

1. Rural radio stations in Cotonou and in Parakou have no way of investigating their audience. No very recent study has been made on this subject. Some studies were made at the time of FAO aid, but no copies of these documents exist at the General Management of ORTB, other than of a study undertaken in April 1988 on the rural radio service during the first phase of the project ('Itinerant local rural radio PIDC/UNESCO/BEN').
2. There are no reliable mechanisms other than letters sent in by members of the audience, gossip and rumour (*radio trottoir*), and rare occasions of live broadcasting.
3. The impact of particular programmes is evaluated by whatever agencies use rural radio; they assess how far the population has been mobilized in terms of the penetration of the themes that have been broadcast or the success of campaigns which are periodically promoted through rural radio. This is what happened in the cases of UNICEF village water supply projects, conservation

schemes, etc. There are no scientific techniques that allow the regular survey of opinion among audiences of rural radio. On paper, a unit, Studies of Promotion and Marketing, was created within the Public Relations division of the ORTB. In fact, this does not exist.

Burkina Faso (Bassirou Diallo)

1. There are no existing tools for measuring or knowing radio audiences in Burkina Faso. Studies that have so far been undertaken on this subject are far from exhaustive; nevertheless, a study was completed jointly by the Ministry of Communications and Culture together with the National Institute of Statistics and Population Studies and UNICEF entitled 'A survey of listeners in the town of Ouagadougou and rural radio audiences in the Ouagadougou region' (project submitted on completion of studies at CIERRO).
2. Mechanisms which enable feedback relating to rural radio include the following: (a) letters from the audience to rural radio – participating in topical debates broadcast (such as female circumcision, family planning, the role of women in society), or asking for clarification of subjects previously discussed; (b) informal exchanges between rural radio employees and listeners when such employees go out to meet them; of particular concern to investigators are the most popular broadcasting times for rural radio, as well as whether the themes discussed meet the audience's interests, (c) feedback is also gathered through the reactions of partner organizations to the broadcasting of their programmes on rural radio; these reactions are often apparent at the end of a campaign, when the target groups for whom the programmes were made come back with appeals for clarification and further information. Unfortunately, these mechanisms have not been formalized but arise spontaneously in the light of the subjects dealt with.
3. Here again, there are no existing means for measuring the impact of programmes, although an experiment was attempted in the course of a German–Burkinabe project in the 1970s and 1980s, with listeners' clubs in regional development centres. The end of the project also marked the end of this initiative. However, some assessments have been undertaken on broadcast campaigns by the partner organizations which sponsored them. The results of these assessments have not been reflected back to the rural radio stations. The documentation on which the assessment reports are based tends to disappear even at the partner organizations. So that rural radio is not always preaching in the desert, it would be better able to fulfil its role if mechanisms were established for gauging audience reaction to programmes. Surveys using the methods and tools of opinion research should be carried out at least once every two years.

Central African Republic (Bernard Yoro)

1. The first audience survey was undertaken in 1988. That study helped to establish the best times for radio transmissions targeted to rural people, and programme scheduling was revised in this light.

2. Audience feedback on rural radio essentially comes from: listeners' letters; fieldtrips; peasant and pastoralist groups; development partners using the airwaves of rural radio; correspondents' reports; provincial administrative authorities (including *préfets, sous-préfets* and mayors), sectoral development workers; telephone calls; and sometimes directly on air.

3. The German development agency (GTZ) has been planning a rural radio audience survey since 1992; but this study can take place only after rural radio has established countrywide coverage. The survey will aim to define methods and tools to measure the impact of rural radio.

Congo-Brazzaville (Etienne Epagna-Toua)

1. No large-scale scientific study of listeners has been conducted since the establishment of rural radio. However, some evaluation of activities in different sectors was made in 1989 (thanks to funding from the Friedrich Naumann Foundation) in the districts of Kellé, Ewo and Boundji, and in the Sibiti and Gamboma regions. Before this, an international evaluation of the rural radio project had been undertaken in 1982. This evaluation allowed the management team of the time to judge, from the reactions of their peasant audience, just how effective were the methods used by rural radio in reaching them.

2. Various mechanisms have been used to establish feedback from the target audience: listeners' letters, phone calls and face-to-face contacts during fieldtrips have provided information which has been analysed at management level. These mechanisms were responsible for the diversification of the themes currently explored in the various branches of rural radio. A case for rural radio to focus more directly upon agriculture was often made; today, these themes are linked to the environment, to health, hygiene, breast-feeding, education, isolation and the rural economy. These are dealt with at great length by rural radio stations.

3. These mechanisms constitute real spaces for dialogue between the public and programme producers. Other methods employed, besides those mentioned above, are public debates. As well as going out into the field, the rural radio teams organized participatory broadcasts with quizzes and prizes. Often, the riddle in these quizzes referred to a theme that had been previously dealt with in a rural radio broadcast. These were the occasions when participants were asked about the names of the presenters of programmes in national languages and in French, and so forth. Today, because of material and financial difficulties, this umbilical cord has been broken and such methods forgotten.

The Gambia (Amie Joof-Cole)

1. The Gambian rural radio audience is heterogeneous in terms of ethnicity, age, gender and social status. Adult education (RBAE) programmes are broadcast to the general public, but more specifically to the adult population in rural communities. More than 70 per cent of the listeners are illiterate, and issues of national concern tend to be directed at urban adults. No nationwide audience research to assess the impact of its programmes has been conducted by RBAE;

in the past it has relied on studies done by its project collaborators. IEC staff and research officers undertook these studies using qualitative and quantitative research methodologies: reports compiled by agencies and institutions in the field; focus group discussions; extended interviews; feedback from organized radio listening groups (RLGs).

2. Programmes related to specific projects are targeted towards a particular group; that group is then assessed for the evaluation of any impact the radio programmes may have had, in providing information or education and in changing attitudes. There are several indicators of the impact of the programmes: the response to appeals as indicated by listeners' letters; person-to-person interviews in the street; feedback through radio listening groups; demand for air time by institutions and agencies since the inception of Radio Gambia, RBAE in particular.

An evaluation of the impact of radio programmes was undertaken during the nationwide campaign for Tetanus Toxoid (TT) immunization conducted by the Expanded Programme on Immunization (EPI) unit of the Ministry of Health. The first phase took place in January 1995. The target was to immunize all girls and women of child-bearing age (between the ages of 15 and 45) who had never had children. Within a patriarchal society, reflected in the gender relations of decision-making, the radio programmes took the form of extended interviews and radio spots, targeted at both women and those men who were able to facilitate the participation of women.

During the first phase, a total of 1,918 village settlements and institutions were covered and 49,792 women were given TT immunization. Out of the total of 1,918 settlements and institutions approached, only seven responded negatively, construing TT immunization as family planning.

The second phase of this campaign occurred a month after the first. Some women came forward for their first TT, having recognized that it was unlikely that 1,918 village settlements would have allowed their women to be given an injection that prevented them from having children. Interviews were also conducted at several immunization sites to find out why people had come forward for the TT. The majority of responses referred to the radio (Radio Gambia) as a source of information and encouragement. There was even one particular young man who said, 'I know the government will do anything that is for our benefit.'

3. Given the extremely high rate of illiteracy in rural areas, letter writing is not the best method to determine the impact of radio programmes. Gambian society relies heavily on oral communication; producers receive verbal feedback after the broadcasting of a particular programme. Phone-in programmes have been introduced more recently, so that listeners from different parts of the country can express their reactions to the issues under discussion. RLGs are targeted for authentic feedback on broadcast programmes. The first RLG was set up in Kembujeh, situated 23 miles from Radio Gambia, in January 1972. The programme 'You and national development' for which the group was formed was aired twice a week. The report I wrote in 1981 suggested that 'after the first six months of broadcasting, the production team did not receive listener reaction from any other area except for Kembujeh. Secondly, the

questionnaires required someone literate in order to fill them out, and they did not accommodate the views of farmers adequately enough. RLG members elaborated on issues when they were interviewed. This method was more meaningful to an illiterate audience.'

An evaluation in 1983 of mass media and health practices in the Gambia, conducted by Stanford University in collaboration with the Ministry of Health, indicated that there was a working radio in 59.3 per cent of all households, and batteries to operate them could be purchased locally in 90 per cent of cases. The report estimated that 78 per cent of the radios were owned by men. In only 25 per cent of the households interviewed did women say that they chose which station the radio was tuned to. Radio Gambia was first choice for the majority of households. Some 70 per cent of the women preferred to listen after 8 o'clock in the evening when household chores were completed. The report also indicated that 60 per cent of these women listened to the health programme Jaata Kendeya and 46 per cent had heard the radio spot on diarrhoeal diseases, and had also learnt something about how to care for children with diarrhoea.

An RLG was also established for feedback on the 'Fakube Jarra' (FKJ) drama series. The first FKJ series started in 1988–9 under the URTNA project in two villages, Munyagen and Mandinari. Thirty-six drama programmes were produced in two local languages: Mandinka and Wolof. The evaluation process consisted of a series of Focus Group Discussions (FGDs) conducted with members of RLGs in the two villages, feedback received from the groups after each broadcast, and the monitoring of service statistics by the Gambian Family Planning Association (GFPA) during the programme period in all seven GFPA clinics from August to December 1988. An evaluation of the RLGs set up for the FKJ dramas indicated that members listed a variety of actions taken as a result of listening to FKJ programmes. A similar evaluation conducted that year reported that 53.3 per cent of new participants who visited the family planning clinics in the target areas were motivated by FKJ and 33 per cent by the radio spots. Some 65 per cent of these participants talked to their friends about FKJ, while only 23 per cent said that they had heard about FKJ from their husbands.

A Women's Bureau 'Media assessment and listenership' survey, prepared in December 1992, stated that 90 per cent of respondents to their sample survey rated radio sources as reliable, and Radio Gambia had the highest reliability score among the listenership.

The pattern of listenership to rural programmes is related to the regional distribution of ethnic groupings and languages. For instance, Wolof programmes have a high percentage of listenership in Banjul, Kerewan and Kuntaur LGAs, while the Fula programmes have their highest percentage of listenership in Georgetown and Basse. Likewise, the Jola programme recorded its highest listenership in Brikama area council. It is interesting to note that Mandinka programmes recorded the highest listenership in all LGAs except for Banjul, probably because of Mandinka's role as a lingua franca in the Gambia.

Ghana (Alex Kuarmin)

1. The Ghana Broadcasting Corporation has an audience research unit which normally undertakes an audience survey roughly every six months, using a panel of about 320 listeners selected to constitute a representative sample from all over the country. For the panel, questionnaires are used which are revised to reflect the objectives of each particular survey. The method used for these surveys is described by GBC as follows.

> Panel surveys: invitations are extended to interested listeners and viewers through radio and TV announcements asking them to complete forms stating their demographic characteristics and programme preferences. Panel members are selected on the basis of geographic location, sex, age, level of education, occupation and language spoken or understood.

In addition to these regular surveys, audience research is undertaken from time to time as may be required for specific purposes. The techniques used for such research are determined by the objectives and targets involved. In most cases, the interview method is used since the selected sample includes illiterate listeners. Interviews may be with individuals or with groups. The method used for conducting interviews is described as follows by GBC.

> Field surveys: samples are taken and interviews conducted by trained personnel on a nationwide basis or in selected regions. Undergraduates from the universities or teachers are trained to conduct interviews during school vacations in their areas of origin to surmount language problems. Interview techniques include involving mass education groups, farmers and members of organized groups with the help of chiefs and other opinion leaders.

2. Research undertaken has included the following.
   i) Radio Forum: research was undertaken as part of the activities of the Radio Forum project. Surveys were undertaken before the start of Forum broadcasts to help determine, among other things, the design of the project and programme content. Other surveys during the early period of the project verified effectiveness.
   ii) Apam survey 1990: an audience survey undertaken in 1990 covered the towns and villages served by the Apam Community Radio Station. It provided the following data: (a) major economic activities in the area; (b) literacy rate and school attendance; (c) radio/TV receiver ownership; (d) audience size; and (e) listening habits. The method used was the interview. The sample size was 500 households.
   iii) URA Radio survey 1990: this survey covered the Upper Eastern Region, part of the area served by URA Radio. It provided the same data as above. Interviews were used and the sample size was 642 households.
   iv) Shepherd boys study: this study was also of the URA Radio coverage area. The objective was to obtain relevant data on shepherd boys of the area for whom the Department of Non-Formal Education was planning to introduce educational radio programmes in collaboration with GBC. Interviews were used.

There is also a private company, Marketing and Social Research Limited, which undertakes media research and with whom GBC has collaborated on at least one audience survey.

3. Results of audience surveys are studied and discussed by senior programme officials at headquarters who use them as guidance for programme decisions. The results are also distributed to the officials in charge of the various stations.

Guinea (Bashir Bah)

1. Audience research has always been a concern for managers and broadcasters of rural radio in Guinea. As a result of inadequate training and a lack of resources, however, research methods are limited to the following techniques: listeners' letters; street interviews; phone-in programmes; the broadcasting of game shows which enable an immediate evaluation of messages put across; showing films of these game shows, made by the Labé and Kankan stations at the sites where UNICEF's FINNATCOM project is in operation (Labé, Dalaba, Faranah and Dabola); the introduction of radio listeners' clubs, in collaboration with partners in the field, for instance with Population Services International (PSI) in Central Guinea (10 groups), Upper Guinea (10 groups) and Forest Region Guinea (10 groups). These groups were given receivers with the idea that they would listen together. Monthly reports are regularly sent to the PSI stations in certain regional administrative centres (Labé, Kankan, N'Zérékoré). With a view to training personnel and improving programmes, two workshops on self-evaluation were organized in 1994 and in 1995 with the support of the Swiss development agency. With aid from the Friedrich Ebert Foundation, whose particular concern is the training of artisans, 16 listeners' groups were established in Kindia from where the Foundation's radio, 4A, broadcasts. At the time, these groups had not had receivers. As an example of feedback here is some correspondence sent by the heads of these group.

> From the Dyers' Group of Kindia: 'We thank you for Wednesday's broadcast "Little ways of making a living". We would like to make a criticism: we women dyers are not many but we too do a lot for Kindia.' (Madame Adama Sow)

> From the Welders' Group: 'We members of the Welders' RLG follow your broadcast every Wednesday with interest. We are very satisfied. But we ask you whether it would be possible to lengthen the broadcast to make it better.' (Therna Mara)

> From the Blacksmiths' Group: 'We follow with interest our Wednesday broadcast on small traders and we are satisfied. But this is what annoys us a little: can we not speak in other languages apart from Soussou, because we do not speak this language well?' (Noumou Diallo)

UNICEF is planning to initiate listeners' groups at the sites of the FINNATCOM project in Central Guinea (Labé and Dalaba), and in Upper Guinea (Faranah and Dabola); these sites are equipped with receivers and public address system facilities.

PSI organized a study in 1993 to measure the impact of the AIDS awareness campaign and the 'Prudence' condom in Central Guinea; it was conducted for six months by the rural radio station of Labé. The results of the study which covered a range of 723 people were as follows.

Number of listeners to Labé rural radio

	Men	Women	Total	%
Listen to rural radio	451	226	677	94
Do not listen to rural radio	21	25	46	6
Total	472	251	723	100

The conclusion of the study by PSI says:

> Since rural radio is the vehicle of communication used to convey the messages of the media campaign, this survey was intended to determine the number of listeners in the population. The listening rate is 94%. Such a figure is not exaggerated; rural radio is seen to be the major means of communication throughout this part of Guinea.
>
> For the Foutah population, it is the only channel of communication which is able to reach a large number of people at one time. Moreover, in a region where the means of communication are relatively difficult, radio is the only form of exchange between people who are far from one another.
>
> In addition, the participatory approach used by rural radio means that the people feel the station belongs to them. The language used, and the messages presented that address the concerns of the people, reinforce this connection and amply explain the high rate of listenership. The impact and spread of the work of Labé rural radio in changing popular behaviour in the face of AIDS should not be underestimated. We recommend the use of all rural radios in Guinea to fight the AIDS pandemic in the entire country. (PSI document)

Guinea-Bissau (Bareto de Carvalho)

1. Hitherto there have been no means of understanding audiences and no study has been conducted.
2. There are no mechanisms which enable feedback from programmes.
3. During four regional meetings within the framework of the TCP/GBS/2251 project, participants expressed an almost unanimous appreciation of rural radio, especially public service broadcasts, and hoped that rural radio would continue.

Kenya (Lucy Mulenkei)

The last audience survey was undertaken in 1995 and the main method employed was the filling out of a questionnaire. In existing rural radio stations, feedback on programmes is obtained through: letters from listeners; demands for participation in programme production by rural communities; increases in commercially sponsored programmes from the business community; increases in demand for the dissemination of information by NGOs and other agencies operating in the rural areas.

Mali (Sangaré Omar)

1. Since 1960, when Mali Radio was founded, up to its expansion into television in 1983, no audience research relating to radio was undertaken. In 1995,

despite the explosion of radio on the national scene, there was still no prospect for research on audiences in this area. This has been due in part to the many, day-to-day, technical and financial problems which state and private radio face, and also to a failure to perceive the need for audience research allied to the lack of specialists in the subject.

2. Whether at national, regional or local levels, rural radio has only two ways of gauging its audience: there are listeners' letters, which even if their reliability may be questioned, are at present the only barometer, or feedback, for rural radio programmes and, thus, the only means of knowing the audience for community radios of the sort found in the rural areas; phone calls – rural radio receives an enormous number of phone calls, as well as mail, from the area around the capital. There is a pressing need for audience research in order to evaluate the existing systems of communication. The only evidence available at the moment comes from Dorothea Schulz, a German sociologist, who conducted a preliminary study in 1994, 'The reception and appreciation of local and national rural radios in the rural and semi-urban context'.

3. Following the production and broadcast of a programme on a well-defined and precisely targeted theme, rural populations very often react by sending personal letters or letters written by associations. Since most of these letters are written in the national language, one is dealing with educated people or with literate farmers. Once these letters have been received by the radio, they are read aloud on the stations, and this makes for the beginnings of a dialogue.

No mechanisms exist for measuring the impact of rural radio in Mali. At the moment, rural radio stations and other stations evolving in Mali are generally not concerned with the impact of their messages. It has been the development projects, the programmes and the technical or ministerial departments which have always managed this aspect. The results of studies, surveys or polls conducted by sociologists are very often left with projects or ministerial departments, and there they remain. This lack of interest in understanding the impact of rural radio is simply a result of the absence of adequate structures to handle the issues.

Mauritania (Halakha Djimera)

1. Rural radio possesses neither the necessary means nor the technical expertise to conduct surveys of the audience. Empirical methods are often used to gain information on the audience, its needs and expectations: opinions gathered during fieldtrips, analysis of public broadcasts, listeners' letters, reports compiled by local administrations, NGOs and other services operating on the ground.

One survey was undertaken in 1994, by the National Programme of the IEC in population studies, on familiarity with audiovisual media in Mauritania. This showed that rural radio programmes are followed throughout Mauritania by one in two people. The ratio is markedly weighted towards women (60 per cent female as opposed to 40 per cent male listenerships). Interest in programmes increases the higher the age group. Listeners to rural radio tend to be drawn from the less educated sectors of society.

2. Fieldtrips are used by rural radio to gauge: the reception quality of transmissions; the frequency of listenership; the types of programmes most often listened to and favoured; and the impact of programmes on changing the life of local populations. These fieldtrips also allow investigators to record local opinions about the contents, form and transmission times of programmes, as well as recommendations for improvement. As complete a dossier as possible is compiled for each locality visited.

Although it is not easy, rural radios do their best to collect reports emanating from local administrations and NGOs operating on the ground. These specialist reports (written by administrators, agronomists, doctors, engineers, sociologists, etc) furnish rural radios with indications of the conditions of life, concerns and expectations of the populations covered.

Rural radio also uses the classic medium of listeners' letters but, because most of the target listenership is not literate, there is not a large mailbag. Game-playing is used to discover evidence that listeners have understood or applied the scientific, technical or practical burden of a broadcast message. Rural radio also tries to discover the deep-rooted reasons for practices to be perpetuated.

Nigeria (Tunji Arokoyo)

While a number of studies have been undertaken in the country on the importance of radio as a communication tool, most have been very limited in scope and coverage. There is a national survey currently (1997) being undertaken by NAERLS/ABU. Audience surveys are done by the various stations, but it cannot be ascertained how vigorously these surveys have been executed. There is a need for an in-depth study to be done in order to determine the impact of radio on rural life in Nigeria.

Senegal (Baba Counta)

1. When rural radio began in 1968, listeners were organized into groups; their collective reactions were gathered by a designated leader, who then took them to the station. Today, with the penetration of the transistor radio into rural areas, listening to programmes has become an increasingly individual activity or, when people do listen together, they tend to be a family group in their courtyard.

The only way of knowing the audience is through letters and the reactions of listeners during broadcasts. From time to time, listeners who live in the rural areas present themselves at the premises of the rural radio in order to give their reactions to a programme that has already been broadcast.

2. Since 1976, no reliable study of a scientific nature has been made of the impact of programmes. However, when conflict has arisen between the promoters of a project and its participants, and these have been brought up during broadcasts, there has generally been the beginnings of a solution to satisfy both parties. It is then that one realizes the impact of rural radio programmes; for example, from the very favourable reactions of promoters to

rural radio following a livestock vaccination campaign or a campaign against bush fires. These bear witness to the impact that rural radio broadcasts have.

For many years, rural radio has made available stamped envelopes (printed with the address of the broadcasting station) available to listeners' groups. Listeners were encouraged to express their reactions promptly, and the radio received no fewer than 35 letters each week.

Tanzania (Sango Kipozi)

Audience research is carried out by preparing questionnaire forms and distributing them to people to fill out. This is done by going out to the rural areas and meeting people. Radio-sets are used to make assessments of signal quality, as well as assessing the number of households who tune in to the station.

Tchad (N.D. Maurice Namodji)

1/2. We have little objective information on which to base an evaluation of how well known are rural radio programmes and what impact they have on the population.

3. Although a dedicated audience study still needs to be undertaken, there are indications that rural radio programmes are much listened to and appreciated by rural people in Tchad. For example, the Ministry of Farming and Pastoral Hydrology has noted a steady increase in the demand for vaccines and drugs from livestock breeders since the broadcasting of mini programmes on the vaccination of herds.

In much the same way, the Ministry of the Environment has noted greater participation by the population in the campaign for reforestation. This topic was similarly dealt with in a series of radio broadcasts, in magazines, round-table discussions and mini-programmes.

Systematic surveys were organized by several ministries, notably the ministries of Livestock, Social Affairs, Environment and Health. The vaccination campaign provided the opportunity for measuring the impact of rural radio programmes. This assessment was undertaken by UNICEF, the Ministry of Health and the Ministry of Communications. As a general rule, the heads of ministerial departments seemed satisfied with the programmes produced and broadcast by rural radio in Tchad. These programmes cover the whole spectrum of concerns linked to rural development. Rural radio in Tchad has become an essential tool for raising awareness in the rural world and for mobilizing people; rural radio has simultaneously popularized national development themes while taking into account the initiatives taken by rural communities and the difficulties they face. This has been done, very concretely, by exploiting personal testimonies and by concentrating on producing 'micro dramas' at grassroots level. The success of rural radio is indisputably tied to this interactive quality, because it is able to raise problems, without being patronizing, and to produce varied and attractive programmes anchored in popular tradition and the cultural patrimonies of the different communities of Tchad.

Zambia (Charles Thingadane)

1. The Zambia National Broadcasting Corporation (ZNBC) has so far conducted three radio audience surveys: the Zambian national survey conducted in 1991; the urban media survey of 1993; and the 'Audience Reaction to Change' of ZNBC-Television and Radio Network News Transmission conducted in 1995. Questionnaires were the main tool used during these surveys. Christian Voice Radio has not yet carried out any audience surveys. During the planning stages the radio station used data from ZNBC surveys to evaluate the impact of radio on Zambian audiences. Christian Voice currently uses proprietary questionnaires distributed to a random sample of potential listeners.
2. Both Radio One (in seven local languages) and Radio Two (in English) have programmes tailored to cater for audience response. ZNBC and its production departments depend to a considerable extent upon listeners' letters for feedback. Queries on programmes are largely dealt with by programme producers. Occasionally, ZNBC responds to listeners' queries through the Public Relations Unit. Some listeners write letters straight to the Director-General of the Corporation, while others communicate through the 'Letters to the editor' columns in the daily newspapers.

Zimbabwe (Jennifer Shibanda)

1. The BBC, with Research International and the Zimbabwe Broadcasting Corporation (ZBC), undertook a radio listenership survey in 1991.
2. Another audience/evaluation survey was carried out by FAMWZ which wanted to ascertain the popularity of the project and to see if there was a need for the expansion of their project to other areas. A consultant from Ghana was hired to do the evaluation with the assistance of Zimbabwean field workers. Evaluation involved the following methods: individual interviews among club members and monitors, as well as key field informants (local teachers and nurses, among others) and key individuals involved in the initiation, management and operations of the project; Focus Group Discussions (FGDs); observation of Development Through Radio (DTR) club sessions; and content analysis, area workshops and a final workshop involving DTR members, ZBC and other partner organizations, government departments, donor organizations and NGOs.

   The relevant methods were pre-tested in a pilot study involving one club from each of the six areas (growth points) in which the project operates. In the actual field research, individual interviews were conducted among the following: a random sample of 225 DTR club members; 21 DTR club monitors, also chosen at random; and 61 key informants. Interviews were conducted in Shona and Ndebele, as appropriate, with responses entered in English in the questionnaire forms. A total of 51 FGDs involving DTR members – 31 in Mashonaland and 20 in Matabeleland – were conducted. Twenty-three 'control' FGDs – nine in Mashonaland and fourteen in Matabeleland – were also conducted. Of the 560 individuals who participated in the FGDs, 397 were DTR club members. The FGDs were conducted in Shona and Ndebele as appropriate and recorded throughout. The tapes were subsequently translated verbatim into English. A total of 22 DTR clubs were observed while conducting their regular listening-and-discussion sessions. These activities were carried out between November 1991 and April 1992. Meanwhile, between December 1991 and February 1992, content analysis was applied to a sample of 83 programmes broadcast to the Mashonaland DTR clubs between March 1988 and May 1991. No content analysis was undertaken on the Matabeleland DTR broadcasts because all DTR programme tapes had been erased.

Progress on the evaluation was seriously hampered by the demise in a car accident in May 1992 of a member of the three-person DTR Evaluation Project Coordinating Committee. The consequent request by the Research Director for a postponement of the remaining items of evaluation (data analysis, management interviews, area workshops, final workshop, write up of report) further inhibited progress. Another blow to the project was the departure of the research director to take up a job outside Zimbabwe before completing the above tasks. The external communication research consultant to the evaluation, who had in the meantime been posted to Harare, agreed to take over from the research director and assembled a team of two to assist him in analysing the data from the individual questionnaires and the FDGs. The following items on the evaluation programme were then undertaken:

- April 1993, workshops involving DTR club monitors and other members in each of the six areas covered by the project;
- May/June 1993, management interviews, synthesis and write-up of content analysis;
- June 1993, final evaluation workshop.

References

Brecht, Berthold (1967 [1932]) 'Der Rundfunk als Kommunikationsapparat', *Gesammelte Werke* (ed.) Elisabeth Hauptmann, Vol. 18, Frankfurt am Main: Suhrkamp, pp. 127–34.
Ilboudo, Jean-Pierre (1992) *La radio rurale du Burkina dans les années 1980: 1'étude des conditions de production du discours radiophonique, du contenu du discours radiophonique et de l'auditoire*, doctoral thesis in Information and Communication, University of Bordeaux III.

4
National & International Broadcasters

Policies & Practices
IBRAHIMA SANÉ, ROGER NOUMA & ELIZABETH OHENE

This chapter brings together the contributions of three professionals representing national and international broadcasting, and is rounded off with the transcript of a plenary discussion of issues relating to the role of international broadcasters in the development of radio in Africa.

Ibrahima Sané[1]: Obstacles to the emergence of a national radio and television broadcasting culture in Senegal

From my position as Director of Senegal National Radio I have been watching with interest the trends both in the development of local radio and in the technological and other changes which international radio has been undergoing within the global information revolution. National radio stations have not only been receiving something of a bad press in certain quarters, their positions are in need of definition vis-a-vis the local and the international arenas. In my view there is a vital role for national broadcasters in 'holding the ring' between, and to some extent standing above, sectional and commercial interests. A first step in understanding the potential of national radio is to recognize the constant pressures to which a national broadcaster is subjected, and the limitations of its resources.

The pressures are of various kinds: political (both the government and its opposition); religious (where society has a diversity of religious groups competing for adherents); administrative (civil servants with expectations of access to the airwaves); language (where a multilingual society produces competing demands

---

1 Ibrahima Sané's contribution, which he has reviewed, derives from a translation of a paper submitted in French and various of his spoken comments.

for representation within the media); and technology. Often competition focuses upon access, and in many societies in Africa radio is the cardinal means of access to the people. A democratic system insists that competitors must abide by rules, both in the process of gaining support and in any processes of transition. The national broadcaster has to appear impartial while negotiating competing demands and trying to satisfy them from a limited budget, frequently with dated technology.

Political parties and civil society lobbies

Political party lobbying is extremely difficult to contend with. Many of the party heads in power consider that the directors of the public services should be party sympathizers, if not active members.

The culture of a one-party state, having taken a long time to become attenuated, still produces certain reflex responses. Even if the state does not intervene officially, sometimes orders are given in the name of the state, often with partisan objectives. A director of public service broadcasting is suspected of being everything: an 'adversary' to be replaced, a 'traitor' who does not acknowledge those who gave him or her the position. When one examines them more closely, such reactions are often no more than the responses of individuals who are looking for support in a competition against a local adversary. To be able to mobilize national radio and television is to be able to demonstrate power. It has to be understood, however, and it is a matter of some good fortune, that the state has not always allowed itself to become implicated. The public service in Senegal has never directly concerned itself with political leanings when recruiting or nominating people to positions of responsibility.

Opposition parties are even more of a headache for the directors of public service broadcasting. They have the opposite mentality from the party in power. For them, it is not the threat of dismissal which is their weapon, but the threat of physical violence. For example, several people who work for the radio have had their houses burnt down by opposition party members. ꞯꞯꞯꞯꞯꞯ

For many militants of the opposition, a journalist of the public service does not tell the truth unless it corresponds precisely to their point of view. If the view differs, then this journalist is a 'sell-out', an anti-patriot, and many other such derogatory terms that come to mind. The most curious fact of all, however, is that these verbal attacks are broadcast on public radio stations: they are reproduced in the name of pluralism of public opinion.

In Senegal, there is an extremely high concentration of civic associations of all kinds; many of them without specific objectives. Many of them consist of only the founders and a small number of family members. The influence that these associations may have depends more on their reputation than on the number of members. This in turn depends on the ability of their directors to invest in the media, above all in the public media. So the first place they go is to the radio in order to get one or several members of the editorial staff interested in their activities. Thus, over the course of the year, these associations can set themselves up as legitimate voices, all in the name of pluralism. It is even better if an association member has a relative or friend who is in government, so that the association can obtain media coverage for all the events it wants, by inviting the government member along.

✗ Religious lobbies

Every week, Radio Senegal covers on average 20 religious events on its seven channels (those used by its central radio station and by its regional stations). To cover each of the events, it usually takes:
- one-and-a-half days of work by reporters;
- 17 litres of fuel;
- a team of three people.

In financial terms, this means CFA francs 31,500 for *per diem* monies (100 CFA francs = 1 French franc), CFA francs 7,735 for fuel, and other sums, altogether amounting to a figure of CFA francs 784,700 in expenses a week (approx. $1,400), without counting the costs of vehicles, material and salaries for the staff employed.

Religious groups are a very sensitive issue in Senegal (Senegal is 95 per cent Muslim). All the *marabouts*, 'religious leaders', consider themselves to be important; they are very touchy and adore the media, especially if they are in the limelight. One can imagine how much time those who are in charge of the public media services devote to this question.

The main way for religious groups to gain access to public broadcasting is through government. Religious groups are very structured and, consequently, the political machine of the ruling party can exploit their strength and influence. The problem in Senegal is not conflict between religions, but conflict between brotherhoods, and it is very difficult to organize them or persuade them into some form of collective agreement. In this sense, it is not easy to implement rules and, although there is a regulatory body (the *Haute Conseil de la Radio et de la Télévision*), nobody really cares what it says. The lobbying of religious groups extends to pressurizing journalists. As far as I am concerned, if my journalists obeyed the orders of a religious leader instead of obeying me, I would give them the sack; they are sure to turn up in a month's time on my doorstep, however, asking to have their job back. Expatriates, among others, are getting fed up with the number of television programmes in Senegal that are predominantly religious, but there is not enough funding to produce alternatives, and so foreign programmes are imported for them.

The public authorities

Everyone sees the public service as their 'thing'. In Africa, everyone believes that they can manage things better than those who are in fact in charge. This is especially true for the civil servants. Public service broadcasting is perceived as an extension of the administration: the government of the day considers the public service to be its tool, and the personnel who work for the public service are natural partners in 'development'. Of course, there is some justification for this, but only on condition that partisan politics do not get mixed up in it.

One way in which civil servants exert pressure upon broadcasters is by withholding information or feeding it to competitors. Ministers do not always feel obliged to respond to requests for information made by the public service media. On the contrary, being afraid of the private media, they sometimes take the initiative in offering them information without being solicited, rather than providing the information to public service broadcasters.

Since the Société nationale de radiodiffusion télévision Sénégalaise (RTS) decided to broadcast an alternative programme on a second channel, one which catered for the interests of numerous expatriates, it has found itself accused of creating this programme in order to fight the influence of those religious groups which have tended hitherto to dominate the screen. This example illustrates the difficulties inherent in the management of public service broadcasting in Africa: most citizens consider the public services to be something in which they should have a say – they are always telling you what to do. And contrary to what one may believe, it is far more difficult to reach forms of accommodation with parts of civil society in general, particularly religious groups and political parties, than with public authorities.

Language

Since public service radio is obliged to broadcast in 12 different languages, it has a certain mission to fulfil (in this sense, it has a lot of potential). Unlike private radio stations, for example, public radio has to talk about health issues. This may chase away listeners, although these issues are important. If such programmes are broadcast in so many different languages, and the contents are boring (one needs to have money in order to make a programme on health issues more interesting), listeners do tend to turn away from public broadcasting.

Technology

Public service radio, badly run in many senses, even in other parts of the world, 'takes refuge' in the rural areas (to paraphrase M. Bernard Felier, Director of Intermedia Consultants). This is despite the fact that it would be very useful in urban areas where there are problems of hygiene, health, security, social harmony. In order to be useful, however, public service radio has to have an audience. On the technical side in general, there has been much delay in modernizing equipment as compared with the competition from the private sector. Equipment is outdated, expensive to run and is always breaking down; it can take anything from two days up to a month before a part is replaced or repaired. The problem is lack of funding: the main backers believe they would be financing political propaganda if they were to finance national radio broadcasting. This is not necessarily true.

Conclusion

The public service has to try to retain its credibility by avoiding too much government involvement (which of course is easier said than done). Despite these problems, those who manage the public service have to be fully aware that they have an instrument in their hands which belongs to all taxpayers without distinguishing on the basis of social class, political or religious leanings. The public service should therefore be the channel *par excellence* of pluralism in political opinion. It should not serve a particular market or those who fund it, but rather it should serve the whole community (within the limits of the constitution and good taste). At the same time, those in authority who retain guardianship should be careful not to exert direct influence. Finally, the opposition should try to resist the desire to demolish the public service, seeing it as being identified with the regime in power; otherwise, hostile relations will inhibit the public service in its continuing move to become more open.

Roger Nouma[2]: The relations between international and local broadcasters

Since their inception, private radio stations in Africa have had to cope with a host of problems (including financial, technical and training) which have been compounded by the diverse lobbying pressures to which they are subjected. Many African public broadcasters face the same problems (as Ibrahima Sané's contribution emphasizes), and they are not problems unique to radio but shared by television and the print media. Will radio liberalization go the way of press liberalization? When the press was first liberalized in the early 1990s, the African continent seethed with new titles. By the decade's end few remained: those few who had managed to solve the sorts of problems that now also face private radio stations.

'Mirror radios'

How do radio stations, especially private radio stations, develop and what role do they play?

Whatever the difficulties they go through and regardless of their status (associative, community, rural, commercial, etc), private local radio stations are communication vectors of a kind I like to call 'mirror radios': they try to reflect the realities of daily life in the environment to which they broadcast. In doing this, local radio stations usually set themselves three goals or missions:

- to promote the musical heritage of the rural areas and the country as a whole; musical programming predominates on many such stations;
- to promote national languages by broadcasting in these languages as well as those of the former colonial powers; thus Bambara and Peul (Fulfulde) are used in Mali, Hausa or Djerma in Niger, More or Dyula in Burkina Faso, Wolof in Senegal – to speak only of Francophone countries;
- to popularize local and national cultures so that the different ethnic and linguistic groups addressed by the station are able to identity culturally with its programmes. Such identification is usually closer where journalists and broadcasters share cultural reference points with their listeners.

2 Roger Nouma's talk was delivered in French, recorded and then transcribed by the author. It was subsequently translated, edited and referred back to the author for correction.

I would like to add a fourth to these three missions:

* to participate in education, development and advice by broadcasting on questions of health, hygiene, agriculture and environment, as well as seeking solutions to the problems that arise in community life.

Because they are close to the people whom they serve, such programmes may be powerful means of cultural renewal and social initiative. They are a type of cement that may help to bind a local community, and to entrench relations between individuals, villages and communities. State-level radio plays an equally important role, but in different domains that are further removed from people's everyday concerns.

Complementarity with foreign radio stations

The landscape of African radio is composed not only of private and national broadcasters, but also of international broadcasters: BBC, VOA, RFI, etc. What is more, these predate private radio in Africa. What is their place and role in Africa? Do they compete directly with local radio stations?

Unquestionably, international radio broadcasters have access to means that local broadcasters lack. Nevertheless, I feel that the relationship between them is one of complementarity rather than competition: unlike international broadcasters (such as my own Radio France Internationale) broadcasters in African countries – whether private or public – play a role that is based on their proximity to their audience. To their side of this complementary relation, the international broadcasters bring two things: an openness to the wider world, not least by virtue of their international correspondents, and a range of forms of cooperation that are less well known to a general public but important. So far as RFI is concerned this has three main aspects as follows:

* Since the early 1960s, RFI has supplied African national radio stations with the current news items they would be unable to gather on their own account.
* RFI has also provided Africa-centred programmes to national broadcasters to enhance the range of their programming. Although this is not a radio matter, I might add that RFI also plays the role of a news agency for the African print media.
* Through its International Training Service, RFI also takes part in both basic and advanced training for broadcasters, journalists and managers working in African radio stations, regardless of whether these are publicly or privately owned.

Elizabeth Ohene[3]: The changing face of the BBC World Service for Africa

Graham Mytton has covered some of the facts and figures of BBC World Service broadcasting to Africa; I want to add something about the changing culture of

---

[3] Elizabeth Ohene's contribution is a transcript of her talk at the workshop lightly edited as a text, and reviewed by the author.

our activities. In my opinion – at least for English-speaking countries – the BBC Africa Service still provides the most comprehensive coverage available to African listeners: there are news and current affairs (my own programme 'Network Africa' is broadcast in the morning and evening), features and arts, drama and sports programmes. Together these provide a rounded picture of what is happening both in Africa and in the rest of the world.

But who are the reporters and where does all this coverage come from? This is an important question because when people talk about the BBC they seem to think of it solely as part of the western media. Just at the level of personnel, this is a simplification. The Africa Service currently has 141 reporters in 51 countries on the African continent. There are more of them in some countries, for instance Nigeria and South Africa, than there are in others; and we still have difficulties finding radio journalists who understand the local languages but can broadcast in English in some of the smaller countries. Of these 141 reporters, I would think that 16 might be described as foreign correspondents, that is, BBC radio reporters sent from London to the field. But some of these 16 would resent being thought of as outsiders: an extreme case would be Tanya Matthews, by now a very senior member of the profession, who has lived in Tunisia for about 30 years and so is not what usually springs to mind when the phrase 'foreign correspondent' is used. She is exceptional, but it is more generally the case that none of our correspondents lacks a long-term commitment to the country on which they report. Postings as reporters generally last 6–24 months. Our journalists are usually of high repute, and many of them have landed in jail, often without having done much to get themselves there. One of our reporters was recently imprisoned for six months in Sudan; it took the entire BBC machinery to get him out, and he has still to be told the charge on which he was held.

At the BBC, we accept that we are judged on criteria that are even more stringent than those applied to other broadcasters; and we rely on reporters who put not just their reputations but even their lives on the line. So, how do they report and who decides what makes the news? Another common misconception is that people sitting in London substantially process or censor what is sent to them. If this was ever the case, it was before my time, and the situation that made considered news-vetting possible no longer exists. First, there are many more non-traditional 'BBC voices' on the air. As a Ghanaian, I do not have what you would call a 'BBC voice' or background. Yet I am on the air much of the time; too much of the time some would say. More generally, news reaches us so fast from the ground that we have to rely on the reputations of the local reporters whom we put on air. And it is not only our reporters who get on air. Africa is notorious for its coups d'états; there was a time when people in Africa immediately tuned to the BBC when there was a coup; I speak from experience having lived through five or six coups in Accra. But now that I work for the BBC I recognize there was some absurdity in the BBC World Service for Africa relaying to Ghanaians news that the BBC Monitoring Service had picked up from Radio Ghana in the first place. But this is to speak about what it was like 10–12 years ago; news management from London has changed entirely. Let me give some instances.

When there was a coup in 1997 in Sierra Leone, our telephones rang incessantly for three days; this could never have happened during the Ghanaian coups I recall. Ten or fifteen years ago, there were few African countries from which one could make international telephone calls easily. Nowadays, people from all the African countries are constantly sending us faxes or ringing to demand to be put on air. The balance of control over news coverage has moved markedly out of our hands. Returning to the 1997 Sierra Leone coup, I then had a very interesting conversation on air with the coup leader, Johnny Paul Koroma. As a result, people phoned to ask why I had not given Jerry Rawlings a similar 'third-degree' interview when he took power in the 1980s. The answer is simple: back then you could not call Ghana after a coup because the first thing to happen was that the international telephone service was disconnected. Nowadays, you cannot pull the plug on a satellite phone.

Here is another example that struck me. If we wanted to know what liberation movements were doing in Africa during the 1980s, we had to despatch a reporter to rendezvous with them. The reporter might disappear for a couple of months before finding a telephone on which to contact us. A year-and-a-half after I began working for the BBC, we had a telephone call from someone claiming to be from the Eritrean People's Liberation Front (EPLF) who said he was 70 miles outside Asmara. We assumed it was a hoax since the line was as crystal clear as if he had been phoning from the Strand.[4] Previously, we had only been able to contact the EPLF through their representative in Brussels; here was a person calling us on a satellite phone from outside Asmara.

This was the first time we had direct coverage from a participant in an African conflict. But it was a short, and quickly taken, step from there to someone starting a war with a satellite phone. This was what happened in the case of Liberia's Charles Taylor, who called the BBC World Service for Africa on Boxing Day 1989 (the day after he launched his invasion) demanding to be put on air. The moral seems to be that if you mean to start a war in Africa today, you get a satellite phone before you get AK47s.

However, there is consolation in that access for warmongers is also access for the public. This was evident when a young woman in The Gambia called us from a public phone-box in her village with the first news that the Farafenni barracks were under attack during the failed counter coup of November 1996, which followed the successful coup of July 1994.

There is a moral to these anecdotes. Changing technology is making control of news from London less and less consequential. Although our news will continue to carry the BBC brand name, not only will we get increasingly close to the ground but, so to speak, that ground will increasingly come to us. The time-scale of our responses to the news is becoming compressed, and this raises difficult questions of editorial control that may be tantamount to the London operation becoming disempowered.

---

4 Bush House, the home of the BBC World Service, is between the central thoroughfares of Aldwych and the Strand.

Discussion

Jean-Pierre Ilboudo began by posing two small questions to Roger Nouma: how would he react to a widespread observation in Africa that people listen to the BBC rather than RFI because they find it more 'objective'? Given that many radio stations in African countries are underdeveloped technologically – some not reaching the whole country – if RFI offers a quality FM service can it really be said to be a complement to the national services? Jean-Pascal Daloz similarly voiced his reservation whether the relationship between national and international broadcasters was complementary rather than competitive. He gave the instance of Cotonou (Benin) where, in his experience, listeners used RFI to the exclusion of the Benin national service because its news service was considered more up-to-the-minute. Graham Mytton added that extensive audience research was usually necessary to know why people listened to the stations they did: in Abidjan it transpired that BBC was listened to as a music station and RFI as a news programme. In Ibrahima Sané's opinion some of these comments were a little harsh on RFI which he thought had reformed itself away from being the voice of the French government towards offering a more objective news service. Wolfgang Bender pointed out another complementarity: the export of Paris-based African music served to raise the technical standard of music production on the continent. Finally, Tilo Grätz wondered why RFI did not broadcast in African languages.

In his response, Roger Nouma took up the question of listening habits in Cotonou. Why is it that people claim only to listen to RFI? Although Benin opted early for a process of political democratization this was not matched by broadcasting liberalization. Given that their national broadcaster had made little progress in its news presentation, it was to be expected that its poorly informed audience would turn to international radio or television. This was unsurprising and applied more generally in the continent where national broadcasters had either failed to respond to people's needs for a diversification of their news sources, or lacked the means to cover inter-African and international news.

The questions raised about people's comparisons between RFI and BBC certainly invited further thought. Finally, RFI was aware of the issue of African-language broadcasting which had been raised internally as long ago as 1965. Although it was still on their agenda, for RFI (like any other international radio station) the decision lay outside the hands of the radio professionals and was essentially one of political will.

Addressing Elizabeth Ohene, Ibrahima Sané wondered whether the BBC and RFI really differed much in their coverage: the BBC most intensively carried current affairs on the old colonies and 'star countries' (like South Africa, Kenya and Nigeria – with the proviso that stars wax and wane). Leave aside a few stringers and people of good will (among whom he included Elizabeth Ohene), and the impression was still that the BBC did not cover Africa systematically and had a counterpart colonial bias to RFI. Malami Buba, with Nigerian experience in mind, asked how the impartiality of reporters was assured, and whether there was any problem of celebrity reporters who themselves became the news.

Elizabeth Ohene admitted that the turnover of reporters in some African countries was rapid, but added that this was attributable to the effects of their lifestyle on their reliability more than a reflection of their capabilities as journalists. Coverage in the non-English speaking countries of Africa could certainly be improved and depended too heavily on the quality of individuals. For instance, the decision in 1993 of one individual to report from Zaire (now the Democratic Republic of Congo) had meant that five or six stories on Zaire were carried in 1994. Graham Mytton added that even in heavily reported countries, individuals were important: there had been three years of poor coverage of Nigeria in the mid-1970s when they had no reliable journalist willing to travel to the country.

Richard Carver asked Elizabeth Ohene whether BBC staff were still vetted by MI5. (Colloquially, within the BBC, this was known as 'Christmas treeing' after the arrow-shaped stamp on a person's file that apparently referred further enquiry upwards.) Graham Mytton thought this had not been the case for at least 15 years.

Aida Opoku-Mensah asked about the role of an international broadcaster, like the BBC, which found itself in competition with proliferating local channels. For instance, by transmitting in FM from Abidjan did the BBC not suppress indigenous initiatives and divert resources and listeners from them? Elizabeth Ohene replied that, although people were accustomed to shortwave radio in Africa, since FM reception was superior it made sense to offer it. In times of crisis, there might be no FM broadcasting (because of its shorter range it could be shut down), then people had to revert to shortwave for their news (as had happened in Sierra Leone). In Ghana, the government subsidized production of radios manufactured with presets for the national stations. It was true that the BBC commanded greater resources than local radio. For instance, if a stringer phoned to say he needed US$300 to cover a story, this could be arranged there and then. Someone working for local radio would be unlikely to be able to call on similar backing. But one could argue that good resources make good radio, and that the BBC should be an example and challenge to other radio stations. Graham Mytton added that the results of audience research showed that, given a choice, people virtually always listen to domestic stations first and turn to foreign stations for some particular reason, such as to get extra information. Elizabeth Ohene was asked a related question about the relaying of BBC programmes by local stations, for instance Joy FM and other FM stations in Accra; she responded that this was commercially attractive because of cash constraints but hoped that Africa-based stations would increasingly be able to produce their own programmes.

Aida Opoku-Mensah further asked whether BBC programmes tended disproportionately to reach the elite and policy-makers in African countries because they were able to understand English. Besides pointing to the mass audiences for the BBC's African language services, Graham Mytton said that 'Focus on Africa', the programme presented by Elizabeth Ohene, had a wide audience despite being in English.

Ibrahima Sané broadened the scope of discussion by suggesting that public broadcasting was frequently treated less than even-handedly. At a time when liberalization of the airwaves was seen as a panacea in some quarters, people still tended to think that public broadcasting was 'Daddy's radio': covering what such and such minister had said or done, and being shut down if it strayed from the party line. This was not wholly true: opposition parties had rights of statutory access to the offices of the Senegalese public broadcaster; for 61 days before an election, journalists were legally obliged to campaign neither for nor against political parties; political parties had their slots (party political broadcasts) in which they were free to insult one another. Senegalese public broadcasting was certainly free enough to attract regular complaints against it from the ruling party. Research supported Graham Mytton's point about local broadcasters being preferred to international broadcasters: RFI lagged well behind public broadcasters in terms of popularity. Local issues were more readily addressed by the national broadcaster (in local languages), and it was more easily held accountable for any bias in its news coverage than a remote international broadcaster might be. However, this argued that public broadcasting remained important, not that those running it could be complacent. The proliferation of private radio stations involved challenges to public broadcasters that concerned both their financing and their radio cultures.

Jeanette Minnie concurred, noting that the independence of professional and community broadcasters raised problems yet to be faced in Africa. Take the position of local representatives in a community radio station. A simple majoritarian way of appointing them, or of their conducting their affairs once appointed, would be likely to militate against minorities being represented, or if represented, getting issues of concern to them onto an agenda. It seemed unrealistic to expect neutrality from 'journalists' who were actually not broadcast professionals but representatives of their communities. A different sort of ethical charter needed to be devised for such organizations to avoid majoritarian tyranny.

Reverting to the BBC, Graham Mytton noted that it is often assumed that declining audience figures are bad in themselves. While the BBC World Service is not looking to disappear, there is some truth in the description someone once made of it as the 'OXFAM of the mind'. The BBC has a similar status in people's estimation to the Red Cross or UNHCR: a supplier in the last resort. Elizabeth Ohene had described how technological innovation is changing the way that the news is reported. Technology invented in the richer countries may be used in ways we cannot always anticipate in the poorest parts of the world. There was need for serious thought about the impact of changing technologies on the future of broadcasting in Africa.

II
Local Radio, Local Radio Culture & the Culture of Radios

5
The Evolution of Radio Broadcasting in Burkina Faso

'From mother radio to local radios'
URBAIN NOMBRÉ

The evolution of radio broadcasting

Radio Upper Volta or 'mother radio'

Burkina Faso has now seen almost four decades of post-independence broadcasting. It has been a rocky path, strewn with setbacks, and dominated until recently by 'mother radio' (the state broadcaster based in the capital). There have, however, been recurrent attempts to achieve broadcasting pluralism: by establishing regional stations, local state-sponsored rural radios, and latterly commercial radios (which made up 22 of the FM radio stations on the air in Burkina Faso in 1997 – a further 10 being owned by the Burkinabe or French states, see Chapter 6). This chapter will briefly outline the development of local radios and the gradual loosening of mother radio's grip on broadcasting in both Burkina Faso and the former Upper Volta. First, a brief characterization of the country.

According to a survey undertaken in 1991, the population of Burkina Faso was 9.2 million, of whom 51 per cent were women and 49 per cent men. Population density was low: Burkina is a vast, mostly flat, country of 275,000 square kilometres. The Burkinabe are a young population, almost half of whom were below 15 years of age in 1991. Most people continue to live in rural areas, where their activities are predominantly linked to the primary sector: farming, herding, handicrafts and fishing. Burkina Faso is one of the world's least developed countries, carrying a foreign debt of 639 billion CFA francs in 1995. There is a low rate of literacy: 38 per cent (again among the lowest in the world); of the numerous local languages found among Burkina's sixty ethnic groups, the most widely spoken are Moore, Fulfulde and Jula. All these factors meant that radio had the potential to play a vital national role.

As in many of the former French African colonies, the appearance of radio

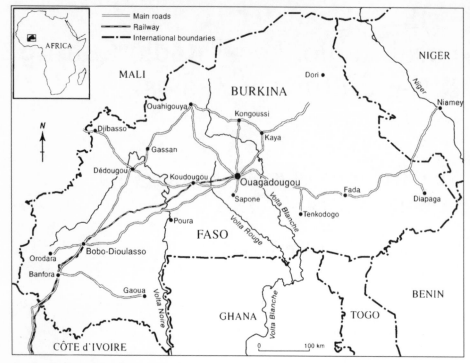

Figure 5.1 Radio in Burkina Faso

broadcasting in Upper Volta (as it was then) coincided with the era of independence. The national broadcaster was established by a decree of 25 October 1959 and was on air by the proclamation of independence (on 5 August 1960) and the accession to power of Maurice Yaméogo at the head of the single political party, the Rassemblement démocratique africaine.

Baptised Radio Upper Volta, the first station was run by the political leaders of the time who considered it an instrument of the 'expression of national sovereignty'. In short, Radio Upper Volta came into being as a state institution within a single-party state. Equipped at the outset with a one kilowatt transmitter broadcasting on mediumwave, Radio Upper Volta put out six hours of (mainly French) programmes weekly which were aimed at the elite living in Ouagadougou, the capital, and its immediate surroundings.

Radio Upper Volta progressively increased its audience by upgrading its equipment, enlarging its staff, and diversifying its programmes, all of which occurred while the state retained its monopoly over broadcasting. As an institution of the state, the radio station stayed under the watchful eye of the Ministry of Information and was almost exclusively financed from the national budget. An instrument of government policy, Radio Upper Volta remained closely linked to the projects and programmes of a succession of governments, quite regardless of changes in its name: Voice of Upper Volta, Voice of Revival, Inter Channel, and so forth.

Radio Bobo Dioulasso

On 2 December 1962, while the country was still under the presidency of Maurice Yaméogo, Radio Upper Volta became mother to the Bobo Dioulasso regional station: a 'daughter' station in the country's second city. Radio Bobo closely resembled its mother in Ouagadougou. In fact, it was no more than a relay station improving local reception for programmes made, for the most part, in the capital. Although it would have liked to play the role of a regional station, Radio Bobo's programmes had little to do with the realities and concerns of its potential listenership. It continues to be little more than an appendage to Radio 'Ouaga' (Radio Burkina), which provides it with staff, financial resources and, above all, programme content. The progressive introduction of national languages with the creation of a rural radio department within the national broadcaster did not materially change this situation.

Rural radio

The second daughter of the mother radio was born on 24 November 1969 courtesy of a presidential decree promulgated by the then military leader, Colonel Sangoulé Lamizana, who had seized power following union-led, popular revolts against salary reductions in 1966. This second child was called 'rural radio'; its main objective was to make programmes in local languages that would persuade rural people to implement development plans hatched by the government. Given widespread illiteracy, as well as the poor development of both communicational and educational infrastructures, it seemed that radio would be the best tool to circumvent linguistic barriers, so as to develop and popularize initiatives taken in relation to agriculture and social education.

The birth of rural radio increased the weekly programme output: 69 hours in 1970 rose to 114 hours in 1974 during the Second Republic under Lamizana. This expansion in broadcasting was linked to the recognition of 17 indigenous languages (*langues nationales*), and was made possible thanks to collaboration with the Federal Republic of Germany which enabled production and broadcasting equipment to be upgraded, staff to be trained, and resources to be devoted to making programmes.

1985 marked the end of the German collaborative project, and rural radio began its decline. Having failed to make any preparations to sustain rural radio financially, governments led by Thomas Sankara (1983–7) and, in the aftermath of the coup in which Sankara died, Blaise Compaoré, presided over both a continuing decline in programming levels and a reversal of production priorities. Starved of funds, rural radio producers were unable to make the fieldtrips which would allow their programmes to reflect the concerns of rural people. Instead they fell back on studio transmissions which largely consisted of the advice of development specialists, the very obverse of their original role.

Following a process of transition to multiparty democracy, and elections in 1991 and 1992, the Fourth Republic, under the presidency of Compaoré, has seen some improvement in the fortunes of rural radio broadcasting. Searching for the means to relaunch rural radio activities, officials of the Ministry of Information negotiated a sum of CFA francs 100 million from the FAO to undertake a project entitled, 'Decentralization and regionalization of rural radio'. Over a two year period, the project was supposed to achieve the following objectives:

• enhance the mobility of rural radio activities by supplying vehicles and equipment;
• train and retrain production personnel;
• put in place systems to plan, follow-up, and evaluate the activities of rural radio stations;
• support programme production;
• train administrative personnel.

The project, carried out between 1990 and 1992, included both rural radio and the two regional radio stations in Gaoua and Bobo Dioulasso. However, the results were not such as to assure the future of rural radio activities. A second phase had to be negotiated, financed this time by the Netherlands development agency with the FAO acting as the agent handling implementation. This second project (with a further budget of CFA francs 100 million) saw as its main objective preparing rural radios to run themselves autonomously within legal and administrative frameworks that would allow them to raise and manage the resources they needed. However, a lack of real political will prevented this objective being met by the time the second programme came to an end in December 1996.

Radio Gaoua and Canal-Arc-en-Ciel (the Rainbow Channel)

I have already had cause to mention the 'third daughter' of Radio Burkina: a second regional station established in Gaoua (southwest Burkina Faso) in 1985. Like Radio Bobo, Radio Gaoua was meant to make and broadcast local programmes; and, just like Radio Bobo, it ended up as an appendage of Radio Burkina, acting as a relay for most of its programmes. It relied just as heavily on the mother radio for its staff and working budget.

Canal-Arc-en-Ciel, effectively a fourth daughter, was the most recent state-sponsored station to see the light of day, in 1991. It transmits on the FM band, and it shares its mother radio's building, staff and budget; its station director works directly under the authority of the national radio director. Canal-Arc-en-Ciel is really no more than a hived-off part of the national radio, created to serve the capital's youth market which was otherwise abandoning the state broadcaster in favour of the programmes offered by the private station Horizon FM. A regional station of Canal-Arc-en-Ciel was subsequently opened in Bobo Dioulasso.

State-sponsored local radio stations

Burkina Faso has undoubtedly been the Francophone West African pioneer in setting up local radios. The first meeting on local radio was organized in Ouagadougou on 4–28 October 1981 as a cooperative venture between the French aid agency (ACCT), the Ougadougou regional school of radio journalism (CIERRO) and the international broadcasting agency CIRTEF. This meeting turned into a training seminar for programme-planners in rural African radio stations. Swapping experiences led them to reflect more theoretically on both the future of their rural radio stations – confronted, as they were, by enormous financial difficulties – and why their programmes provided so little space for the authentic voices of rural people. Were there solutions to these dilemmas?

In response to these reflections the sponsors (ACCT, CIERRO, and CIRTEF) organized a subsequent workshop in 1983. This took the form of a training session devoted to the production of local radio programmes. The key module of the workshop, between 21 March and 8 April, involved an experiment with local radio in Toudou, a village about 60 kilometres from Ouagadougou. The results of this second meeting subsequently furnished a series of recommendations. Rather than just reiterating that local rural radio should be envisaged as a way of involving local communities in radio programming and management, these recommendations focussed above all on the hard question of insufficient funding and what to do about it.

In October 1984, under the revolutionary government of Thomas Sankara, a project to establish radio stations was conceived within the framework of a 'popular programme for development'. This resulted in the progressive creation, from 1986 onwards, of six local radio stations in the *départements* of Kongoussi, Gassan, Djibasso, Orodara, Diapaga and Poura (p.89). Their original statutes declared that the objective of these local radio stations was to become 'useful complements' to national radio broadcasting. They were placed under the authority of administrative heads and, oddly enough, were to be managed by committees representative of the social and professional composition of their locality. Additionally, their activities were to be coordinated by an overall rural radio directory. The ambiguities in these statutes doubtless had a lot to do with the subsequent poor performance of local radio stations (that I noted earlier) which was characterized by:

* financial and technical problems;
* lack of staff training;
* lethargic management committees;
* absence of community participation in the planning of programmes.

These factors led to the closure of some stations for longer or shorter periods, or to their surviving as little more than juke boxes or public telephones.

Private local radio stations

Leaving aside the commercial radio station Horizon FM (which was set up in Ouagadougou in December 1987 and ten years later had nine local stations, see p. 89),[1] private radio stations have been established only after adoption of the 2 June 1991 constitution, which began the process of democraticizing public life in Burkina Faso. While retaining control over the allocation of frequencies, the state set conditions under which the creation of FM stations was authorized. By 1997 there were 24 such stations in different parts of the country, 3 of them foreign-owned (RFI had stations in Bobo as well as in Ouagadougou where the Gabonese

---

[1] For a profile of Horizon's founder, Moustapha Thiambono, see Panos Institute 1993 *Radio Pluralism in West Africa*, pp. 31–4.

Africa No. 1 had also set up). These stations differ in orientation and therefore programming: from predominantly commercial stations, to religious stations, and *radios associatives* (run by non-profit-making associations, like NGOs).

Perspectives on the present situation

The current radiophonic landscape of Burkina Faso is characterized by the coexistence of three gross types of radio station.

State radio stations are created by governmental authorities and placed under the care of the Ministry of Information. Other than the local radios, they are run by civil servants and financed from the national budget. As creations of the state, their role is to popularize the government's choice of political alternatives and development options.

Local radio stations are also created by the state, but they are mostly run by local volunteers. They have statutes (*un cahier de charges*, see Myers p. 92) and a management committee. The state gives them a grant to buy production materials. The national directory of rural radio looks after coordination, as well as the maintenance of equipment and staff training.

Private radios belong to individuals, to associations, or to religious communities. These radio stations, especially those created as part of the democratization process, exist in what is almost a legal vacuum; they are hardly regulated and notably lack the statutory obligations of local radios. True, there is a law for the press and a regulatory body, the Conseil supérieur de l'information, but we would do well to recognize that the slackness of the current regulatory framework already discourages qualitative competition, and it could easily lead to a situation of anarchy.

Since January 1997, the Ministry of Communication and Culture has undertaken vigorous measures to instill some new dynamism into the media generally. The framework envisages: the organization of a forum on communication; carrying out a study with a view to transforming the statutes of the state media (which were to become public services with semi-autonomous management in 1998); preparation of laws on advertising; equitable access for political parties to the state media.

List of FM radio stations broadcasting in Burkina Faso

	Name	Frequency	Location	Owner/Director
1	Horizon FM	104.4	Ouagadougou	Moustapha Thiombiano
2	Horizon FM	98	Banfora	Moustapha Thiombiano
3	Horizon FM	100.4	Ouahigouya	Moustapha Thiombiano
4	Horizon FM	102.7	Dedougou	Moustapha Thiombiano
5	Horizon FM	102.7	Bobo	Moustapha Thiombiano
6	Horizon FM	98.7	Koudougou	Moustapha Thiombiano
7	Horizon FM	96.1	Kaya	Moustapha Thiombiano
8	Horizon FM	104.6	Dori	Moustapha Thiombiano
9	Horizon FM	97.6	Tenkodogo	Moustapha Thiombiano
10	Radio Taamba	98.4	Fada	Fada Diocese
11	Radio Palabre	92.2	Koudougou	Benem Nooma
12	Radio Maria	91.6	Ouagadougou	Cardinal Paul Zoungrana
13	Lumière Vie Développement	98.1	Ouagadougou	Pastor Samuel Yameogo
14	Radio Evangile Développement	93.4	Ouagadougou	Joanna Ilboudo
15	Radio Energie ABGA	103.4	Ouagadougou	Inoussa Sankara
16	Africa No. 1	90.3	Ouagadougou	M. Mapangou (the state of Gabon)
17	RFI	94	Ouagadougou	France
18	Radio Notre Dame	105.8	Koudougou	Koudougou Diocese
19	RFI	99.4	Bobo	France
20	Canal-Arc-en-Ciel	96.6	Ouagadougou	D/RNB (Burkinabe state)
21	Canal-Arc-en-Ciel Plus	89.8	Bobo	D/RNB (Burkinabe state)
22	La Voix du Paysan	97	Ouahigouya	
23	Radio Notre Dame Kaya	88	Kaya	Abbé Laurent Balma
24	Radio Pulsar	94.8	Ouagadougou	Claver Yameogo
25	Radio 'Vive le Paysan'	107	Sapone	André-Eugène Ilboudo
26	Radio 'Salankoloto'	97.3	Ouagadougou	Roger Nikiema
27	Radio Orodara	105.5	Orodara	Burkinabe state
28	Radio Poura	88.2	Poura	Burkinabe state
29	Radio Diapaga	95.8	Diapaga	Burkinabe state
30	Radio Djibasso	91.2	Djibasso	Burkinabe state
31	Radio Gassan	94.6	Gassan	Burkinabe state
32	Radio Kongoussi	93.2	Kongoussi	Burkinabe state

6
Community Radio
& Development

Issues & Examples
from Francophone West Africa
MARY MYERS

What is community radio?

Definitions are not easy. In West Africa a variety of names have been used recently to denote small-scale local broadcasting initiatives. These include '*radios libres*' (free radios), '*radio rurale*' (rural radio), '*radios associatives*' (radios created and run by non-profit associations) and '*radios de proximité*' (literally radios which are 'close by' and figuratively radios which are part of the landscape of everyday life). Opoku-Mensah (Chapter 11) sees community radio as having four salient characteristics: ownership by people, access by people, participation and non-commercial/non-state dependence.

However, in West Africa, particularly Mali, there are numerous examples of community-type stations existing on a commercial basis. There is also the question of religious affiliation; some would discount confessional stations altogether, while others would see them as an organ of 'community' par excellence. The extent of state and donor involvement is also a question. In Mauritania and Benin, for example, there are a number of new, successful community-oriented radio stations owned and operated by the government for the community. Furthermore, if a radio's establishment and running costs are underpinned by an international NGO like OXFAM, is it truly community-owned?

In this chapter I shall define community radio in a flexible way, taking it to mean small-scale decentralized broadcasting initiatives which are easily accessed by local people, actively encourage their participation in programming, and which include some element of community ownership or membership.

A typical example of community radio on the West African model is Daande Duwansa (The Voice of Douentza) in the Mopti region of Mali. This tiny solar-powered studio, housed in a mud-brick building, broadcasts on FM at a radius of about 125 kilometres to a listenership of approximately 120,000 people. It is staffed by six local 'animators' and operates on a shoestring budget of about £25,500 per year (Myers 1997; Rolt 1995). Its equipment is basic (everything is recorded and edited on audio-cassette), its sound is relatively amateurish, but it enjoys huge local popularity. Radio ownership in the local town of Douentza and the surrounding villages jumped 140 per cent in its first half-year of operation (Rolt 1995).

Daande Duwansa's output is mainly in the local languages of Fulfulde and a dialect of Dogon, and it prioritizes local music and news. Initiated in 1993 by a local NGO, called NEF (Near East Foundation), it has so far received core funding from the British development agency, OXFAM. But it has always had a strong element of local ownership too. It has a large group of contributing members and is governed by a steering committee of local notables and villagers, both men and women. Its main raison d'être is to fulfil a developmental function. Eighty per cent of its talk programmes are on health, education, agricultural and social (particularly women's) issues. Its staff believe fervently in 'opening the microphone' to as large and diverse a cross-section of local people as possible to stimulate debate and help people make informed choices about their lives and livelihoods.

It is these sorts of radio stations we will be looking at – not exclusively rural and not all totally independent of the state – but all attempting to wrest broadcasting away from large state concerns to make it local, relevant and people-centred. We will be looking at the particularities, successes and problems of community radio in the context of development.

The independent radio explosion

Since the early 1990s there has been something of a broadcasting – or microcasting[1] – explosion in a significant number of West African countries, where the democratization process has made radio pluralism possible. Mali, Benin and Guinea and to a lesser extent Burkina Faso, Mauritania and Senegal are cases in point. However, it is in Mali[2] and Burkina Faso where the climate has been particularly favourable to the spread of independent radios. Almost three-quarters of the newly created radio stations are in these two countries (Bouhafa 1997) with 77 independent studios in Mali and 24 currently operating in Burkina Faso.

The primary reason for radio being the mass medium of choice is easy to appreciate, given that the populations of all of the Francophone states in West Africa are overwhelmingly rural, non- or semi-literate, and possess a strong oral tradition. Particularly in the desperately poor and arid regions of northern Mali and Burkina Faso there is no competition from television or newspapers. The extent of sharing of radio sets is not statistically proven, but must be very significant, given that figures for individual ownership of transistors is not, in fact, particularly high by African standards in general (officially 44 radios per 1,000 people in Mali, compared with an average of 149 per 1,000 for Sub-Saharan Africa as a whole (UNDP 1997)).

---

[1] Microcasting is defined as 'broadcasting for a more narrow and often homogeneous population through use of low cost and lower range FM transmitters' (Bouhafa 1997).

[2] For a discussion of the role of radio in the democratization process in Mali, see Myers (1998).

Several other factors have contributed to the independent radio explosion, all to some extent linked with democratization. One of these was structural adjustment and private competition. As Bouhafa (1997) puts it:

The adjustment process [World Bank-promoted SAPs] also forced governments to privatize previously state owned and operated mass media. Along with the democracy movement, the net result has been guidelines and enabling legislation to free the media. This in turn has generated a new pluralistic media landscape, in which many new players are competing for the interest of the citizen.

Another reason for the growth of independent media has been donor support. In the same way that democratization was actively encouraged by pressures from outside the region – notably from France – independent radios have been hailed and encouraged by bilateral, NGO and United Nations donors as a powerful force for community development and the promotion of human rights. UNICEF and FAO are the big UN supporters, while the French Agence de coopération culturelle et technique (ACCT), Americans (USAID), Canadians (CIDA), Swiss and Germans (GTZ) have funded significant sectors of the public service broadcasting structures. For example, German money has kept the CIERRO radio training centre in Ouagadougou alive and UNICEF has a nationwide programme of training and infrastructure support in Mali, including a motorbike donated to every community radio station to facilitate reporting from the field. Another interesting initiative in Mali is a mobile technical repair and support team funded by USAID, in conjunction with the independent broadcasters' union, URTEL (personal communication, Dennis Bilodeau, USAID, Bamako).

Donors have also been attracted by the developmental success of early radio projects. Radio Kayes, for instance, was a pre-democracy example of a community radio in Mali which had some relatively well publicized success with local literacy campaigns and with encouraging local initiatives such as the building of wells, schools, dispensaries and mosques. Supported initially by an Italian NGO, Radio Kayes has proved enormously popular with the local Soninké-speaking population and their relatives working as emigrants in France. The financial support of these emigrants is now proving useful for the long-term financial survival of the station.[3]

The establishment of a legal framework to help facilitate the development of radio has been crucial. Again, donors have been instrumental in this area. For instance, the Panos Institute in conjunction with local journalists' unions helped organize a West Africa-wide conference in 1993 at which the 'Bamako Declaration on Radio Pluralism' was signed. This document, endorsed by the Malian president, Alpha Oumar Konaré, recommended to the states of West Africa:

The drafting, adoption and effective implementation of the legislative and administrative frameworks for information pluralism, and especially for radio pluralism [and] the establishment of independent regulatory authorities ... (Bamako Declaration, Panos Institute and West African Journalist Association, September 1993)

At the same time President Konaré called for a new type of radio 'that is close, shares the same roof, becomes one of the family, with which one identifies, an

---

[3] For more information on Radio Kayes see Berqué (1992).

ally; radio that provides the anchor for local democracy' (Panos 1994, quoted in Bouhafa 1997).

The new legislation legitimizing local radio which was passed by Burkina Faso in 1995 is typical of a rash of similar laws which came into force in the region (such as in Senegal, Benin, Mauritania and Mali) around the same time. The text of the Burkina law bears witness to the prevailing feeling that local or community radio is a force for development:

> Article 2: Local radio is a participatory tool held in common by all members of society for the development of the region concerned ...
> Article 3: Local radio's main objectives are to:
> • Liberate the voice of the peasantry by being an instrument of communication, *animation* and *dynamisation* of the community with a view to its well-being
> • Reinforce cultural identity
> • Value knowledge and traditional wisdom as well as the cultural heritage of grassroots communities
> • Promote the use of local languages (*langues nationales*) as part of the rural development process
> • Stimulate people's participation in it and management of it
> • Support and encourage development initiatives and activities of a socio-economic and cultural nature
> • Inform, animate and entertain
> (Ministry of Communication and Culture, Burkina Faso, Arrêté No. 036, 21 August 1995 (my translation).[4]

Community radio and development

Self-help and self-expression through radio

Powerful evidence that radio is an outlet for self-expression at the grassroots is provided by instances of villagers starting 'home-made' radio stations on their own initiative. Many in the region still operate illegally. For instance in Mali 'there are dozens if not hundreds of unofficial radio "stations" consisting of jury-rigged portable radios converted to transmit signals over a simple wire antenna, and covering one or two kms' (USAID 1997). Some were started before the new wave of democracy began. A specific example, again from Mali, was in the region of Bankass in the south-east:

> In April 1993 several pirate radio stations started to broadcast in Bankass ... Having visited the village of Tori where an illiterate radio electrician had set up a radio station, I had witnessed the enthusiasm of the villagers for 'their' station. The local school headmaster as well as the village headman confirmed the usefulness of village radio for education and communication. Nobody had to move from house to house anymore to inform citizens on local developments or venues for meetings ... However, somehow Bamako became aware that 'Radio Tori' emitted without a licence, and the gendarmerie got orders to close down all 'clandestine' radio stations. (Sturmheit 1993)

In some ways the clandestine nature of such popular initiatives has worked in favour of community interests. In the above case, a British-based NGO, SOS Sahel UK, decided to fund a legitimate community radio, Radio Seno, for Bankass, once

---

4 Courtesy of Urbain Nombré who supplied copies to the workshop in 1997.

free radios had been legalized in Mali. At Radio Kayes in the western part of the country, which began before the 'revolution', there had always been a hidden agenda:

> The unstated political purpose of the Kayes station included support for peasant organi-
> zations and, at the same time, a transformation of the authoritarian nature of relations
> between the local communities and central authorities. (Berqué 1992)

Even now that many more are legalized, the 'anti-authority' character of community radios seems to have attracted NGO donors. For instance, the radical urban radio Bamakan based originally in Bamako has not been short of donors, although it has been temporarily closed down on several occasions by the Malian government.

At Daande Duwansa (Mali), an on-air democratization campaign began in 1995, designed to educate local people about their rights in the run-up to the 1997 elections and the decentralization of government. This was, in fact, a multi-media campaign which combined radio with theatre, leaflets and newspaper articles. It produced some interesting instances of 'people power' against authority. The following is an extract from the evaluation which followed the campaign:

> 'You opened our eyes' was the reaction from Mondoro [village]. In Gono village, a
> newly literate man said 'the booklets, the plays, the radio programmes helped us a lot
> to understand the law on decentralization; we understood that those villages that wish
> can join together to form a *commune* ...' in Tieécouraré, Prye, Dansa, the inhabitants
> declared they were no longer frightened to speak up [against persons in authority].
> 'Even in the Commandant's office we say what we think; that's democracy too!',
> Seydou [a man from Boumbam village] said, 'Before we didn't know much about laws
> and we were made to do a lot of things by force, but now if it's not the law we don't
> agree and we say so clearly and freely'. (NEF 1996) (my translation)

Apart from popular self-expression, what also attracts donors about community radio is a tangible expression of communal effort. Radio Seno, for example, was built by local labour and with donated local materials. From an NGO point of view, if broadcasts can also foster public works such as well-digging, savings groups and literacy classes, then so much the better; this is reportedly the case at Radio Kayes (Berqué 1992). In Fissel, Senegal, from where Radio Penc-Mi (Radio Meeting-Place) broadcasts, locals say that the women's programmes have helped spread news about the activities of local women's groups and has boosted membership (Myers 1997).

In many cases community radios have grown out of pre-existing peasant associations or community groups. This is the case, for example, with Radio Penc-Mi in Senegal, which was started by three local peasant associations in order to extend news of their meetings and activities to a wider public; it is run by Ousseynou Gueye who comes from the local area and was formerly secretary to one of the associations. La Voix du Paysan (The Farmer's Voice) in Burkina Faso is another example, where an established local NGO, in this case the well-known Naam movement, decided to extend its reach by going 'on-air'. Since the Naam communications team had been using audiovisual aids since 1983 to facil-itate discussion in village meetings, the radio idea seemed like a natural extension of pre-existing communication efforts. As Bouhafa describes:

The broadcasts are linked with animation and inter-personal communication activities. This is currently done by fourteen technical teams employed by the federation of Naam groups who are in charge of interventions in communication, water, sanitation, forestry, credit, marketing and women's development. Teams include a small number of technicians and announcers from the village. (Bouhafa 1997)

Broadcasters as development agents

On the old model of state-run radio, broadcasters were civil servants trained to extend government policy to the rural masses. By contrast, in community radio, broadcasters are from the local area themselves and see their jobs more as midwives of rural self-expression. In Francophone development parlance, this is the difference between the old 'vulgarisation' and the now more acceptable 'animation'.

Ilboudo in Chapter 3 draws a parallel between good rural radio and PRA as currently practised by development workers in the agriculture or health context:

> In the way that they collect information both PRA and rural radio put familiarity with the rural world, and the knowledge of villagers, first. They share the thesis that peasants know their countryside better than experts coming from elsewhere. (p. 57)

Significantly, rural radio methods predate PRA, showing how the Anglophone development world is only now becoming alert to the participatory approaches which have been used in the Francophone community for some time. One of the most influential writers on rural radio is François Querre, whose book A Thousand and One Worlds (1992) is a rural radio handbook setting out a comprehensive methodology which integrates radio with participatory development. Central to Querre's methodology is the broadcaster as development agent:

> The [radio] producers will create the right environment for broadcasting and a way of thinking familiar to rural life. Dialogue will be genuine and real. Concrete solutions to concrete problems can be discovered together ... They will preserve the cultural identity of their audience and hand back to them their right to be heard. (Querre 1992: xi)

Querre writes in the context of relatively large rural radio departments run by state radio. These broadcast in local languages, but are run centrally from major urban capitals such as Ouagadougou, Niamey, Bamako and Dakar. This is the typical structure funded by the FAO, which from the 1960s to the early 1990s was the prevailing 'peasant' radio model. Now the airwaves have been 'liberated', his methodology is being adopted by community radio practitioners and trainers. His model of the broadcaster as rural animateur is now even more appropriate and applicable.

The very local nature of community radio begins and ends with the producers/ presenters, who call themselves animateurs/animatrices, in common with grass-roots development workers. They must, if they are to have any credibility with the audience, be from the area. In Douentza (Mali), the presenters on Daande Duwansa are a young farmer, a former literacy-worker, a former assistant nurse and couple of energetic secondary school-leavers with a little technical know-how. Their mother tongues are Fulfulde and Dogon, the languages of the locality. Listeners know them by name, and no doubt many have family ties with them. The almost constant presence of the presenters at the radio station, even when not on-air, means they are always receptive to the regular stream of visiting locals who come to deliver requests or to record announcements; market day in Douentza is especially busy.

Some broadcasters have become such well-known figures that they have a certain authority – even those who would normally be disadvantaged by their age and gender. For example, at Radio Penc-Mi (Senegal) one of the young (female) *animatrices* says:

> Since I started doing my programme [about food hygiene] the fried fish sellers and the doughnut hawkers in the market-place cover up their wares because they are ashamed when they see me passing through the market on my way home from the studio. (personal communication, Marie Magdalen)

A question many of these presenters must confront is the extent to which they can be didactic on matters relating to development. Some know the influence they wield, and do not hesitate to adopt a teacherly approach, as in the case above of Marie Magdalen's dire warnings about the dangers of fly-infested food on sale in the dusty market place. On the other hand, because they are locals, albeit educated above the average, *animateurs* are rarely so out of touch with local mores that they are likely to cause offence or, worse, to be ignored, as was so often the case with national radio presenters broadcasting from the capital to 'ignorant' peasants.

When quizzed on their treatment of sensitive issues (for example local politics, gender relations, religious questions), most community radio presenters will say that they try to present both sides of the argument and leave it to listeners to make an informed choice on the evidence (personal communication, Diawara, of Radio Daande Duwansa). Nevertheless, it is clearly difficult for them to resist being prescriptive on occasion. A case in point is the question of female circumcision (or female genital mutilation, FGM). For example, in Burkina Faso the national rural radio held a seminar for community radio producers to educate and convince them about FGM's negative consequences (most attendees were male from relatively traditional rural backgrounds). Clearly this was felt to be necessary in order that these presenters, in turn, passed on this message to their listeners. In this case no open choice was advocated – rather a toeing of the line; after all, as one participant put it, 'FGM is against the law'.

In many cases, neutrality is a difficult tightrope for community radio broadcasters to walk. Some assiduously accord equal airtime and charge the same advertising fees to all parties, particularly for competing political parties at election time. Others, particularly the more radical urban radios in Mali, do not even make the pretence of so doing. This is easier when the radio station is more commercial, or privately owned. Indeed, stations like Kayira, Bamakan and Liberté have created loyal listener-bases by virtue of controversial debate. However, there are obvious dangers in this, not the least of which is to fall foul of national regulatory authorities, or even the police.[5]

---

[5] For example, in 1993 Radio Kayira in Bamako was accused of inciting armed revolt as groups of students occupied the state radio station in March and massive demonstrations were held against the government's economic policy in April. There is some anecdotal evidence that the allegation about Radio Kayira's involvement are true. Kayira's broadcasts were jammed in 1995 and again

Another dilemma is the extent to which broadcasters can truly fulfil the role of development workers. There is, for example, the perennial problem of lack of sufficient funds to visit outlying villages, even for gathering 'vox pop', let alone recording longer musical performances or the ambitious 'public game shows' which Querre and other practitioners of his rural radio method advocate (see Querre 1992). Most outside broadcasts, if they are done properly, require several days worth of per diems, fuel, vehicle spare parts (two punctures per day in the harsh environment of the arid scrub are not uncommon), batteries, cassettes and, of course, the initial investment in the appropriate recording equipment. Few small community radios in rural areas can afford to make such programmes, and so they adhere, instead, to the relatively improvised, live DJ-style where developmental advice or discussions are interspersed with local music.

A further problem is a lack of training among broadcasters. Few have more than secondary education, so their ability to respond correctly to listeners' questions on matters such as agriculture, health, legal rights and so on is perforce limited. The most conscientious will consult specialists – like the local health worker. However, there have been instances of misinformation and rumour being spread by amateurish presenters.[6] The other problem with training is that many community presenters, once trained, are lured away to better paid and more secure jobs with national radio in the capital city.

Furthermore, many of the available training opportunities tend to be more journalistic than developmentally oriented. The more *animateurs* are trained, the less likely they are to bring the fresh spontaneity and local flavour to their manner of presenting, as they will invariably have been schooled in the style of the BBC or RFI where pre-recorded and carefully edited production is the ideal.

Evidence of developmental change

Listener surveys and impact assessments in West Africa are infrequent and have not been done methodically or over a wide range of radio stations and countries (see Chapter 3 Appendix). Nevertheless, there are a gradually growing number of documented examples which show the positive influence of radio on developmental behaviour change among listeners.

One of the larger studies is carried out by the US Demographic Health Survey on a regular basis. The 1996 survey found that in Mali radio was the principal source of AIDS information for men (75 per cent of the sample) and women (50 per cent). Interestingly, on this particular topic, the radio outstripped other more usual sources of health information such as friends, relatives and health workers

---

[5] (cont.) on the occasion of a student strike in January 1996. In September 1997, international alerts were issued by Reporters sans Frontières in defence of two Radio Kayira employees, arrested because they were members of the opposition SADI party. Staff of other radios such as Klédu and Guintan have also been the subject of harassment, interrogations, even beatings on occasion (see Myers 1998).

[6] For example, staff of the NGO PLAN International in Bamako have noticed with disquiet that some young people claim to have heard on the radio that condoms (which are distributed free as protection against HIV/AIDS) are actually infected with the AIDS virus and are being donated by agencies as part of a conspiracy by the West to control the Malian population (personal communication, PLAN international staff member).

(DHS 1996). Again on AIDS, in Mali at a more local level, a survey by the NGO Save the Children Fund in the Mopti region found by means of a KAP study of 2,000 respondents randomly selected throughout the region that 95 per cent of the sample had heard about the existence of AIDS and that the principal source of their information was the radio (SCF Malian Ministry of Health1994).

AIDS may be a subject to which radio lends itself particularly well, being a topic that is more easily articulated by a young DJ over the air than by health workers in a face-to-face situation, which might entail more embarrassment. However, there are examples of health education success on other subjects. For example, in Mauritania, in an area where guinea worm was rife, the local station Radio Barkeol seems to have achieved a significant drop in rates of worm infestation in its catchment area:

> After eight months of operation ... the radio programmes had a large following, and the evaluation suggested that the change in hours of broadcasting (from afternoon to evening) could increase the number of listeners even more ... The programmes devoted to guinea worm and vaccination helped 80% of the mothers (in an area where women outnumber men) to better understand the disease and change their behaviour [i.e. filter their drinking water]. In addition UNICEF reported that the numbers of children being immunized multiplied by five. (Bouhafa 1997)

Successful behaviour change can be achieved on environmental subjects as well as on health, although these are often more difficult to evaluate given the long time-frame necessary before environmental changes become noticeable. In Mali in 1995 a project run by Cranfield University initiated a successful experiment with Daande Duwansa which was designed to measure the impact of a set of tailormade radio programmes on the theme of preserving and encouraging the growth of indigenous trees:

> After the broadcasts a high proportion of respondents within the FM 'footprint' showed increased awareness of how to mark (or *visualise*) the young tree (2 out of 35 before, and 15 out of 35 afterwards), and furthermore were putting the advice into practice by marking the shoot with old cups or calabashes as the radio programmes recommended. There was a jump in the numbers of those aware of the correct spacing required between trees in fields (9 out of 35 before, and 28 out of 35 after) and also an increased awareness that pruning permits do not need to be paid for ... Overall 60% of the sample demonstrated that they had heard our programmes and remembered them in some detail. (Myers *et al.* 1995)

Other developmental issues, such as girls' schooling and community literacy, have also been the subject of surveys. For example, in Senegal, Radio Penc-Mi is credited with having helped achieve a rise of 40 per cent in girls' attendance at the local secondary school in one year, following a broadcast campaign featuring young girls who were still regularly attending school, despite already being married.[7] In Douentza, after Daande Duwansa went on air, the demand for places on local literacy classes, as 'advertised' on the radio, jumped by nearly 120 per cent (Rolt 1995). Even conflict can be resolved or prevented by radio, as shown, again in Douentza, by the radio carrying notices from farmers about precisely when their fields will be harvested and when they will be free for browsing by migrating herds of cattle. This prevents the – often bloody – conflicts between

---

[7] Girls marrying at 13 years and upwards is not uncommon in this area.

farmers and herders which are liable to break out in certain seasons when pastoralists' herds are accused of trampling farmers' crops (personal communication, staff of Radio Douentza).

All the above examples arise from discrete education campaigns on the radio. These are relatively attractive to donors who like to see results emerging from a well-defined number of hours of sponsored airtime. However, the long-term effects of regular slots on health and hygiene, women's rights, education, environmental conservation, folk wisdom and farming must also be having a positive – though more intangible – effect in the long term. This is the daily and regular diet of community radio listeners.

By whatever measurement, the cost-effectiveness of community radio cannot be disputed. For example, Bouhafa (1997) quotes a WHO study which costed out HIV/AIDS education strategies in developing countries and found that educational programmes through mass media (television and radio) were far cheaper than reaching people through schools or person to person: 'The cost ranged from 0.07 to 0.041 US cents per person' (Bouhafa 1997). At Daande Duwansa, the costs are also extremely low: each programme hour costs approximately £7.50 (sterling), which per listener is about 0.00009 pence.

What future for community radio?

Despite the cost-effectiveness of small-scale radio in terms of development impact, one of its perennial problems is financial sustainability. State-owned rural radio has always received subsidies, usually through bilateral aid, but community radios are expected to survive without the benefit of public money. If they look to the commercial sector instead, rural community stations in particular have a problem attracting advertising revenue. Unlike their urban counterparts rural stations cannot count on commercial interest in metropolitan buying power. Music requests, birth, marriage and death announcements and on-air 'lost and found' announcements bring in only a tiny income, because they are designed as primarily a community service rather than a money-making exercise.

For most community radios, sponsorship by development agencies presents the best hope of sustained support. It would seem that UN and NGO agencies are, for the time being, pleased with the results they obtain from the support they provide. But the funding of core costs, as opposed to discrete campaigns, is urgently needed. As Bouhafa (1997) says: 'Stations need policy support, training and equipment', and he sees an expanded role for the state:

> Development banks could support the policy reform that is necessary to ensure that community radio is supported by governments and that the national radio budgets pay as much attention as possible to the most vulnerable groups. (Bouhafa 1997)

There are other possible options, such as twinning with community radios in Europe and support from expatriates overseas, both being options that Radio Kayes has successfully taken (personal communication, Many Camara, Radio Kayira, Mali).

A mix of a number of these alternatives is probably the best strategy. Meanwhile, it is significant that despite the community radio explosion in countries like Mali, 'since 1991 there has not been one station that has stopped broadcasting for want of funds' (Bouhafa 1997). It would seem that somehow radios find ways of surviving if they are truly popular with local people. Membership fees from listeners' clubs and sponsorship from local traders have helped numerous stations stay afloat despite the poverty of the populations among whom they operate.

The popularity of community radio is ultimately also its means of survival. Unless it is truly representative of local people's interest, it will not receive community and donor support. The negative precedents set by some of the rural radios in Burkina Faso present a case in point. A number of rural stations such as La Voix des Lacs in Kongoussi were established by the central government Rural Radio Department in the 1980s to serve the local community. But these ultimately were, and are, initiatives made on behalf of rural people rather than by them; and many have failed as a result. La Voix des Lacs has encountered major financial and management difficulties with even the radio station's motorbike being commandeered by the management committee for use by the local tax collector, rather than being used for community broadcasts (Myers 1995). As Bouhafa says:

> The extent to which this potential [for community empowerment] can be realized is directly related to the extent to which the community participates in the management and therefore the content of the material that is broadcast. (Bouhafa 1997)

In making any assessment there remains the problem of defining what the community actually is. Development discourses warn that too great a reliance on the homogeneity and cohesion of any social grouping is dangerous. There will be splits in any community: of a religious, caste, class, gender, age, income-related nature. Radio stations are all too aware that powerful local influences, for example the dominant political party, often would like to monopolize the airwaves. The influence of the ruling ADEMA party in Mali is an example, where radio stations such as Daande Duwansa have to be extremely careful to accord equal airtime to all. In his study of community-type radio in Benin, Grätz (Chapter 8) details some examples of external political, ethnic and personality conflicts which have put considerable pressure on Radio Rurale Tanguiéta.

The survival of community radio is also dependent on a favourable political climate. Even in Mali, where growth has been phenomenal, and where the process of democratization and decentralization seems relatively well established, there is always the shadow of censorship and clamp-down by the authorities. For instance, the supposedly neutral regulatory body appointed to advise the Malian government on the granting of broadcast licences, the *Conseil Supérieur de la Communication* (CSC), has recently been charged with partiality because its Secretary-General was not elected by CSC members, but was appointed by the government instead (Radio-Actions 1996).

Conclusion

Having reviewed some of the unique characteristics, successes and problems of community radio in West Africa, we must ask: is community radio a positive force for development? The record would indicate yes, with some reservations. Successes have been patchy and sustainability is a significant problem.

The growth in community radio does not follow a uniform pattern. As Bouhafa (1997) remarks: 'Media pluralism does not automatically translate into community empowerment. There have not been equivalent results in all countries [of the region].' Senegal, for example, despite having liberal press laws, has only one example of an independent rural station (although there are several urban ones), whereas, as we have seen, Mali boasts dozens. Does this mean that Mali's rural people are more empowered? Or perhaps, quite the reverse, Senegal's peasantry is better organized into associations, and therefore does not need the aid of radio.

What is certain is that the best community radios are more than just 'juke-boxes and public telephones', as Nombré (Chapter 5) says of some of the less successful state-funded community-type stations in Burkina Faso. Outfits like Daande Duwansa (Mali), Radio Penci-Mi (Senegal), La Voix du Paysan (Burkina Faso) and Radio Barkeol (Mauritania) are having a real developmental impact. This can be measured, as we have seen, in terms of behaviour change on health and other issues. Positive impact is also demonstrated by the very fact of the survival of these radios against the odds in very impoverished communities.

Finally, we can turn our question around and say that development is a positive force for community radio. The two go hand in hand. Without some of the decentralized structures such as peasant associations, local NGOs and community organizations which are becoming more common in the region, many community stations would not have a basis on which to exist. The macro-political and economic environment creates a context for decentralization and human development, which, in turn has made community radio possible.

References

Berqué, P. (1992) 'The hard lesson of autonomy', in Bruce Girard (ed.) *A Passion for Radio*, Montreal: Black Rose Books.

Bouhafa, M. (1997) 'Grassroots media and community empowerment in West Africa', paper presented to the International Conference on 'Media and Politics', Katholieke Universitet, 27 February–1 March, Brussels.

DHS (Demographic Health Survey) (1996) 'Enquête démographique et de la santé – Mali 1995–96', Calverton, USA.

Myers, Mary (1997) *Media Monitoring Visit to Senegal and Mali*, Report to the Creative Radio Initiative of the International Centre for Humanitarian Reporting, Geneva.

—— (1998) 'The promotion of democracy at the grassroots – the example of radio in Mali' in Vicky Randall (ed.) *Democratization and the Media*, Ilford: Frank Cass.

Myers, Mary with Adam, G. and Lalanne, L. (1995) 'The effective use of radio for mitigation of drought in the Sahel', Cranfield University, Royal Military College of Science.

NEF (Near East Foundation) (1996) 'Rapport narratif des activités du programme d'appui à la démocratie et à la décentralisation', internal report, Mali: NEF.

Querre, F. (1992) *A Thousand and One Worlds – A Rural Radio Handbook*, Rome: FAO.

Radio-Actions (1996) No. 10, December, newsletter published by Institut Panos, Dakar, Senegal

Rolt, F. (1995) *Evaluation Report Radio Daande Douentza*, Oxford: OXFAM.

SCF/Malian Ministry of Health (1994) 'Rapport de l'enquête CAP sur les MST et le SIDA dans la région de Mopti', November, Mali: Save the Children Fund.

Sturmheit, P. (1993) 'The priority of priorities: a free radio for Bankass', unpublished paper, London: SOS Sahel.

United Nations Development Programme (UNDP) (1997) *Human Development Report*, New York: UNDP.

USAID (1997) 'A community radio success story', press release by Dennis Bilodeau, Bamako, Mali.

7
Radio
in Niger

Central Control
versus Local Cultures
CHRISTINE NIMAGA CEESAY

Communication technology is going international, creating an ever-growing number of gadgets for the global talking shop: satellite technology, e-mail, internet, video-conferencing, and so on. However, in the shadow of this process of globalization, radio in West Africa is going local. More and more local radio stations are being set up whose links to the larger networks of government-controlled media or public service broadcasters are becoming less and less important. Local radio (called by a variety of names – regional, local, rural or community) gains its strength and appeal from its geographically limited nature: it thrives within boundaries instead of trying to break them down.

These local stations usually have the support of big organizations, albeit not the likes of CNN or other commercial broadcasters. They are often supported by development agencies like the FAO, ACCT, OXFAM, or GTZ.

An example of this kind of cooperation in West Africa has been a project entitled 'Regionalization of radio in Niger'. Started in 1988 with the assistance of GTZ, the project is due to end in 1999. Its aim was to decentralize radio and give more power, more transmitters, more airtime and more resources to local people; the idea was to enable them to determine their broadcast culture as part of their regional development. The multi-million dollar project established and equipped six regional FM stations in the provincial capitals of the Republic of Niger. Each of the stations covers an area of 60–150 kilometres radius around the sites of transmitters and retransmitters.

The attempt to cover a country as large as Niger with a network of local FM stations can only be described as bold. With the Sahara desert constituting two-thirds of the country where population density drops to less than 1 person per square kilometre, the technical side of the project was a real challenge. FM transmitters with a power of between one and two kilowatts cover an area of 100 kilometres radius on average. Areas of this size are like isolated islands in the vastness of a country like Niger which stretches for more than 1,500 kilometres from east to west and from north to south. In spite of this geographical context, a growing number of local radio stations see themselves as part of a much bigger network of FM, mediumwave and shortwave stations.

Almost all radio listeners in Niger have a wide range of stations to choose from: besides the national radio which broadcasts on mediumwave and short-wave, there are a host of other stations from the sub-region (such as Nigeria, Algeria, Mali) and of course the international broadcasters like the BBC World Service from London, RFI, the Voice of America, among others. Yet despite this choice, only the FM station induces the listener to talk of 'my' or 'our' station. It is the exclusiveness of coverage that makes people proud of their own station.

The project in Niger ran into many difficulties, from technical problems to political squabbling and endless bureaucratic hurdles. But the moments when listeners came forward to express their appreciation of their own new radio station, where presenters spoke their own language and dialect, where programmes talked about the price of millet that farmers had grown in the area, and where the music spoke of their legends and heroes – these moments far outweighed all the problems that the project had to endure.

The popularity of the local stations was even more surprising when one takes into account the fact that they broadcast only three or four hours a day and operate on a shoestring budget, with limited personnel, vehicles, tapes and equipment. Audience research carried out in 1995 for the two oldest of the regional stations, namely Zinder (launched in 1992) and Tahoua (launched in 1994), showed that more than half the listeners in the area covered by the FM station were regular listeners (85 per cent regular listening in Zinder, 65 per cent regular listening in Tahoua).

Indeed, the regional station in Zinder was so popular that it became the favourite station in the area. Some 56 per cent of all people living in the target area preferred listening to the Voice of Zinder. Less than a quarter of the same group preferred the BBC World Service (in Hausa, which is spoken as a lingua franca in and around Zinder). Most surprisingly, the national radio came only third, with 15 per cent of the audience listening to the strikingly named La Voix du Sahel, the Voice of the Sahel. The audience research was carried out by two local consultants and came as a surprise to the local radio producers and their managers (De Campos and Mahanman 1996). It was hard for them to accept that the national radio was losing its status as *la radio de référence*.

The rising popularity of regional broadcasters at the expense of national stations follows a trend already well established in many industrialized countries. National stations may see their audience figures drastically reduced when the number of regional and local stations increases (provided that the regional stations still supply essential national news). In the case of Niger, one could well imagine that the national radio may become superfluous to people living in areas covered by FM stations. Their need for local and national information would be satisfied by the regional and local stations (radios of proximity), while the need for inter-national information would be catered for by the international broadcasters (on shortwave, or re-broadcast on FM by local stations) who have the necessary means to cover events all over the world. La Voix du Sahel cannot compete with

either of these: it is too far removed from local events, and it does not have sufficient means to cover international events from a Nigérien perspective.

As all six regional stations in Niger are part of the public service broadcasting
network ORTN, their activities are regularly influenced by political manoeuvring.
De jure, ORTN has been separated from the Ministry of Information and
Communication, but *de facto* it is still the extended arm of the ministry. All the
senior radio producers are *fonctionnaires*, i.e. civil servants who are answerable to
the political authorities and whose career chances depend on the goodwill of their
superiors.

For many *fonctionnaires* sent to the provinces by ORTN, working in a regional
station in 1992 was a major challenge: instead of being close to the Director-
General of ORTN, or indeed the Minister of Information, they were now close to
the audience and received immediate feedback from rural people.

Before 1992, locally produced radio transmitted on a regional level simply did
not exist in Niger: all programmes were broadcast from the capital Niamey on
mediumwave and shortwave. Correspondents' reports from the regions were
recorded and edited in, and controlled by, Niamey. Even today, when people
mention the national radio, they say 'That's Niamey broadcasting', because the
output of the national radio is still controlled by the ruling political class in the
capital.

In 1992, the first local transmission went on air in Zinder, Niger's second
largest city in the east of the country. Many Zarma politicians in Niamey must
have watched with trepidation as this predominantly Hausa region was given its
own voice. Fears of secession surface easily in Niger. Three decades of one-party
rule, domination by the military and a lack of resources have created a political
culture which leaves little room for harmonious pluralism. If, with the Voice of
Zinder, the Hausa had got their own medium for mass communication, what
about the Fulani, the Kanuri, not to mention the Tuareg who were involved in
an armed rebellion against the government, demanding more autonomy?

Controversy surrounded not only the question of which region would receive a
radio station or a retransmitter site, but also the question of the languages in which
the stations would broadcast. The people involved were aware of the power of
communication: during election campaigns, the government regularly tried to
increase the number of languages per station; ethnic minorities hoped to gain
wider recognition by having their language broadcast to a whole region; proponents of dominant languages like Hausa were not keen on linguistic diversification on the airwaves, arguing that their language was the lingua franca understood by most listeners.

The network of regional stations was created in a society of two opposing
political cultures. The first is the culture of post-independence: a French-oriented,
strongly centralized society which works on the assumption that the government
in Niamey decides and the *fonctionnaires* execute the orders, while the rest of the
country is expected to obey. Disobedient regions could be punished by the central
powers by not getting their share of national revenues, mainly development aid.

The second political culture was born at grassroots level when the people of
Niger started protesting against the one-party state and military domination, and
forced the government to hold a national conference in 1991. Democracy and

decentralization are the key words of this political culture which also gains support from the development partners of Niger, donor agencies and NGOs. These organizations, having seen how much past development money disappeared into the overblown bureaucracy of the centralized state, have decided to get closer to the people and bring them closer to the national wealth. Naturally, this meant going regional, if not local. The second culture is also linked with traditional regionalism, emphasizing cultural boundaries that are older than the newly created concept of Nigérien democracy, older than the one-party state and older than colonialism.

Not surprisingly, these two different cultures often clashed during the implementation of the project entitled the 'Regionalization of radio in Niger'. On the one hand, the central government was interested in using the regional station for its propaganda; on the other hand, the GTZ and the rural population were interested in decentralizing broadcasting and empowering local citizens.

Two examples highlight the problems involved. The first concerns a weekly press review broadcast as a digest by the national radio. There are a dozen independent newspapers in the country published in the capital. The papers often publish heavyweight analyses of current politics, occasionally mixed with criticism of the government. The papers, as well as the broadcast digest from the Voix du Sahel, are all in French, Niger's official language, spoken by about 10 per cent of the population.

A proposal to translate the review of the press into vernacular languages for local stations triggered a storm of protest from the *fonctionnaires* in charge of the stations' schedules. Their main argument was that a programme like a press review was not made for 'those illiterate country people', and that too much information was doing harm to farmers. The most surprising aspect of the debate was the vehemence with which the *fonctionnaires* argued their case. This was not just about avoiding the newspapers' criticism of government from spreading; there was a deep-rooted wish to control the intellectual world of rural citizens. For the *fonctionnaires*, control could translate into promotion or financial reward for the 'controller', a system often exploited by the state during election campaigns.

In the eyes of the *fonctionnaires*, development of the rural regions was necessary. But for them this meant programmes that would preach and teach. By so doing, radio would ensure that rural people continued to think of themselves as being 'under'-developed. Programmes of this nature abound at ORTN. A typical opening might be, 'Hello dear listener, dear herder, today we are going to tell you how to herd your cattle. Here's our expert on the matter, Mr XYZ, and our first question to you is: how do you define cattle herding? ...' To many *fonctionnaires* at ORTN, development and programme-making still had to come from the top and be given out like alms.

The above discussion may sound harsh, even unfair, given that many journalists work very hard for their regional programmes and honestly believe that the didactic approach is the key to regional development. A producer from the regional radio in Zinder once described people's reactions to his programmes: 'If only the people were listening to me! Since our station was launched four years ago, I've been telling them about family planning and that we have to change our ways. But look at our birth rate, so high! They just don't listen!' These journalists have a lot of potential and enthusiasm, but they follow the example of the *fonctionnaires* in thinking of themselves as members of an educated elite which has to enlighten the ignorant masses.

Certainly, the traditional culture of Niger makes it easy to adopt this hierarchical approach. Traditionally, the elite advised the common people in the form of a monologue. Who would dare to interrupt or enter into a public dialogue with an emir, a king or even a village chief? And is not local broadcasting all about keeping alive customs and cultures?

Programme-makers in local radio often find themselves squeezed between two philosophies: on the one hand, they want to protect local cultures and customs, and on the other, they want to promote 'development' which is often equated with 'change'. In addition, the lack of a clear definition of what 'development' means and where it is supposed to lead widens the gap between the 'Old' (traditional culture) and the 'New' (development culture). The traditional old might not work any longer in a changing and deteriorating environment (pressure on water and land due to high population growth). But the Old is the familiar system in which the pride of the people is invested. The New is difficult and complicated (the language of the New is sometimes difficult to fathom – family planning talks of 'birth spacing' rather than 'reduction' as a result of criticism by Muslim clerics), and, moreover, the New is not generated within the community and remains foreign and strange to many.

Many programme-makers of regional radio stations are (often unconsciously) caught between the Old and the New, unable to bridge the gap because their self-perception is just as problematic as the reality around them. They themselves do not know where the development of their region should lead. This confusion often results in programmes which are unable to link the two cultures. Programmes about the Old can sound out-of-date, while programmes about the New can sound complicated and strange. Inevitably, the complicated and strange programmes do not constitute favourite items for the audience. Audience research in Zinder in 1995 showed that a typical development programme like the one produced by the Radio Club of Zinder was actually the most disliked programme broadcast by that station.

A second example relates to an intra-cultural dialogue on such issues. Despite conflicting philosophies and approaches, a bridge can be built between the traditional values of a society and a changing environment requiring changes in behaviour. To show that it can be done, I want to describe a radio spot which was produced by a regional station in cooperation with a family health project. These spots are comparable to commercial radio advertisements; they contain short messages produced for daily repetition over a period of several months.

The audiences of these spots (Hausa, Zarma) live in cultures where wisdom is often conveyed by story-telling, citing proverbs or solving riddles. So the radio spot would start with a jingle for the family health project, followed by a grandmother saying, 'What is this?' Since this opening is a fixed cultural phrase and requires a fixed response from the audience, some seconds of blank tape have to be inserted here. 'You do your best to get a lot, in order not to have anything!' A chorus of voices would then answer by shouting 'Collected money is the remedy for sickness!' Then a farmer tells a short story of how his village collected money to buy a stock of malaria medicine. If somebody fell sick, they did not have to go to the nearest pharmacy which was some 40 kilometres away. With the stock of medicine, and with the grace of the Almighty Allah, many lives were saved. At the end the grandmother is heard saying: 'You see? You do your best to get a lot of money, in order not to have any sickness!'

The example shows how radio can establish a dialogue with the audience. Not only does the spot pick up a classic form of Hausa and Zarma dialogue, the riddle (see Abdulkadir, p. 137), it also uses a farmer's voice, his vocabulary and the images a rural audience is most likely to associate with the topic. All this creates a channel of communication between the listener and the radio message.

Radio is the ideal medium in which to exploit established patterns of communication in an oral culture. Apart from riddles, there are tales, proverbs, jokes, poems and songs. But a genuine dialogue is established only if radio also takes into account those things that remain unsaid: taboos, prejudices and deeply rooted misconceptions. If radio does not incorporate them, it does not enter into the world of real dialogue with the listener.

The expert who is filling airtime with his monologue is not communicating with the mental world of the listener. Therefore, he cannot make people change their lifestyles, be it a matter of using condoms, considering family planning techniques or applying a new kind of fertilizer to their fields. The message has to reach out to the mental world of the listener, the more specifically the better. Only local radio can make full use of the wide range of expression in a community. If a programme tries to go beyond cultural boundaries, any dialogue with the listeners' mental world becomes increasingly more difficult. Within the boundaries, local radio can work like the village palaver tree and reach everybody who wants to participate in the communal dialogue.

This technique of creating a dialogue between the radio message and the listener by talking culture, talking taboo was shown to yield results. The same family health project did a series of radio spots on cholera protection. They were broadcast at the beginning of the cholera epidemic in Niger in 1996. By the time the Ministry of Health sent out their extension workers to explain to the villagers how to protect themselves against the disease, everybody had heard it all before on the radio. At the end of the year, the Ministry acknowledged a relationship between the radio spots and a reduced number of cholera deaths compared with previous epidemics.

Creating a dialogue and reaching out to the practical and mental world of the listener demands an intimate knowledge of the audience. However, this knowledge is not as easily acquired as many radio producers tend to think. The results of some audience research undertaken in 1995 came as a big surprise for many programme-makers at ORTN. The study showed that in Zinder, widely regarded as being part of the conservative heartland of Hausa culture in Niger, twice as many women as men preferred to discuss politics. Also, the percentage of women discussing religion was slightly higher than that of men. The programme schedule of the Voice of Zinder had not reflected these preferences at all: all newsreaders were male, and most interviewees were men. The religious programmes were exclusively male-dominated.

The research also revealed misconceptions among programme-makers about the type of work their listeners were involved in. In Zinder, for instance, there were more female than male stockbreeders. This fact produced disbelief and even anger on the part of the (mostly male) programme-makers who insisted that Niger was still a male-dominated (agri-) culture in which men looked after huge cattle herds on the wide plains of the Sahel. None of the programme-makers had ever thought of the large and growing number of women breeding domestic animals in their compounds and about the type of information that would be of interest to them.

The research also showed that both men and women had very clear ideas about the type of information that would be useful for them. Instead of looking for help on 'How to solicit the aid of an office or a project' (4 per cent of people questioned), more than half the people questioned wanted information on 'How to increase my capital' and 'How to increase my production'.

All told, the results of this piece of audience research dented some of the programme-makers' editorial preconceptions. After the study had broken up their 'ignorant masses' into specific target groups, it was impossible to continue with the time-honoured approach of feeding the rural population on a diet of centrally controlled material.

The same study also showed that the regional stations are among the most popular broadcasters in their respective areas. This popularity, combined with the potential of local radio as an educational tool, has had two effects in Niger. On the one hand, it has opened up a new source of income for the permanently underfunded local stations. The donor agencies constitute a big market in an economy like Niger, even if the usefulness of a market that depends on outside investments is debatable. After establishing marketing departments within the regional stations of ORTN, a large number of sponsorships and cooperation contracts were secured. The extra revenue also gave the regional stations more political weight vis-a-vis the central administration in Niamey. If the Voice of Zinder was earning good money for ORTN, how could Niamey tell it to change its programmes?

On the other hand, the government was always aware of the usefulness of the local stations as propaganda tools. Especially during election campaigns and official visits of senior politicians to the regions, the output was heavily affected. Journalists sometimes had to adapt to changing circumstances very quickly: from a training course on impartial reporting, financed by the project, they would be called into the studio to announce the arrival of the 'Great Prime Minister, the Far-Sighted, the Powerful'.

ORTN is not the only institution establishing regional or local stations in Niger. Some of the commercial stations which exist in the capital Niamey have started to expand into the interior of the country. In Niamey, the private sector has already put up a challenge to the public service broadcaster. The first commercial radio went on air in 1994, a year after RFI had broken the monopoly on the airwaves held by ORTN. In mid-1998, people living in and around the capital were able to listen to a long list of stations on FM: three commercial stations owned by Niger citizens (Radio Anfani, Radio & Musique, and Radio Souda), two foreign broadcasters who set up their own FM stations here (RFI, Africa No.1), the national radio La Voix du Sahel, and a host of international broadcasters who have their programmes re-broadcast on one of the private FM stations (BBC, VOA, Deutsche Welle).

La Voix du Sahel did rather badly in this competitive environment. Programmes on the private stations are less wordy and presented in a more relaxed style to appeal to a relatively young and more educated urban audience. Against this background, the character of the national radio was exposed more clearly than ever: It was informative, educative and dry. It was a radio made by and made for the administration and its *fonctionnaires*, and as such it could not become the day-to-day companion of the ordinary listener. As a consequence, La Voix du Sahel lost a big share of the Niamey audience after the deregulation of the airwaves.

The reaction of programme-makers at ORTN indicted that the public service broadcasting station lacked identity and had no long-term concept for its different branches, the national and regional stations. For instance, a new programme schedule proposed by the national station in reaction to developments in the capital would have increased the amount of French language programmes by almost 20 per cent to around 70 per cent (at the expense of vernacular programmes). The idea was to modernize the image of the national station by using modern language. Fortunately, this proposal was not put into practice (as mentioned earlier, only 10 per cent of Niger's population speaks French).

As the private stations are only just beginning to move to the provinces, little can be said about the new dynamics they will create in the rural areas. In theory, the regional stations of ORTN stand a good chance of retaining their popularity because they not only possess the equipment and professional experience of regional broadcasting but also know exactly (because of the audience research undertaken in 1995) what the audience expects. Whether in the end they have the creativity to turn machines and documents into lively radio programmes remains to be seen. Creativity needs space and cannot thrive if the central administration tries to exert too much control. It may be that competition from commercial regional stations will help listeners to gain a voice in the programme-making process. With more broadcasters competing for audiences, radio stations can no longer afford to serve only political interest groups.

Reference

De Campos, Pascal and Mahanman, Malam Baba (1996) 'Etude de l'auditoire des radio régionales de Tahoua et de Zinder. Evaluation de leurs performances auprès du public-cible', Niamey: Projet Radio Régionale ORTN-GTZ.

8

New Local Radio Stations
in African Languages & the
Process of Political Transformation

The Case of Radio Rurale Locale Tanguiéta
in Northern Benin[1]
TILO GRÄTZ

This chapter examines the processes involved in the establishment of new local radio stations, broadcasting in African languages, in Benin. One such station, Radio Rurale Locale Tanguiéta, is discussed at length. With reference to this case study, I aim to show the specifically political processes at work in: the struggles to appropriate and negotiate management of the community radio project by actors on the local and national scene in Benin today; the impact of the radio broadcasts – as symbolic resources – on local listeners and local-level politics; and finally the potential – and limits – of local radio stations as a means of forging a new civic consciousness in the process of democratization promoted by different development agencies and donors.[2] I begin with a summary of the general situation of local broadcasting in Benin and of the problems facing new community radios.

General problems in setting up local radio stations
in Benin

Local radio stations broadcasting entirely in African languages have existed in Benin since 1994. They were the very first independent stations in the country, enlarging the variety of media in the process of the so-called *renouveau démocratique*,

[1] The chapter is based upon field research, carried out in Tanguiéta in 1995–6, as part of my doctoral research on political transformation in Northern Atacora, Benin, while a student at the Graduate School of Sociology and Social Anthropology, University of Bielefeld. My research was supported by the Deutsche Forschungsgemeinschaft. Comparative sections of this chapter derive from the researches of Erik Voss (Berlin), who worked in 1996 with the radio station in Banikoara, as well as evaluation by the Institut Kilimandjaro (1996), on behalf of Coopération Suisse and the Centre Afrika Obota (CAO), both of which are active in this field.
[2] Independent radio stations are often simply assumed to have a positive impact on the process of democratization (e.g. de Souza 1996), a judgement I temper below.

or 'democratic renewal', that had been going on in Benin since 1990 (Raynal 1991; Allen 1992; Kohnert and Preuss 1992; Bierschenk 1994; Bierschenk and Mongbo 1995). Promotion of local radio stations was designed to improve access to information for the rural population, especially in African languages, and to promote development initiatives; a project on these lines was requested by the Ministry of Culture and Communication and financed, in the main, by ACCT in close collaboration with other donors. The project was developed together with the Benin national radio service ORTB.

ORTB, the state-owned national broadcasting agency, had already established a service promoting African languages in the 1960s, under a programme called 'Radio rurale' with equipment supplied under German technical assistance. Hours were scheduled in the programming of Radio Cotonou and Radio Parakou, which previously broadcast only in French, for emissions in each Béninois language. These programmes, broadcast on both FM and shortwave,[3] were unanimously judged to be insufficient and difficult to receive; their programmes, which tended towards monologic lectures, were considered remote from the needs of the local population. Therefore, a project to create community radio stations began early in 1994.

Initially four (now five) relatively remote communities were chosen: Lalo, Ouèssè, Banikoara, Ouakè and, later, Tanguiéta. The stations, were designed to cover large rural zones by transmitting in FM; for instance, Radio Lalo covered a radius of about 100 kilometres. The stations were set up in different parts of the country with very basic equipment consisting of transmitters, solar panels (and batteries) and a small studio (basic installation costs ran to about Canadian $100). Each station was meant to broadcast in two languages to serve the multi-lingual situation of its locality (*département*).

The five community radio stations (radio rurale locale) and their départements in Benin by 1996

RRL Tanguiéta	Atacora
RRL Ouèssè	Zou
RRL Banikoara	Borgou
RRL Lalo	Mono
RRL Ouakè	Atacora

In status and administrative structure, these associative radios were to be strictly independent, related neither to the state nor to political groups, and were not to be run as private enterprises. Each radio station was to be managed by a local association and supervised by an elected committee, the *comité local de gestion* (CLG; sometimes called *comité de gestion communal*, COGEC) headed by a president other than the station director. Each community radio was to be run by a staff of five employees:

---

[3] Initially, Radio Parakou was planned to broadcast only in African languages, but later turned mainly to French.

- two local radio presenters (*animateurs*), one for each language;
- two technicians, recruited by test and then trained in a special programme in Ouèssè and paid for by their committee;
- one experienced and specifically trained director (*chef de station*), chosen and paid by the national broadcasting service (ORTB).[4]

The committee and its president were meant to be elected by a general assembly, including representatives of all local groups and associations, and to consist of a representative of the station itself, the director of the station, and representatives of as many *sous-préfectures* (administrative units) as were covered by the radio. The programmes were to be free from political statement or comment (I shall discuss the reality later). The buildings to house the radio station were to be erected by the local population which was also asked to collect money to defray the costs of setting up the station. The finance for continued operation was to flow from payment for programmes by development agencies, from other funds (especially support by foreign political foundations), and money raised from charges for public announcements, commercials, greetings and any other messages requested by the local population.

However, since 1994 the process of establishing these radios has been beset by general difficulties and specific conflicts (Coopération Suisse 1995) for which there have been two main causes. The first is the prolonged absence of official regulations, legislating articles and statutes that have been discussed thoroughly and received the consent of all those involved. The second derives from the general process of reorganizing radio and public media in Benin. This has involved radical restructuring at the national radio, new legislation and the establishment of the national media-supervising board, HAAC. New laws governing the operations of independent radio and television stations have only just been passed by the Benin parliament after prolonged debate and controversy.

Benin, seen widely as a good example of democratic transition, was a latecomer to reform compared with other former socialist, Francophone countries such as Mali and Burkina Faso (Panos Institute 1993; Bourgault 1995; Nombré Chapter 5; Ilboudo Chapter 3). Currently, some reorganization of several of these radio stations is under way, due to the intervention of a special programme of assistance (*programme d'appui à la communication*) headed by the Swiss development organization (Coopération Suisse). But the process of reform is far from complete, and a variety of problems, from the sustainability of funding to technical hitches, persist.

In the case of Radio rurale locale Tanguiéta, I shall focus particularly on the structural difficulties of local management. My account involves the relations between the local actors in this newly emerging arena of public negotiation in Tanguiéta (Bierschenk 1988).

The establishment of Radio rurale locale in Tanguiéta

The region of Tanguiéta, consisting of the three *sous-préfectures* of Tanguiéta, Materi and Cobly, represents a remote area – consisting of a sort of a triangle –

---

[4] All the *chefs de station* were trained at CIERRO in Ouagadougou, Burkina Faso.

between Burkina Faso and Togo and Benin. It is a plural social and cultural setting, composed of a variety of linguistically distinct peasant groups, Fulbe herdsmen, immigrant craftsmen and Muslim traders. The town of Tanguiéta, a French colonial foundation dating from the beginning of the century, is a regional centre of trade with about 20,000 inhabitants. This region behind the mountains is neither covered by television nor reached by newspapers. The first radios (called *walesehun*, wireless, in Biali) were brought there in the 1950s by migrants returning from Ghana and demobilized soldiers. Before the installation of Radio rurale locale Tanguiéta, the main stations, received on shortwave with poor reception, were Radio Cotonou and Radio Parakou. In this respect, Tanguiéta was a highly appropriate location for a communal radio project; broadcasting started in July 1994.

The staff of Radio rurale locale Tanguiéta in March 1996

Sandros Tigri	technician and interim director
Nicaise Yokossi	technician
Dacosa Sahgui Sarré	presenter Biali
Ahmadou Méchanou Bukari	presenter Dendi
Robert Tiando	presenter Waama
Firmin Kpakpari	presenter Nateni
Léon Kenati	presenter M'belime
Bello Blanquit Adam	temporary presenter Fulfulde, 1995

Radio rurale locale Tanguiéta was originally supposed to be located elsewhere, in Ouaké. It was as a result of disputes between the two neighbouring communities of that region about the location of the radio that the donor agencies and state authorities decided to relocate the radio and all its equipment (which, by that time, was ready to be installed elsewhere). They chose Tanguiéta (for reasons I shall touch on later); but the relocation came in some ways unexpectedly and without adequate preparation. The local state administrator, the *sous-préfet*, charged the existing Community Development Association, the Association de développement de Tanguiéta, with responsibility for the radio. The *sous-préfet* of the time was on good terms with the president of the Association, Séraphin Syéri N'Dery, who was elected President of the first management committee, the *comité de suivi*; other leading members of the Association similarly took over positions on the *comité*.

The major problem, once the radio station and its interim structures, by now called the *comité de gestion*, CLG, were founded, was the absence of any process to define the functions of the committee and its collaborative relations, and to establish a system for financing the radio; this situation persisted until the end of 1995 (Coopération Suisse 1995). The absence of statutes, mentioned earlier, caused problems at several levels. It was up to the local committee to create its own unwritten statutes; a fact which subsequently gave much room for manoeuvre to local actors to define their own positions and to impose their own regulations. Several conflicts over the management followed.

The first problem for the Tanguiéta committee resulted from the official preference for two local broadcast languages. The choice of Biali[5] and Nateni was seen by speakers of other languages in the community to be overly restrictive. Their demands were agreed by the President, who authorized broadcasts in six languages, adding Gurmancema, Mbelime and Waama (local Gur languages), and Dendi, the language of the local trading community and lingua franca of the north of Benin. Additional presenters were recruited who, although not formally trained, nevertheless claimed a salary. This was approved by the committee, though their salary was smaller than the trained presenters. Some months later, the financial situation of the station worsened; as a consequence the committee lacked funds to pay all the presenters. By the end of 1995, no salaries were being paid to the presenters at all, a situation which caused profound conflict between the president and the presenters, and provoked disputes about the different statuses of the two trained presenters and the newcomers. All the presenters related better to the station director than to the president and his committee, and they expressed a wish for greater independence, as befitted professional journalists rather than volunteers in a community project.

Another conflict involved the president and the station director. The president of the CLG, Séraphin Syéri, a former politician and influential member of the MNDD party (represented in parliament at the time, and with a minister in the governing coalition), entrusted the station director with administration of the budget of the radio station. In mid-1995, Syéri accused the director of nontransparency and embezzling funds for his own use, writing a letter of complaint to ORTB and the donors. Syéri, or 'the old Séraphin' as he is called by followers and opponents alike, was supported by representatives of the region in parliament and government. The station director quit the station, returning to a position in the ORTB and appointing one of the technicians as interim director.

Yet a third conflict had already arisen during the first year, concerning one of the ways of fund-raising: a general collection, or *cotisation*. The population of the *sous-préfecture* of Matéri collected less money than others, arguing, first, that the radio transmissions did not cover the whole region[6] and, secondly, that they had already collected a lot of money in three recent *cotisations* for other projects, all of which had required either funds or active participation (*participation communautaire*). Only a third of the anticipated sum was raised. Later, relations between the representatives of the *sous-préfectures* of Matéri and Tanguiéta were to become even more strained.

At the beginning of 1996, the Swiss Mission for Technical Cooperation embarked on a programme (*programme d'appui à la communication*) to promote reorganization and improvement of the management of local radio stations in Benin. They enlisted a domestic NGO, Institut Kilimandjaro, to carry out this task, which was meant to bring together all involved persons to elaborate a new management structure and set up new statutes for each radio association, as well

---

[5] Biali is the language of the Byerebe, also known as Berba in French. Biali and French were the languages used in my research.

[6] The radio presenters later made several tests attempting to prove this was not the case. However, they made these tests with more powerful receivers than those used locally, which undermined their case.

as to reestablish cooperation between local radios, the ORTB and other institutions. Meetings and discussions were initiated in each of the communities involved as well as at national level.

These discussions, designed to ameliorate the situation, had the unanticipated effect of renewing older tensions between ethnic groups in the region and refocusing these on Radio rurale locale Tanguiéta. People in Matéri, Tanguiéta and Cobly, which differ in linguistic composition, tend to see themselves as engaged in competition for the allocation of available resources in the region. The inhabitants of Tanguiéta, a town privileged since colonial times and which remained the sole administrative centre until 1975, were regarded with envy, and their official representatives considered overweening. More than anything else, the actions of the president, Syéri, provoked criticism. Despite his 70 years, he remained very active politically, and claimed a role as promoter of local culture and history. A sort of local 'big man', he was criticized for accumulating too many functions (he presided simultaneously over the Community Development Association, the Nateni Alphabetization Committee and the Association of the Parents of Tanguiéta School Children); as president of the radio committee too, he was accused of being an obstacle to the radio's better management.

A meeting (*assemblée générale*) held in June 1996 to discuss and vote on the new statutes, revealed how far these tensions had accumulated (Adéniyi 1996b). The representatives of the *sous-préfectures* of Matéri and Cobly demanded better representation on the CLG, as well as limitations on the mandate of the president. In the ensuing discussion, the president was supported by his friend and political party crony, the mayor of Tanguiéta, Albert Yomboleny. In preparation for the meeting, they had already invited more persons from Tanguiéta than elsewhere. Before the vote could commence, the invited participants were listed and any other people present had to leave the meeting. The organizers, representatives of the Swiss agency, tried hard to mediate between the factions and eventually reached an agreement about the station's statutes, which was finally voted through at the beginning of 1997. The *assemblée générale* then elected a very large committee, 19 in all, with additional representatives of all the communities; and the president's period of office was limited to a single term. To oversee day-to-day functioning, a smaller executive bureau was elected, of which Syéri was also made president. He seemed to come out of the affair well, but discussion of the radio station, and of his role in it, was not over, especially among younger people and his political opponents in Tanguiéta.

Clearly, the project of Radio rurale Tanguiéta had become the object of symbolic action and dispute in the local political field. Over and above the routine problems of fund-raising and remuneration for the presenters, the process of establishing the radio station created a field for negotiation and vivid struggle in local politics concerned above all with the appropriation of its management. Since this does not offer direct material benefits, I see it as the acquisition of symbolic capital in the form of a highly esteemed public role, one which in the long run is a potential resource in the struggle for political power in the wider social field of the region. The symbolic and political aspect of control over the management of local broadcasting becomes more evident in the question of programming in African languages, a field of symbolic struggle linked to questions of local identification (and the creation or maintenance of ethnic boundaries) and to tensions between interest groups in the region.

The impact of radio broadcasting in Tanguiéta

Types of programmes

Three different types of radio programme on Radio rurale Tanguiéta can be distinguished:

* *concerts d'auditeurs* request shows, playing music plus greetings (for which listeners pay CFA francs 100 per *disque demandé*, or request);
* programmes offering advice, services and carrying advertisements;
* information and discussion broadcasts.

Especially with respect to the final type, local radio works together with various development agencies and foreign donors, as well as local NGOs. I shall give examples of two different types of influence such programmes may have. This impact is often overestimated in statements uncritically celebrating radio, as if it were a means to 'globalize' access to the free flow of information and promote democratization *per se* (Thiam and Sy 1996; de Souza 1996). As an element of liberalized mass media, and especially by broadcasting in African languages, radio is expected to improve popular consciousness in ways auspicious for development. Studies have revealed the limitations of these expectations (Kunczik 1985; Jazbinsek 1992). This must be conceded, but it is still the case that the introduction of local radio broadcasting represents a new medium, and this can reconfigure the local political field in a variety of ways. Development agencies may begin to promote radio, and members of local communities themselves come to express demands for programmes closer to their interests and the life of their community. Genres of programme may have different public impact; in what follows I examine three cases: the programme of civic education (*programme d'education civique*) that ran throughout 1996; request shows (*concerts d'auditeurs*); and news coverage of a local event, the Natemba rally, in October 1995.

The programme of civic education

The programme of political education was initiated in collaboration with two radio stations by the NGO CAO and financed by a German political foundation, Konrad-Adenauer-Stiftung (Centre Afrika Obota 1995; Mehler 1996).[7] The programme

---

7 Convention de partenariat entre le Centre Afrika Obota (CAO), et Radio rurale locale Tanguiéta:
La présente convention porte sur la production d'émissions radiophonique d'Education civique. Cette émission est répartie en 104 éditions en deux langues à savoir: Langue Biali – 52 émissions, langue Naténi – 52 émissions. Les buts visés par la production de l'émission sont les suivants:
* créer un cadre de discussion entre pouvoirs publics et citoyens
* susciter des débats sur les problèmes de développement au niveau local
* renforcer la capacité et la confiance des citoyens dans la recherche de solutions endogènes
* encourager l'esprit d'initiative de citoyens et des communautés aux actions civiques.
Tous objectifs concourent au renforcement de la démocratie pour un développement dans un contexte de paix sociale (CAO, January 1996).

began in January 1995 following a three-day seminar (Centre Afrika Obota 1996) to discern the local problems to be addressed and to develop a series of broadcasts together with the presenters and a selected number of representatives of different communities: often teachers and collaborators (*animateurs*) of development agencies. Subsequently, a monitoring workshop (*comité de pilotage*) was held every three months to discuss past programmes and propose the next. The NGO sent out two members to work out the programmes with the president of the association, the station director and two presenters; to assess transmissions together with a so-called *cellule d'écoute*, or monitoring group; and to supply financial means.[8] The broadcasts (104 transmissions in all, half in each of two languages, Biali and Nateni, and lasting half an hour a week) treated diverse subjects related to the social and political life of the region. There were domestic problems that occurred within and between the households, such as early or forced marriage, and advice on hygiene. But there were also such public issues as poaching in the nearby game reserve (Parc national du Pendjari), the use of trees and the protection of the environment. The responsibilities of local authorities, as well as of the local population, were pointed out; during the period of the presidential elections, information was given on how to vote. The range of subjects was wide and designed to enlarge the local population's knowledge and awareness.[9]

The most interesting aspect of the programme was the form of broadcast the presenters initiated. These predominantly consisted of discussions conducted by the presenter with participants in different villages, and concluded by his own remarks that corrected previous opinion or pointed to the 'correct opinion', either offered by the presenter himself or by a specialist (a school director or member of the local administration) who proposed the 'correct conclusion'.

But this controlled framework was often subverted when debate led to controversy in relation to sensitive local issues. For instance, the presenter might propose that poaching be suppressed, but the listeners and participants pointed out that gamekeepers commonly practised poaching. The roles in community life of such functionaries as local chiefs, village head and the mayor were frequently controversial, and presenters struggled to respond to the proposals that arose when debate occasionally took an unexpected direction. For example, a discussion (in Biali) about the right way to vote included a participant who complained of having been abused and imprisoned during the 1995 parliamentary elections. He had been accused of taking a second voter's card after losing his first, and did not know he should have declared this fact officially at the polling station. He gave a shocking report of what happened to him afterwards: recounting how he had been physically abused in prison, and subordinated to rules established by hardened prisoners designed to initiate him into criminal behaviour. During the discussion, the presenter at first tried to treat him as a salutory example from which others might derive better knowledge of the election process. But as the

---

[8] Funding of CFA francs 2,256,400 was released by a convention in January 1996 (CAO 1996: 3). Since devaluation in 1993, the CFA has had a fixed exchange rate of 100 CFA francs = 1 French franc.

[9] In Biali, this programme of education was called *bi kanseke pwam dii ke iibu*, 'a curious child wouldn't eat his own totem' (that is, transgress his own dietary taboos; a person can manage his life better with fuller knowledge). I shall not offer a full evaluation of this programme here.

debate went on, the excesses of his treatment said more about the state of civil rights in that region of Benin than it did about any inadequacies in the poor man's knowledge. Finally, the presenter was at a loss how to link this example with his intention to stress the importance of taking part in elections as an element of political education.

Similar cases came up often. In another example, a presenter who was supposed to discuss the responsibilities and obligations of the local authorities was confronted with quite contrary realities. The inhabitants of a village near Dassari quoted the case of a young boy accused of stealing a sheep who had been coerced by his village head, *chef de village*, in keeping with his formal responsibilities, to give himself up to the Gendarmerie. The youngster was imprisoned and so mistreated that he died. The parents of the boy accused the *chef de village* of direct responsibility for their son's death, supporting their case by the fact that the sheep had been found in the meantime and its owner had dropped charges against the boy. The *chef de village*, they said, should have tried the case within the village, and negotiated ways of restitution.

As these two cases show, the hiatus between the rhetoric of 'democratic renewal' and its local realities became obvious during discussion programmes. This, to my mind, is an interesting effect, but not one intended by the donors; and the effect was made more obvious by a technical consideration: lacking editing facilities, the presenters had either to present the entirety of what they had taped or nothing at all, in which case they needed to make another programme. Transmissions of civic education programmes were widely followed; they offered a forum for discussion, and their reports were sometimes done well, although in a style that tended to the didactic. Compared with other programmes, those on civic education were novel: local problems were put on the agenda, and new styles of broadcasts tried. The most popular transmissions were those concerned with such problems as traditional marriage: particularly the position of women in exchange marriage (*cigeru* in Biali), a crucial social problem in the region and responsible for antagonisms between generations. After request shows, the programmes on civic education transmitted in Nateni and Biali were the most appreciated by listeners.

Concerts d'auditeurs

Request shows are interesting because, by revitalizing local culture in particular ways, they contribute to the process of collective identification. Going out in all the six languages used by the radio station, they address listeners as members of communities defined by language and as inhabitants of one of the zones covered by the radio station's transmissions.

The languages spoken in this region of extreme diversity have not yet been studied in any depth, although a few vocabularies have been collected. Nevertheless, language practice is assuming wide significance. Some languages have attained greater importance than others by virtue of their use as a medium for the songs and tales presented almost daily on the radio. Here is a flavour of what went into a request show broadcast in Biali:

29 February 1996, 7 p.m., in the studio of Radio rurale Tanguiéta: The request show in Biali is on air. The presenter, Dacosa, is greeting the listeners in his usual way: '*n'yebe nii-i peem*', 'good evening fellows'. He's passing on greetings and announcements to the Biali-speaking population, which means the regions of Dassari, Materi, Gouandé, Tanguiéta, etc. 'Sambieni is greeting his great brother Yuomfe in Tanguiéta, and the people of Mamoussa (*Mumusu yebe*)'; 'a funeral (*humum*) is to take place in Materi'. At the beginning of the broadcast, the studio is hosting one of the 'sons of the village', Monsieur Raphael Windali N'Ouéni,[10] known to listeners by the name Kwake Wendai, which he long used as a presenter of the first radio programme in Biali at Radio Cotonou during the 1980s. Today, as director of the National Board of Functional Alphabetization, he has come to Tanguiéta in the company of the minister, Alassane Tigri (*Natemba*), a 'son of Tanguiéta', who is campaigning for President Soglo. Together with the 'guest of the evening', the young Gnammi, Richard de Materi, they are talking about the need to take part in the polls, the right way to vote, and so forth.

Windali does not propagandize overtly, but listeners know his political persuasions. There follows a song by Pauline, a woman of Gouandé, evoking the burial of Daniel Tawema of Materi, a friend of Windali, who was another 'big man' of the region, former minister and parliamentary deputy (1991–5). Then Dacosa sends another series of greetings and announcements across the airwaves: 'The Mayor of Materi invites the villagers to clean the market place', 'a meeting of war veterans is to take place', and 'the white student, Sambieni Tilo, is greeting his colleague Annette in Kotari'. Dacosa now motions the technician to play a song by a blind singer. The song concerns a violent dispute over a woman; the singer berates someone for denying his real lineage identity to avoid being beaten in a dispute, such denial being a sort of sacrilege for Byerebe. After several invitations (mainly concerning burials, *humum*, which are the major festivities among Byerebe), some women's songs requested by people of Tanguiéta are played. Later that same evening, Dacosa reverts to the subject of 'Byerebe heritage'. Some wise elders discuss dietary taboos, *iibu*, among the Byerebe ...

The greetings exchanged by members of this language community highlight a particularistic set of kinship and neighbourhood relations: there are invitations to family events, public festivals and 'liberation' parties;[11] announcements about marriages and funerals; greetings to relatives living in different villages; and perhaps the opportunity to hear one's own voice in songs recorded by the presenters (and the anthropologist as well). The dimension of language difference is only one of the ways that collective awareness might be fostered in the same social field, but there could be other ways: emphasizing the socio-professional and religious division between traders and peasants, focusing on the solidarities of generations, or stressing political affiliations. Official sociolinguistic perspectives on ethnicity go back to the pioneer works of missionaries (Chantoux 1949; Prost 1973) and the later activities of the *commissions linguistiques* as well as the alphabetization campaigns of the socialist period (CENALA 1983, 1990). These cultural projects of the state were similar to others in West Africa of that period (Fardon and Furniss 1994), but they offered town-dwelling intellectuals and politicians ways to strengthen clientelist ties to their home regions; these processes are of renewed importance today. Ethnic features of difference and identity have become prominent in public negotiations in recent years, a symptom of the re-emergent ethnic discourse in Benin (Kohnert 1997). The impact of these

10 Raphael Windali N'Ouéni died in a car crash in November 1997.
11 A literal translation of the local French term for a neo-traditional ritual which accompanies the presentation of a professional diploma on the completion of an apprenticeship.

processes is but slightly visible as yet. But one could think of similar developments elsewhere, such as the Kalenjin of Kenya whose name (derived from the formulaic greeting 'Kalenjin' used in radio broadcasts) has become a group identity (a group of which the Kenyan president, Daniel Arap Moi, is the most prominent member; see Kipkorir 1973). How radio stations are appropriated, and their broadcasts understood, in the culturally and socially plural local spaces of Benin may transpire to be of equal significance.

Coverage of community events

I have already underlined the dangers of overemphasizing the influence of broadcasts in shaping the consciousness of a population, a regrettable tendency common to different initiatives and organizations that discover in radio a quick fix to promote development. Before jumping to this conclusion, I have argued that it is necessary to undertake more detailed study of all the processes involved in the establishment, control and impact of radio stations. To indicate some of the complexities in the ways that radio programmes follow local events, and are complicit in the formation of opinions, I want to go back to an event that occurred in 1995.

One day in late October of that year, peasants from Taiacou in Natemba region showed up unexpectedly in the centre of Tanguiéta, marching, singing and demonstrating against iniquities perpetrated by some Fulbe herdsmen of their village in general, and against the ill treatment meted out by the local *chef de brigade* in particular. They had come to present their problem to the administrative representative of the state, the *sous-préfet*, and demand he solve it. The Nateni-speaking radio presenter went immediately to cover events on the spot and conducted interviews with a number of participants in the march, as well as recording the refrain they were singing: *CB tuulo, CB tuulo*, 'The *chef de brigade* is a thief, the *chef de brigade* is a thief'. The following morning he produced a long news broadcast on the subject with several excerpts from his interviews. It transpired that the accusations were not specifically being made against Fulbe herdsmen; relations between them and the peasants in the region were routinely strained, apparently because the Fulbe were poorly paid for tending cattle on behalf of peasants who owned them, and were therefore often tempted to work on their own account. The particular object of the peasants' displeasure was rather the local chief of police, the *chef de brigade*, who was responsible for the application of basic law. He was accused of being corrupt, and of finding cases in favour of those who offered him bribes. Later the same day an abbreviated version of this information was included in news flashes in other local languages, so that everyone came to hear of the incident. The song was aired too; '*CB tuulo, CB tuulo*' was heard in each of the other five local language news bulletins. Immediately, children picked up the refrain and sang it constantly. '*CB tuulo, CB tuulo*' could be heard all around town, expressing the solidarity of large sections of the population with the demonstrators. During the days that followed, the case was transferred to the court of Natitingou and judged in favour of the peasants. Pressure on the *chef de brigade* persisted, however, and soon after these events he was transferred from his office.

The role of the community radios in changing the political field in Benin

Radios Ouakè and Tanguiéta

I want to go back to the problems of setting up Radio Ouakè as a way of demonstrating the more general impact of radio in Benin. The radio station was initially destined to be installed in Badjoudé; however, the inhabitants of the greater neighbouring community of Ouakè claimed that, because they were more concerned with the project, it should be sited in Ouakè. That dispute in Atacora region actually prevented its being set up at all in the first instance. It was reported that a deputy from the region had vigorously criticized Benin's President Soglo and his wife in the parliament and, apparently as a form of presidential revenge, the government withdrew the project from Badjoudé and offered it elsewhere. Subsequent discussions were reported to have rumbled on in the departmental capital, Natitingou, in presence of representatives of the Ministry of Culture and Communication. Other places were proposed, but the choice of Tanguiéta seems to have resulted from manoeuvring by one of its sons, a *fils du terroir*, Bertin Borna, an experienced lawyer and politician, and a parliamentary deputy. At the time, his party supported the president, so he would have been the first to be asked whether there was a building suitable to accommodate the radio in Tanguiéta. By coincidence, a short time previously just such a building had been constructed by community subscription to serve as the community's guest house.

Whatever the precise sequence of events, Borna seems to have seized the opportunity to act as mediator and gain reputation as the person who 'brought the radio to Tanguiéta', as his supporters later recounted in versions that probably exaggerated his role.[12] Together with the omnipresent president of the management committee, 'the old Syéri', a fellow member of the MNDD party, Borna strove to convince public opinion of his achievement. This must surely have contributed to his victory in the subsequent parliamentary elections of March 1995 (Bako-Arifari 1995; Degboe 1995), since his constituency, consisting of the four *sous-préfectures* of the region, is largely covered by the transmissions of Radio Tanguiéta.

Radio Banikoara

Comparing the circumstances of Radio Tanguiéta with other local radio stations in Benin reveals both similarities and differences. Here I draw upon the work of Erik Voss (Voss 1998). Radio rurale locale Banikoara, in the north of the Borgou

---

[12]To quote an opposed opinion: 'Borna a fait sembler que c'était lui qui a amené la radio à Tanguiéta. En vérité, il n'y a rien fait. Le bâtiment était déjà là, construit par la population. Et la radio n'était pas prévue pour Tanguiéta. Sur tous les paquets était écrit "Badjoudé"' (Antoine Dayori, 10 March 1996). 'Borna made out he was the one who brought the radio to Tanguiéta. In truth, he did nothing. The building was already there, built by the people. And the radio was not planned for Tanguiéta. "Badjoudé" was written on all the cartons.'

region, also possessed a driving force in the person of its influential director, Mohammed Alidou. He used his radio activities to advance the projects of his own association APEM (Association pour la protection des enfants malheureux), producing publicity and attracting donors for it. As a local 'big man' he also acted as mediator in local conflicts. Radio programming, as well as the radio's budget, were predominantly under his sole management. Appropriation of the local radio was relatively easy for him, since he had gained experience from working for Radio Parakou. In his several television and press interviews (such as *Le matin* 1995) he laid public claim to great influence on the development of the region which he attributed to radio broadcasts.

The president of the CLG in Banikoara is also director of the local primary school. Although he claims to exercise a predominant influence over the radio's affairs, the station director responds by emphasizing the importance of his role as a broadcasting professional. Unlike Radio Tanguiéta, both the members of the CLG and the presenters at Radio Banikoara defend the choice of only two languages (Baatonum and Fulfulde) for broadcasts; but this causes inter-ethnic friction, since it is interpreted as a means to maintain the hegemony of these languages over other languages of the region (Gurmancema, Boko, Dendi).

The general quality of broadcasts on Radio Banikoara seems to be poor. Although many transmissions resemble *communiqués* in style, the most popular programme departs furthest from this norm: a live presentation of riddles and folktales in which up to six old men are gathered in the studio and embark on a round of storytelling replete with the traditional rhetorical devices of such performances – noises, answers, affirmations and so forth. It seems likely that the programme owes its success to employing a rhetorical mode closer to that familiar from oral communication in everyday life. Other programmes follow its format to a lesser degree. The financial resources of Radio Banikoara are much greater than those at the disposal of Radio Tanguiéta. This is a cotton-producing region and, at the outset, the local producers' association, USPP, offered to pay for the building and start up costs of the radio, so no general *cotisation* was needed. Additionally, the Station Director attracted paid contracts for religious broadcasts, worth CFA francs 400,000 per year, from each of the three major religious communities of the region.

Although the situation of Radio Banikoara differs in some respects from those of Radio Tanguiéta and Radio Ouakè, like these two it has been differentially appropriated by local actors for their own ends. Its work provokes tensions in the region, and it has become involved as the subject (and forum) for negotiations of social status and of influence. This would appear to be quite generally the case, since similar processes have been reported from the radio station in Ouèssè (Adéniyi 1996a).

The presidents of the local radio associations now belong to a new association, the Fédération des radios rurales (FRR). Their deliberations on strategy anticipate the passage of effective laws decentralizing and liberalizing control of the media. They have agreed an uncompromising stand for independence from the national broadcaster, ORTB, and hope to make this a reality thanks to direct aid from donor agencies. In response, ORTB representatives argued that sooner or later the local stations would face technical problems they could not solve alone (interview,

Dewanou, 10 March 1997). They may have a point: Radio Ouèssè was out of action for a time when its transmitter broke down, while Radio Banikoara was broadcasting at half of its transmitting capacity. Nevertheless, the president of the Tanguiéta CLG argued that his station was experiencing no problems, despite the absence of a director. Meanwhile, as the representatives of the Swiss task force attempted further mediation between FRR and the ORTB, most of those involved seemed to be awaiting final release of the new media laws (eventually passed by parliament on 12 August 1997), and the end of the restructuring process at the ORTB, before matters could develop further.

The radio project in the context of political transformation

Radio stations in Benin are important local symbolic resources subjected to competition from influential local political entrepreneurs, but they also have a wider political impact, particularly in multilingual regions where relations between language groups are politically fraught. Even more generally, Benin is undergoing a comprehensive remodelling of the landscape of its mass media, particularly its network of radio stations. Although the Benin parliament did eventually pass a law to liberalize the media, as noted above, this law also set limits to the degree of freedom of political expression permitted. This in turn provoked a great debate on the national political scene which is still going on.

In October 1997, independent commercial and associative (communal) radio stations were given broadcasting licences (Gnangon 1997; L'autre Afrique 1997). Fifteen stations were licensed, among them seven communal religious stations. As a consequence of this, and the activities of the press,[13] the landscape of the media in Benin is clearly set for further radical change. HAAC (Vogt 1996: 735) has been established as a broadcasting supervisory board and, after some initial misjudgements, has developed into an important, independent and wise agency. Through it, all the local radio stations are represented in the political negotiations which bear especially on the process of establishing of a multiparty system. A variety of very locally based political parties have emerged (like the MNDD mentioned earlier), sometimes drawing their support from populations that are narrowly circumscribed in terms of their social or linguistic features. The candidates of these parties are presented as *fils de terroir*, sons of the region, capable of representing and mediating local interests at higher political levels. They are brokers (in Olivier de Sardan's sense, 1995: 159) who compete for support by bringing 'projects' to their region.

This resurgence of intermediary actors is closely linked to processes of reconstruction and politicization of local identities. In the case of Tanguiéta, several candidates presented themselves at the parliamentary elections in March 1995, each from a different *sous-préfecture*. Supporters tended to be mobilized by stressing the sociolinguistic characteristics that united candidate and followers,

---

[13] A full survey of the mass media in Benin would need also to take into account the impact of new, independent, and successful newspapers like Le matin, Les échos du jour, Le citoyen, etc.

and necessarily differentiated them from the followers of other candidates. Because these differences could be keyed to the languages of radio broadcasts, control over the managing structures of radio became an increasingly important subject of negotiation and cultural entrepreneurship. But political parties and parliamentary elections are not the only factors shaping the regional field of political action and discourse. A future project of decentralization is already under discussion (Bako-Arifari 1997); laws decentralizing political authority and strengthening local communities will be voted on soon in parliament. These are to lead to the election of communal councils early in 1998 with far greater powers and responsibilities, including financial powers, than current local administrators possess. It is not difficult to foresee that an intensified struggle of interests over the project of Radio rurale Tanguiéta will also form part of this process.

Reorganization of the media in Benin, their legislative frameworks and management structures, is going on as I write. I have mentioned the very recent authorization of independent radio stations as an important instance. My aim in this chapter has been to show just how difficult it is to establish radio stations as community projects that work for the interests of a local population independently of both state control and commercial interests. Participants have divergent interests, and they generally lack experience not just of broadcasting but of what is involved in the whole process of establishing a civil society, as implied in the Béninois *renouveau démocratique*. This is not to suggest that either the technicians or presenters lack ability, only that they face problems for which they have no precedents. At best, their efforts will contribute to the diversification of the media system and enable the expression of multiple and new local 'voices' after the demise of dominant state ideologies. If they can create new forums for the exchange of opinions and information which contribute in the long run to liberalizing public communication in their local communities, their efforts will have been well spent.

Appendix: Radio rurale locale, Tanguiéta: extract from programming schedule in March 1996

Within the general framework distinguishing types of programme, the content of what is transmitted is more flexible than might be suggested by such programme schedules as I reproduce here.

Monday
MORNING
7.00 : Ouverture d'antenne
7.05 : Réveil musical en Biali
7.20 : Apprenons à lire et à écrire en Fulfuldé
7.40 : Conseil santé en Biali
8.00 : Variétés musicales
8.30 : Musique du terroir
9.00–11.30: Market day information in
          different languages:

9.00 : Métè yobu (market day morning) + publicité
9.30 : Kaadi naadi (market day morning) + publicité
10.00 : Kara lai (market day morning) + publicité
10.30 : Katé daari (market day morning) + publicité
11.00 : Ki dagui tié lédé (market day morning) +
      publicité
11.30 : Variétés musicales
12.00 : Fin des émissions

Thursday
MORNING
7.00 : Ouverture d'antenne
7.05 : Animation musicale en Naténi
7.20 : Conseil santé en Fulfuldé
7.35 : Conseil santé en Naténi
7.50 : Conseil santé en Waama

8.05 : Conseil santé en Gulmancéma
8.20 : Conseil santé en Dendi
8.35 : Animation musicale en Dendi
9.00 : Fin des émissions

EVENING
17.00: Ouverture d'antenne
17.05: Animation musicale en Biali
17.20: A l'écoute de la CLCAM* en Dendi
17.35: Echanges techniques agricoles en
      Gulmancéma
17.50: Environnement et développement en
      Waama
18.05: Echanges techniques agricoles en Biali

18.20 : Conseil santé en M'bermè
18.35 : Contes et devinettes en Dendi Gulmancéna
19.00 : Concert des auditeurs en Biali
20.00 : Concert des auditeurs en Gulmancéma
20.40 : Environnement et développement en Biali
21.00 : Fin des émissions.

Friday
MORNING
7.00 : Ouverture d'antenne
7.05 : Réveil musical en M'bermè
7.20 : Echanges techniques agricoles en Waama
7.35 : Echanges techniques agricoles en Naténi
7.50 : Echanges techniques agricoles en M'bermè

8.05 : Famille et développement en Naténi
8.20 : Regard sur l'école en M'bermè
8.35 : Variété musicale
8.45 : Publicité et communiqué en Dendi
9.00 : Fin des émissions

EVENING
17.00: Ouverture d'antenne
17.05: Animation musicale en Biali
17.20: A l'écoute de la CLCAM en Biali
17.35: A l'écoute de la CLCAM en M'bermè
17.50: A l'écoute de la CLCAM en Naténi
18.05: Intermède Musical
18.10: Famille et développement en Biali
18.25: A l'écoute de la CLCAM en Waama

18.40 : Contes et devinettes en Naténi ou en Biali
19.00 : Concert des auditeurs en Naténi
20.00 : Regard sur l'écoute en Dendi
20.15 : Famille et développement en M'bermè
20.30 : Plantes et pharmacopée en Biali
20.45 : Variétés musicales
21.00 : Fin des émissions.

* Caisse locale de crédit agricole mutuel.

Sunday

MORNING

7.00 : Ouverture d'antenne
7.05 : Réveil musical en Naténi
7.30 : Regard sur l'école en Biali
7.45 : Regard sur l'école en Waama
8.00 : Regard sur l'école en Gulmancéna

8.15 : Environnement et développement en M'bermè
8.30 : Plantes et pharmacopée en Naténi
8.45 : Rythme de chez nous
9.00 : Fin des émissions

EVENING

17.00: Ouverture d'antenne
17.05: Animation en Biali
17.30: Apprenons à lire et à écrire en Waama
17.50: Regard sur l'école en Naténi
18.05: Point de rencontre en Biali

18.25 : Point de rencontre en Naténi
18.45 : Apprenons à lire et à écrire en Biali
19.00 : Concert des auditeurs en M'Bermè
19.45 : Musique pour votre détente
20.00 : Fin des émissions.

References

Adéniyi, Philippe (1996a) 'Radio rurale de Ouèssè. Une association de promotion est née', *Le matin*, Wednesday 26 June, 20.

——(1996b) 'Radio rurale de Tanguiéta. Tamaco! Connaissez-vous?', *Le matin*, Wednesday 3 July, 20.

Allen, Chris (1992) 'Restructuring an authoritarian state: "Democratic Renewal" in Benin', *Review of African Political Economy* 54: 42–58.

L'autre Afrique (1997) 'Bénin: Les ondes enfin libres?', *L'autre Afrique* 27, 26 November–2 December, 49.

Bako-Arifari, Nassirou (1995) 'Démocratie et logiques du terroir au Bénin', *Politique Africaine* 59, *Le Bénin*: 7–24.

——(1997) 'La décentralisation au Bénin: aperçu sur la réforme et les recherches', *Bulletin de l'APAD*, May, 13, 167–75.

Bierschenk, Thomas (1988) 'Development projects as arenas of negotiation of strategic groups: a case study from Benin', *Sociologia Ruralis* 38: 146–60.

——(1994) 'La démocratie au village: état, démocratisation et "politique par le bas" au Bénin', in Thomas Bierschenk (ed.) *Les effets socio-politiques de la démocratisation en milieu rural au Bénin*, pp. 1–12. Stuttgart: Université de Hohenheim.

Bierschenk, Thomas and Mongbo, Roch (1995) 'Le terroir en quête de la démocratie. Avant propos', *Politique Africaine* 59: 2–6.

Bourgault, Louise M. (1995) *Mass Media in Sub-Saharan Africa*, Bloomington: Indiana University Press.

CENALA/Commission nationale de Linguistique, Benin (1983) *Les Gulmanceba du Bénin* (*approche sociolinguistique*), Cotonou: DRST.

CENALA (1990) *Alphabet des langues nationales*, Cotonou: CENALA.

Centre Afrika Obota, CAO (1995) 'Stratégies de mise en oeuvre du programme d'émission radiophonique d'éducation civique', Cotonou: CAO, manuscript.

——(1996) 'Convention de partenariat entre le CAO et la RRL Tanguiéta', January, manuscript.

——(1997) 'Mission d'auto-évaluation du programme d'éducation civique sur la Radio Rurale Locale de Tanguiéta', Cotonou, June, manuscript.

Chantoux, P. (1949) 'Les missionaires et les langues', *Echo des missions africaines de Lyon* 6: 78–9.

Coopération Suisse au Bénin/Bureau de Coordination (1995) 'Mission sur les radio rurales locales. Rapport', September, manuscript.

de Souza, Serge (1996) 'Radio rurales au Bénin: De puissants outils de développement', *Les échos du jour*, 56, Tuesday 22 October, 6.

Degboe, Kouassi A. (1995) *Elections et réalités sociologiques au Bénin*, Cotonou: Intermonde Editions.

Fardon, Richard and Furniss, Graham (eds) (1994) *African Languages, Development and the State*, London: Routledge.

Gnangon, Pintos (1997) 'Libéralisation de l'espace audiovisuel au Bénin: 29 dossiers de radios et télévisions privées reatenus', *La Nation* 1843, 22 October: 2.

Institut Kilimandjaro/Bureau de Coordination de la Coopération Suisse au Bénin (1996) 'Programme d'appui à la communication (PAC), atelier d'élaboration des statuts et du règlement intérieur de la radio rurale locale', manuscript.

Jazbinsek, Dietmar (1992) 'Radio in Benin', Exkursionsbericht Institut für Ethnologie, FU Berlin, manuscript.

Kipkorir, Benjamin (1973) *The Marakwet of Kenya*. Nairobi: East African Literature Bureau.

Kohnert, Dirk and Preuss, Hans-Joachim A. (1992) 'Vom Camarade zum Monsieur: Strukturanpassung und Demokratisierung in Benin', *Peripherie* 46: 47–70.

Kohnert, Dirk (1997) 'Benin', in Rolf Hofmeier (ed.) *Afrika Jahrbuch 1996*, Institut für Afrika-Kunde, Opladen: Leske und Budrich, 94–9.

Kunczik, Michael (1985) *Massenmedien und Entwicklungsländer*, Köln: Böhlau.

Le matin (1995) 'Entretien avec M. Mohamed Alidou, chef de la station rurale locale de Banikoara', *Le matin*, Thursday 1 September, 16.

Mehler, Andreas (1996) 'Chancen der Demokratisierungshilfe in Westafrika: Eindrücke und Überlegungen zum Beitrag der deutschen politischen Stiftungen', *Afrika Spectrum* 96(1): 27–36.

Olivier de Sardan, Jean-Pierre (1995) *Anthropologie et développement*, Paris: Karthala.

Panos Institute (1993) *Radio Pluralism in West Africa. A survey conducted by Panos Institute, and l'Union des Journalistes de l'Afrique de l'Ouest*, Paris: Panos Institute and L'Harmattan.

Prost, André (1973) 'Les langues de l'Atacora', *Bulletin de l'Institut Fondamentale de l'Afrique Noire*, Dakar, series B, 35(4): 444–511.

Raynal, Jean-Jacques (1991) 'Le renouveau démocratique béninois: modèle ou mirage?', *Afrique contemporaine* 160(4): 3–26.

Thiam, Cheikh Tidiane and Sy, Demba (1996) *Breaking Monopolies. Legalism and Radio Pluralism in West Africa*, Paris: Panos Institute and L'Harmattan.

Vogt, Achim (1996) 'Medienentwicklung, regionale Journalistenverbände und Medien Kommissionen in Westafrika', *Nord-Süd Aktuell* 4: 727–37.

Voss, Erik (1998) 'Radio in Banikoara', Lehrforschungsbericht, Institut für Ethnologie, Free University of Berlin, manuscript.

9
Popular Culture in Advertising

Nigerian Hausa Radio
MANSUR ABDULKADIR

This chapter examines how, in spite of their apparently commercial message, Hausa radio advertisements written by Bashir Isma'ila Ahmed and broadcast on the FRCN contain a heavy dose of Hausa literary and popular culture forms. I also argue that the advertisements reflect the contents of many other programmes of the radio station, and can therefore be seen as a development of the Hausa literary and popular cultural forms that represent the emergence of a new or hybrid Hausa genre of popular culture.

The Federal Radio Corporation of Nigeria (FRCN)

The present FRCN was established in 1962 as Radio Kaduna. In the late 1970s the Obasanjo government commissioned an American company to carry out audience research for the FRCN. The government doubted the accuracy of an earlier survey, carried out by a Swedish organization, which had come up with a figure of 35 million listeners at any given time within Nigeria, but added that if listeners from neighbouring countries were taken into account, the figure would rise to 50 million. The American research confirmed the figure of 35 million as the average listenership of the station within Nigeria. The most recent research I know of was carried out by a Lagos-based company in 1991. It suggested a figure of 40 million listeners at any given time, and concluded that the FRCN had the most listeners of any radio station not only in Nigeria but in the whole of Sub-Saharan Africa.

It was in 1961, immediately after independence, that the premier of the Northern Region, the late Sir Ahmadu Bello, Sardauna of Sokoto, dissatisfied with the then national radio, Nigeria Broadcasting Corporation (NBC), and realizing the power of radio to mobilize opinion, spearheaded the establishment of the Broadcasting

Corporation of Northern Nigeria (BCNN). This station initially combined radio and television and was known, and still remembered, as Radio Television Kaduua (RTK). In the words of Alhaji Ibrahim Biu, Nigeria's Minister of Information (1960–4),

> According to the ordinance that established the NBC, the corporation was enjoined to be impartial and to present all shades of opinion on any issue and should reflect the culture, characteristics, and opinions of the people of each region. Unfortunately, NBC failed to carry out these duties correctly. The NBC was neither fair to the North nor was it able to give coverage to the government of the North and party programmes. The NBC's lack of fair play and weaknesses were reasons for the Premier of the Northern Region and Sardauna of Sokoto to look for an alternative source of readily accessible mass media. The Northern Nigeria Government was convinced that the NBC could not be relied upon to sell the government's and party's programmes either at the regional level or national level. It was confirmed that the NBC was too centrally controlled to be sensitive to Northern Government's peculiar needs. As a result of this failure of NBC, the Sardauna of Sokoto firmly resolved that the Northern Regional Government would start its own Radio and TV because the Government had lost confidence in NBC because it gave little time to the NPC's National programmes and to Northern interest and culture. It discriminated against the North. (Biu 1992: 9)

Once the BCNN started operating, Alhaji Ibrahim Biu writes that the 'Sardauna used the media to protect and defend the North. The media also projected the image of the people of Northern Nigeria' (Biu 1992: 10). As a result, according to Alhaji Saka Aleshinloye, Baba-Isale of Ilorin, BCNN's Head of News 1962–8,

> The BCNN's editorial policy had been closely identified with the social, cultural, economic and political development of Northern Nigeria. Its radio and television services were intertwined with the hopes and aspirations as well as the fortunes and misfortunes of the people. (Aleshinloye 1992: 15)

Garba Abdullahi concurred:

> The ideals behind setting up the corporation which among others include the protection of the culture of its immediate environment are still being protected. The Station is today the watch dog of the teeming population in the Northern part of this country and beyond. This is so because most of its programmes are produced in local languages and the programmes to a large extent, serve various classes and interest groups. (Abdullahi 1992: 25)

BCNN's focus upon particular groups and classes (and the use of local language) can be gauged from a listing of some of its transmissions, many of which were given idiomatic Hausa titles:

News magazine programmes: '*Labarun Duniya*', 'News of the world', '*Barka da Yau*', 'How's today?'; political programmes, such as '*Sinadari*', 'Flux', '*Dandalin Siyasa*', 'Political platform', '*Alkawari Kaya ne*', 'A promise is a load' (it must be fulfilled, as the load must be put down).

Educational programmes: '*Halittun Gida da na Daji*', 'Domestic and wild creatures', '*Matambayi ba ya Bata*', 'He who asks, will never be lost'.

Agricultural programmes: '*Noma Yanke Talauci*', 'Farming ends poverty', '*Nomau Dan-Takarda Mai Tabaron Hangen Nesa*', 'Nomau, the educated one who has the glasses that see far away', '*Nome Karkara Magajin Garba*', 'Turn the countryside into farming land, heir to Garba', '*Taba, Sa Farin-cikin Aljihu*', 'Cigarettes make the pocket happy'.

Request programmes in which popular music is played: *'Zaben safe Zaben rana'*, 'Morning choice, daytime choice', *'Zaben robb'*, 'Robb's choice,' and *'Zaben Kabo-air'*, 'Kabo-air's choice'.

Radio drama and comedy programmes: *'Zaman Duniya Iyawa ne'*, 'Living in the world requires expertise', *'Dagurasa'*, 'Is a cake available?', *'Duniya Budurwar Wawa'*, 'The world is the fool's damsel', *'Basafce Dan Malam Dogara'*, 'Basafce son of Malam Dogara', *'Samanja Mazan Fama'*, 'Sergeant major, the brave warrior'.

Variety programmes: *'Jakar Magori'*, 'Mixed bag'.

By far the most popular of FRCN programmes are the dramas. Impressed by their success in the Hausa programmes, the station introduced a multi-channel broadcast in Fulfulde, Kanuri and Nupe in the 1980s. Programmes in these languages are transmitted on the same frequency as the English-language programmes, since the station broadcasts programmes on two different frequencies: an English service and a Hausa service. The station transmits for 19 hours every day, from 5.30 a.m. to 12.30 a.m. The English service-programmes are largely news magazines, current affairs and political programmes. The English dramas and enlightenment programmes usually concern modern urban problems; even the entertainment programmes play foreign, especially western music and other cultural forms. Indigenous cultural forms are found only in the Hausa programmes.

Thanks to the FRCN, radio listening is not only a habit for an overwhelming majority of the Hausa-speaking inhabitants of northern Nigeria, but they see it as a Hausa cultural value. International Broadcasting Audience Research for the BBC in Hausa-speaking areas of Nigeria, Niger and Ghana, has maintained that in Nigeria the BBC weekly audience in Hausa is 24 per cent of all adults, which means about 11.5 million listeners. The research noted that, 'although men outnumber women in the Hausa weekly audience by six to four, the proportion of women in the Hausa listenership is substantially higher than that found in other regional languages (Arabic, Somali, French, English and Swahili)' (Eggerman 1996). A BBC survey in 1993 found that 93 per cent of urban Nigerian households owned a radio set, 52 per cent owned a television set and 11 per cent owned a video-cassette recorder (Eggerman 1996). It also found that listeners tuned to Radio Nigeria Kaduna, the BBC Hausa service, the VOA Hausa service, Radio Peking Hausa service, Radio Deutsche Welle Hausa service, the former Radio Moscow Hausa service, in that order of importance. The Hausa services of the international radio stations carry predominantly news and current affairs from all over the world. The FRCN carries similar international news in its magazine programmes, but the predominant material in the very popular drama and request programmes is local social and political news. Local popular cultural genres, such as proverbs, catchphrases, jokes and funny stories abound, while whatever people are talking about on the streets regarding fashion, personalities and events – in short all of current popular discourse – form the stuff of chat shows and other discussion programmes. Bashir has now brought similar material into his Kabo-air and other advertisements.

Bashir Isma'ila Ahmed

Bashir Isma'ila Ahmed is an experienced journalist who has worked for various radio stations at different times for 26 years between 1968 and 1994: the FRCN, 1968–72, 1978–86 and 1989–90; VON, 1987–9; KSMC, 1990–4; and the BBC World Service (Hausa Section) 1974–7. He was appointed Kaduna State Commissioner for Information in 1994. He established his advertising company (Bismad Media Ventures) in 1990. He has produced advertisements for an airline, commercial and community banks, candidates for political posts, private businesses, and government public enlightenment campaigns, among other things.

Bashir has put his training and experience, as well as his understanding of Hausa culture and society, to work in his advertisements. It was during a journalism course at the London School of Journalism that Bashir began thinking about advertisements. His premise was that, if the purpose of advertisements is to attract and hold the attention of an audience, then the way in which that can be done should differ from one society to another. So he began thinking of ways in which it could best be done in Hausa society. This is why, in his advertisements, Bashir presents the products and services he advertises in a way that is integrated into the cultural universe of the audience. In doing so he exploits values, beliefs and practices that appeal to, entertain and inform his audience; Bashir seeks to reinforce this cultural universe, while admonishing and mobilizing his audience.

The rich and vibrant tradition of oral and written literature in Hausa makes it possible for Bashir to do what he does. Over the years many of the Hausa oral and written literary forms have been extensively deployed by national and regional media such as the FRCN, the daily newspaper *Gaskiya ta fi Kwabo*, 'Truth is worth more than a penny', and various other radio stations owned by state governments, to the extent that they have gained such wide currency as to become truly popular culture. These forms include Hausa literary genres, such as *waka* or 'song', *wake* or 'poetry'; *labari* and *tatsuniya*, prose narratives contrasted as 'presumed real' and 'fictive' respectively; *wasan kwaikwayo* or 'drama' (a very fundamental part of the last three is stereotypical characterization and typical interactions between the characters); short-form verbal arts such as *karin magana*, 'proverb', *kirari*, 'epithetic speech', *roko*, 'begging', *habaici*, 'innuendo'; also *kama*, 'catching', that is, 'burlesque art' (Furniss 1996: 96) and *gambara* or 'strolling minstrelry' (Kofoworola and Lateef 1987: 94).

The popular essence of Bashir's advertisements is captured in the words Berger uses to describe the character of popular culture genres:

> The very essence of popular culture is its ability to provide its public with a sense of the familiar, while at the same time also infusing this with enough variety to ensure continued interest. All forms of popular culture walk the fine line between what the scholar John Cawelti has called 'conventions' and 'inventions.' The conventions ensure that the subject matter falls into a recognisable and comfortable category, while the inventions provide the surprise (which can be either in the narrative or in the aesthetics of presentation) which differentiate this item from the many others competing for the public's attention and money. To succeed, popular culture can not stray too far from the recognisable formula, or categories, because the audience will experience difficulty in relating to it; but it must also constantly provide an interesting variation on the theme. (Berger 1992: vii)

My contention is that it is within the context of these recognizable categories, or genres, that all of Bashir's advertisements are created. His subtle innovations do not stray so far from these genres as to become unrecognizable. Taking the various forms I have mentioned above in turn, I shall explain them and show how Bashir uses them in his advertising.

Waka, 'song'

The Hausa term *waka* distinguishes any consistently rhythmically patterned language from ordinary speech. When qualified by the word *baka*, 'mouth' (*wakar baka* 'song of the mouth') it refers to oral song and, when modified by the word *rubutacciya*, 'written', it implies written poetry.[1] In practice, however, there is reciprocal influence between the two genres (Muhammad 1979: 87–9; 1980). The traditions of poetry and song are long-established in Hausaland, both dating back to the early nineteenth century. Poetry was a favourite weapon in the hands of the cleric class in Hausa society both before and after the Jihad of Usman Dan Fodio (see Last 1967). They used it as a medium for the communication of Islamic ideas to local populations. It was therefore one of the 'key weapons in the battle for the hearts and minds of the ordinary people' (Furniss 1996: 197). The role of the oral singer also dates back to the post-Jihad class structure of society based upon a differentiated aristocracy, a merchant class, a cleric class, a peasantry, craft guilds and agricultural slave populations. Although that structure may have given way to a pattern of integration into occupations and statuses derived, through western education, from participation in the modern society of the nation-state, with its middle classes of professionals, civil servants, military and business elites, the role of the oral singer in sustaining such an elaborate status system still persists. This persistence is indicated by an interview Dandatti Abdulkadir had with a popular oral singer, Alhaji Mamman Shata, in 1973, and quoted in Furniss (1996: 126–7), in which Shata presents himself as instrumental to the fame of certain individuals in his status-conscious society.

There are traditionally two types of singer: the 'freelance singer' and the 'tied singer'. While the former can offer their services in return for material reward to any patron, the latter are tied to a single patron, usually a royal family. The functions of songs and singers in Hausa society are, however, not restricted to singing the praises only of individuals. Purposiveness is perceived as a legitimate part of the social role of the singer and the poet. Alhaji Mamman Shata, in the interview referred to above, points to two types of discourse: that which keeps track of important events in society (he mentions the change from driving on the left to driving on the right as an example), and more general exhortation (songs about education and health and against corruption). The latter songs are intended to present to a listener 'a moral vision, sets of values' (Furniss 1996: 129).

[1] See Muhammad (1979) who has described the distinction between the two forms. In public performance song is usually instrumentally accompanied, often sung by a group with lead singer and chorus, and is performed without reference to anything written down; poetry can be chanted publicly without accompaniment but is often simply read in silence. The process of composition also tends to differ; where poetry is written and reworked by the individual poet, song is often composed within a group and re-performed from memory.

The view of his functions expressed by Alhaji Mamman Shata is one that would be shared by the majority of his fellow freelance singers. There are many freelance and tied singers in modern Hausaland. A few of the most famous, besides Alhaji Mamman Shata, are the late Alhaji Musa Dan-Kwairo's group, the late Alhaji Dan-Anache's group, the late Jankidi, Dan-Maraya Jos, Audu Karen-Gusau, Garba Sufa, Audu Wazirin Dan-Duna, Sarkin Taushin Katsina, Sani Sabulu, Marafa Dan-Bawa Kaura, Sa'idu Faru, Haruna Uji, Dan Lami Nasarawa, Binta Zabaya and Barmani Choge. They, and others, perform on social, sporting and ritual occasions; their songs are played on television and radio stations to wide enjoyment. The singing styles of these singers vary considerably; some of them use a lead singer and a chorus, others sing solo, yet others take it in turns to sing (for examples see Furniss 1996: 126–91).

Bashir uses this rich, vibrant tradition of song in his advertisements in a variety of ways. The most popular songs by noted performers are played for a few seconds at the beginning of some of his advertisements: Garba Sufa's *kukuma* music associated with *aikin gayya*, 'communal work',[2] is played in 16 of a corpus of 101 of Bashir's advertisements that I have collected. A particular phrase recurs: *Hobbasa, hobbasa, hobbasallera* which is an expression from Garba Sufa's song that is typically used by porters when picking up their loads, or by any other person realizing the heaviness of an object or the toughness of a job, like ploughing, for example. During communal work, *aikin gayya*, people use the phrase a great deal, in this and other songs.

The following line in Shata's *kalangu* music is used in eight advertisements:

Shata:	*Yawan mutane shi ne kasuwa,*	Shata:	The number of people is what
	Ni ku raba ni da tarin rumfuna,		makes a market. Do not tell to me
			about the number of amassed stalls
Chorus:	*Isyaku, ka dawo lafiya!*	Chorus:	*Isyaku,* safe journey!

Dan-Maraya's *kuntigi* music is used in three advertisements; Abdu Wazirin Dan-Duna twice and Shantu music once.

Initially Bashir chose existing songs by these singers, but later, as the fame of Kabo airline (thanks to the advertisements) gradually grew and some of the singers adopted the owner of the airline as their patron, Bashir was able to use new praise songs at the beginning of either the conversational or the narrative advertisements.

In other advertisements Bashir chooses songs that relate to the locality or target audience of the product being advertised. In the advertisement for Bakori Community Bank, for example, he uses the music of Atta Dabai, a popular drummer who hails from Dabai village (in Bakori Local Government Area) and who plays his drums while rolling on the ground. Just the sound of his drums is

---

2 Communal work is a well-known part of especially rural Hausa society that is, however, fast dying out. In small traditional villages a particular farmer may distribute invitations to the able-bodied members of the village calling them to gather together and work on his farm. His responsibility on that day would be providing lunch for the workers. It also used to be the practice for the young men of a village to organize to work on the farm of a deceased person who has left a large family behind or on the farm of a very old man who has no children of his own. On all such occasions there would be special communal drumming by a special drummer to cheer the workers on.

enough to draw the attention of the people, especially people of his locality, who are the potential customers of the bank. Bashir uses a similar strategy in the advertisement of Harco Textiles, where the *algaita* (reed wind instrument) music of the tied singer of the emir of Zazzau is used to attract the attention of particularly *Zazzagawa* (natives and/or residents of Zaria), because Harco Textiles is located in Zaria. In other advertisements such as those for Afribank, M.G. Cable Network Systems, Nigeria Universal Bank, and for the launching of a book on IBB (Ibrahim Badamasi Babangida, former Nigerian head of state), he used songs by famous singers who had been commissioned by these institutions to sing their praises.

Even when there is no appropriate song by a popular singer, Bashir uses the song genre to make the name of the product easy to remember. There are occasions when he has used the voices of people who are not singers to chant impromptu songs in the studio, about the products he advertises, such as in the advertisements of Borgu Community Bank and Allied Bank, and the advertisement of the 1983 presidential candidate Mahmoud Waziri.

By using these songs as Bashir does, he has been able to link the product with the pleasure that people experience when they listen to the songs of their favourite singers; a pleasure which might otherwise dissipate when a song is interrupted to make way for an advertisement. Bashir does not allow that to happen; he sutures the familiar pleasures derived from popular culture genres into the texts of his advertisements.

Labari, 'story'

In the past, the Hausa term *labari* has meant a narrative that was 'presumed real'. It contrasted with *tatsuniya*, a 'purely fictive' narrative. Recently, however, 'the word *labari* has tended to be used as a very general term, implying any kind of narrative, whether overt or hidden behind a proverb or other referential device' (Furniss 1996: 56). A major collection of Hausa oral narratives (Edgar 1911–13) was reorganized and translated by Skinner (1969). Skinner's translation grouped the *tatsuniya* stories, into animal stories, caricatures – ethnic and other stereotypes, moralizing stories, men and women, young men and maidens, dilemma tales and other content-based categories. The popularity of this genre is attested by a 15-minute radio programme '*Shafa Labari Shuni*', 'Spice up the story', on the FRCN, in which listeners are invited to send in stories of their own invention, or those they have read and enjoyed so much that they wish to share their pleasure with other listeners. The stories sent in are read over the radio in a series.

Hausa stories are dominated by larger-than-life stereotyped characters. At the core of the moral, religious, social and political didacticism, as well as the humorous entertainment the stories provide, is the interaction of the characters. Elements of content and intention come out primarily through the dialogue, the story-teller's art focuses on dramatized dialogue and action.

Bashir's familiarity with this tradition allowed him to build up, as Furniss (1996: 24) says, 'the logic of character and motivation [which] takes precedence over any pretence of verisimilitude'. His advertisements draw on this tradition and develop the characters in such a way that the audience quickly grasps the potential of the situations he establishes. During rehearsals Bashir pays particular attention to voice as the medium of characterization for the roles in his radio advertisements.

The same two character types are used to advertise a variety of different products: 'Malam' (the Islamic scholar, a figure at the centre of Hausa society), and the more fluid character 'Manu', who is capable of assuming many different personalities. Bashir himself plays the part of Malam, and the part of Manu as second voice is played by Usman Yaro, a junior employee of Kaduma State Media Corporation (KSMC). I call him a second voice because voicing the advertisements is literally all he does. Bashir writes the text and directs all aspects of the production of each of the advertisements. When he is satisfied with a script he invites Usman for rehearsal. He rehearses the script with Usman very intensively, his directorial insistence on particular tone and intonation causing many a quarrel between them during rehearsal.

The advertisements involve encounters between the two characters. It is possible for them to say the kind of things they say whenever they meet, because of who they are. Malam (teacher, cleric) is a custodian of knowledge and wisdom, both religious and worldly, so he can explain practically anything to Manu who is always confused about one thing or another and seeking explanation or advice. Because Malam is wise and cunning he dips into the cultural pot to find appropriate forms with which to dress up his explanations in impressive language, rich in cultural connotations. Let me give a few illustrations.

There is an airline advertisement in which Bashir had Manu say, '*Malam ina da tambaya amma ina gudun ka yi min dariya*', 'Malam, I have a question, but I am afraid you may laugh at me'. This is the manner characteristic of a country bumpkin, who, while conscious of his ignorance, is also sensitive that he could be laughed at when it shows. But curiosity overcomes reticence, so he asks what may well be a stupid question. As well as curiosity and fear of ridicule, Manu also has the down-to-earth realistic attitude of a country bumpkin. Malam's reply, '*Manu, ai mai dokar barci ba ya gyangyadi*', 'Manu, he who warns against sleep should not be caught drowsing', portrays the paternal admonition of a wise guide (a malam), a voice easily recognized in a society where didacticism is so common.

In another advertisement Manu, as a merchant, is asked by Malam what is in the sack that Manu always carries. '*To, wai meye a buhun nan Manu?*' 'Well what is always in that bag Manu?', to which he answers, '*Asirin mu ne na 'yan kasuwa, Malam. Idan kana son lakanin, kawo tikitin Kabo-air zuwa ko ina, sai in ba ka*', 'It is our secret, we merchants, Malam. If you want the magical clue, bring a Kabo-air ticket to anywhere, then I will give it to you'. Manu thus tries to reverse positions with Malam, since it is usually malams who give merchants secret magical clues to boost trade and prosperity. So Malam quickly rejects this reversal, '*A'a rike asirin buhunka Manu*', 'Oh no, keep the secret of your sack, Manu', and reasserts his position of power by invoking what gives him the power, or knowledge, thus, '*Ni na san in zan shiga Kabo-air ...*', 'I have the knowledge that if I wish to board a plane of Kabo-air ...'.

In another airline advertisement Malam refers to Manu as 'Mister Manu' and Manu reminds him that he prefers the more prestigious title of 'Alhaji', '*Malam ba fa Malam Manu nake ba yanzu, Alhaji ne nan guda ...*', 'Malam I am not just "Mister" now, I am a complete Alhaji ...' (even though he has yet to earn the title by performing the pilgrimage by air): '... *mai jiran gado*' '.... in waiting'. This has resonances for the audience of the very common joke about a Fulani man who had been to Saudi Arabia to perform the pilgrimage so many times that when he was referred to by the title 'Alhaji', he thought he must have gone way beyond that, and asked why he should not be entitled, *annabijo*, 'prophet-ette'.[3] In this way Bashir uses the speech styles of character types in Hausa stories to paint recognizable personalities in his advertisements.

By using a particular language style to develop these familiar story characters, Bashir has not only caught his audience's attention with something they know, but he has also created suspense by raising their expectations of further entertaining and creative dramatic encounters between characters.

Wasan kwaikwayo 'game of imitation, theatre/drama'

The term *wasan kwaikwayo* in Hausa means drama or theatre. Radio drama has established a range of stereotyped central characters that dates back to the 1950s (Magaji Wando 1985). When Bashir Isma'ila Ahmed produced a drama series for the FRCN, known as '*Basafce*' and aimed at farmers, it set a trend in humorous radio soap operas for following generations. But Bashir was not alone: Adamu Gumel produced a popular series entitled '*Dagurasa*'; and in the 1960s there was '*Zaman Duniya Iyawa Ne*'; while in the 1970s Usman Baba Fategi produced and starred in '*Samanja Mazan Fama*', which along with his other production '*Duniya Budurwar Wawa*' is still a regular radio feature on the FRCN, with '*Samanja*' transferring to television on NTA Kaduna. According to Kallamu (1992), by 1992 practically all local radio and television stations in the northern states of Nigeria had Hausa drama shows of great popularity. This remains the case today. Other popular television dramas include '*Kuliya Manta Sabo*', 'The law does not reckon with familiarity', on NTA Kano, and '*Idon Matambayi*', 'The eye of the enquirer', on NTA Sokoto.

Bashir draws on his extensive experience of this tradition of Hausa drama to reproduce in his advertisements the humorous interactions between stock characters, the graphic wit and the comic action that has made the dramas so popular. These can be illustrated, again, in the recurrent encounters between the two principal characters of Malam and Manu: Manu is often portrayed as a fool, a clown. In one encounter, for example, after innocently expressing what he feels, Manu is referred to by Malam as *angon bante*, 'a greenhorn', a characterization that immediately evokes laughter, since the image of such characters is fixed and very easily recalled. The dramatic irony when Manu, thinking that someone has done something funny, wants to share the laughter with Malam but ends up being the laughing-stock himself, is a similar instance of the reversals of fortune that are the stock-in-trade of serial dramas. Manu is always carrying a sack on his journeys instead of a bag or a briefcase: when he tried using a briefcase it ended in disaster, his air ticket became locked inside when he forgot the key

---

[3] In other situations this may be regarded as blasphemous, any blasphemy is overlooked and may be laughed at in the case of an ignorant Fulani herdsman who spends his life in the bush with his cattle.

combination, an incident which made him 'sweat like a leper'; consequently he abandoned that symbol of modernity and reverted to using his sack. He walks around with big stains on his clothes 'big enough for even the blind to see', and in such a hurried and careless manner that he keeps 'hitting his toes'; his flowing gown 'ending in tangles around him'.

Elsewhere, Bashir uses Malam's superior knowledge, or Manu's linguistic inability, to portray the latter as a fool. By pointing up the foolishness of Manu's utterances, Malam (or Bashir) demonstrates his superior knowledge and mastery of the Hausa language. Bashir makes further use of the character Manu to engage with the audience, inviting them to participate by using the interactive genre of *kacinci-kacinci*, 'riddles'. In one advertisement Malam asked Manu the question, *'Wanne ya fi zaki tsakanin mangwaro nunar sama da nukin daka?'* 'Which one would be sweeter, between the mango that ripens on the tree and the one that is plucked unripe and allowed to ripen artificially by fermenting it and storing it?', and promised him a reward for producing the correct answer. The strategy is double edged: it effectively expresses the idea that Kabo-air is superior to other airlines (the mango that ripens on the tree) and also engages with the audience, leading people to begin to solve the riddle. Malam does not provide the answer immediately; he sends the conversation off at a tangent to give the audience time to figure it out before he finally provides the answer. Malam says, *'ba ni amsar in ji'*, 'let me hear the answer'. Manu then provides, not yet the answer but, a clue 'to help the audience': *'Ai ba ma za'a hada ba Malam, tsakanin wanda ya tsiro, ya tofu, ya goge, san nan ya nuna a tushensa, da wanda aka tsunko yana sharaf aka cusa a duhu'*, 'There is no way you can compare, Malam, between the one that germinated, flowered, grew strong, and ripened on its roots, and the one that was plucked raw and pushed into darkness'. When the answer finally comes, *'Dangarama shi ne nunar sama, sauran kuma nukin daka'*, 'Dangarama is the one that ripens on the tree, and the others are the fermented ones', we realize that all the positive description of natural ripening relates to Kabo-air while the negative description of artificial ripening relates to its competitors. The word 'roots' has further connotations of origin – Dangarama has its roots here (in the north).

A dramatic dimension is added to the advertisements by the way Bashir gives continuity to his characters, suggesting to the audience that they are listening to the people who featured in previous encounters in other advertisements. The advertisements assume the character of a soap-opera. In one place Manu says to Malam, *'Malam, ni dai yau ba zan yarda ba, sai ka fassara min maganar nan da ka ce sai darasi na gaba'*, 'Malam, today I insist that you must interpret for me that expression (of the other day) which you said you would explain in our next lesson'. Malam refers to a previous lesson before giving a new one, *'Ka fadi sunayen jiragen sama da na fada maka lokacin da ka yi mafarki'*, 'Tell (me) the names of the aircraft that I gave you when you had that dream'. The audience's memory is refreshed as they also remember the encounter from a previous advertisement. Similarly, when Manu says, *'Malam, ni kan so in yi tambaya, amma ba'a na ke gudu'*, 'Malam I keep wanting to ask questions, but I am scared of mockery', the audience is being directed to recall the humour in the mockery to which Malam had subjected Manu in previous advertisements. (There are other such instances of recall and continuity.)

In this re-creation of typical dramatic characters and encounters, as well as the interactional games in vivid and colloquial language, Bashir draws upon his experience of the popular tradition of Hausa *wasan kwaikwayo*, 'drama', as he does with other short-form verbal arts, such as *karin magana*, 'proverb', *habaici*, 'innuendo', and/or *zambo*, 'ridicule', and *kirari*, 'epithet', and/or *take*, 'drummed equivalent of praise epithets', considered in the next section.

Karin magana, '(folded/broken speech) proverb'

Bashir appeals to the collective wisdom of *karin magana* in his advertising in a variety of ways. In some cases he simply affirms the wisdom that the *karin magana* contains and attributes it to the product he advertises. Among the devices he uses as associational tools to achieve attribution is the linguistic linker *sai* 'only', in the form of 'X *sai* Dangarama',[4] where X stands for the desirable attribute contained within the *karin magana*,

> *Hakin sama sai rakumi*
> Only the camel (can reach) the high grass

> *Tafiya a jirgin sama sai Dangaraman jirage*
> Only the Dangarama of planes (Kabo-Air) can accomplish a journey in a plane

Once Bashir has linked his voice, the *karin magana*, and a product in the minds of the audience, he can then use the proverbs in the expectation of evoking the product without naming it, as in:

> *Susa ba ta maganin karara, yadda tutu a ciki ba shi maganin yunwa*
> Scratching can not be the remedy for 'cow-itch' (the climbing plant), just like a stool retained in the stomach can not be the remedy for hunger

> *Ruwan gulbi kaza ya kan ba tsoro, agwagwa ko Bahar-Maliya ka kai ta, ta yi maka iyon iyawar gado*
> The water of the river can only scare the hen, as for the duck even if you take it to the Red Sea, it will demonstrate its inherited swimming skills

> *Hantsal-batsalu, tufkar mai koyo, ya karanta hanci ya sabalta igiya. Igiyar rike ingarma sai gwani*
> Wobbly wobbly is the weaving of the learner, he shortens one end of the rope and makes another too long. Only the expert makes a rope to hold a steed

Habaici, 'innuendo' and *zambo*, 'ridicule'

The Hausa term *habaici*, 'innuendo', relates more to the functional aspect of an utterance, speaker intent or illocutionary force, than to its literal meaning. It relies upon hidden meaning, and is typically applied to short fixed phrases. But *zambo*, 'ridicule', is applied to a series of utterances that may contain *karin magana* and *habaici*, usually in a song in praise of a patron, where the *zambo* would be

---

[4] Dangarama means a form of protection or reliable support, and here stands as a laudatory epithet for the airline, Kabo-Air.

directed to the patron's or the singer's enemies: for example, '*ni ba ni waka ina dafe kunne, don ba kokon bara garan ba*', 'I do not sing with my palm placed over my ear, because I am not holding out a begging bowl'. While *habaici* is commonly used by all segments of the society, especially women, *zambo* is more identified with praise-singers. Furniss (1996: 180) quotes Zagga who writes that 'the praise-singer is the protection between the patron and his enemies' and that 'in praising the king, the singer must surreptitiously attack the princes' (Zagga 1980: 16, 72).

In my sample of adverts, Bashir used *habaici* and *zambo* four times each in reference to other airlines. The terms *kyandir, carki, dan-kunya, yamutsa-hazo* and *bigi-bagiro* all contain innuendo against existing airlines in the country. *Kyandir*, 'candle', refers to Okada airline, the planes of which are beautifully decorated. The name, however, reminds the audience of the Hausa proverb '*kyandir mai kyaun banza*', 'The beauty of a candle is worthless' because it eventually burns out. *Dan-kunya*, 'the shy one', is a reference to Hold-trade airline which is partly owned by the Sultan of Sokoto, 'the most highly revered emir in Hausaland'. So Malam is shy in pointing out its faults. *Carki*, the name of a small bird (starling), refers to Harco airline (now known as Harka airline) whose small planes are meant for domestic services. Here Malam is implying that they are too small for any good purpose. *Bigi-bagiro*, 'Big for nothing', is a reference to Nigeria Airways (owned by the Nigerian government), which notoriously fails to provide satisfactory service in spite of the federal government resources at its disposal.

Kirari, 'praise epithets', and *take*, 'drummed equivalents of praise epithets'

The term *kirari* means 'praise epithets', and *take* means 'drummed equivalents of verbal epithets'. In actual usage, however, *waka*, 'song', the extended text that incorporates both verbal epithets and their drummed equivalents, can also be a *take* of an individual, an office or an occupational group. It is possible to refer to both short-form verbal epithets and their drummed equivalents as someone's *take* (Powe 1984). This identification of a *take* as belonging to X happens only when a particular *take* text gains wide currency and becomes easily recognizable as such. But *kirari*, 'praise epithets', vary considerably in length. They can be made up of a short or a very long string of epithetic phrases. They are typically deployed by a *dan ma'abba*, 'praise-crier',[5] for a purpose: to praise, incite or to exhort on occasions of physical sporting contexts such as boxing and wrestling, especially before or after a boxing or wrestling bout. In the past they were used to embolden warriors in battle or to praise them after particular acts of bravery. The combatants can also shout their own *kirari*, to summon courage,[6] in which case the singer(s) and spectators keep quiet and listen, although a *dan ma'abba*, if present, may interpolate speech as he normally does during singing. When singer(s) intend to incite or exhort a combatant, they beat his *take* and sing his

---

[5] Other terms for this function are *maroki* and *sankira*, while the feminine term is *zabaya*.

[6] Powe (1984: 248) explains the way in which *kirari*, when shouted by the combatant himself, works like sympathetic magic, a sort of a word magic in which, at the level of common experience, language and reality are fused. In short it constitutes, for the combatants, a verse formula that is believed to be magically effective in manipulating people or things.

praise. This means that the entire song can function like *kirari*. Combatants, in sports or in war, professionals, such as *mafarauta*, 'hunters', *makera*, 'blacksmiths', usually shout their own *kirari* following a singer's singing of their *take*. *Kirari* of important personalities, be they traditional rulers or office holders, military officers, politicians or wealthy businessmen and women, are usually shouted by a *dan ma'abba*, 'praise-crier', at social occasions such as marriages, naming or graduation ceremonies, launchings and inaugurations, to elicit monetary reward from the addressees. If the personalities are famous, their *kirari* will be fixed and known; if, however, they are new entrants into the social class, the *dan ma'abba*, 'praise-crier', will have to use his knowledge of the form to invent a new *kirari* for them. This type of *kirari* of important personalities is also known simply as *yabo*, 'praise', as well as *washi* or *tumasanci*, both meaning 'flattery'. On similar occasions singers may also drum or sing an extended song in praise of important personalities with similar intents. So both *take* and *kirari* (of combatants, professionals or VIPs) can be made for one person by another (a singer or a praise-crier). While a combatant or a professional can shout their own *kirari*, a VIP will not do so. *Take* can be drumming, or spoken epithets, or both.

Thus a *take*, as an identificatory catchphrase, is like a personal badge, a socially approved way in which performers and singers publicly praise and say something about a person or an institution. A *kirari* is also such a badge, and a socially approved way for a certain segment of the society (verbal specialists) to say what they want to say about themselves and others.

Both *take* and *kirari* contain phrases displaying the characteristics of ellipsis, metaphor and the internal patterning typical of such phrases. In terms of content they are not restricted to praises; they may be taunts, ridicule, humour and scorn, most often in the form of an ingenious use of metaphor or *karin magana*, 'proverb'. As Furniss (1996: 76) writes, this use of language is personally directed:

> even more direct and directed is the notion of *zuga* 'incitement/encouragement' where there is an open conative intent, trying to make the target do something, particularly something requiring an effort or involving danger, which is why *zuga* is the primary characteristic of the deployment of *take* and *kirari* in wrestling, boxing and other combative activities, including in times past, hand-to-hand combat on the battlefield.

In terms of their form and content *take* and *kirari* are ideally suited for use in advertisements. What is novel in the use Bashir makes of them, however, is his creative adaptation of the occasions on which, and the purposes for which, they are used, as well as his ability to create new ones to suit his purposes.

An example of some widely known *kirari* he uses are those relating to the destination cities on the routes that Kabo-Air flies. Flight QNK 601 starts,

> *Daga wurin 'na shehu larabawan bidi'a' zuwa 'ko da me kazo an fi ka', zuwa 'ku da zagezagi tushenku guda ne' sannan ka dira 'garin kabo da adabo'*

> From 'the Shehu's people, Arabs of those who excel in merry making' to 'whatever you come with there is someone who surpasses you at it' to 'you and Zaria people are of the same origin' then you land in 'the city of welcome and goodbye'.

Na shehu larabawan bidi'a, 'the Shehu's people, Arabs of those who excel in merry making' is one of the *kirari* of the Kanuri people, so the destination referred to is

Borno, the capital of that region and where the Shehu resides; *ko da me kazo an fika*, 'whatever you come with there is someone who surpasses you at it' is the *kirari* of Kano city, the commercial centre of northern Nigeria; *ku da zagezagi tushenku guda ne*, 'you and Zaria people are of the same origin' is the *kirari* of Abuja, the new federal capital of Nigeria; *garin kabo da adabo*, 'the city of welcome and goodbye' is the *kirari* of Lagos, the commercial and former political capital of Nigeria.

Bashir displays an impressive repertoire of this genre, which even a profesional *dan ma'abba*, 'praise-crier', must envy, when he deploys *kirari* for the Dangarama (Kabo-Air) or its owner, Alhaji Adamu Dan-Kabo Jarman Kano,

> *Kome saurinka babu ya Dangarama, jigo kafuwar Allah, madara gamin alheri idan kai ba ka sha ba, ka ba yaro, rigiza daya da rabi kan dauka, jifar alheri fada kan asalinki*

However much in a hurry you are, there's none like Dangarama, a pillar that is put in place by God, milk a healthy mixture, if you do not drink it you can give it to a child, a large sackcloth mat can be carried only by one and a half porters, whatever is thrown up in goodness, will fall back down on its originator.

Some advertisements contain a string of praises:

> *Jigo kafuwar Allah, a tashi ko ba riba, don wani sakamakon yana gun Allah, Kabo mai kabo da adabo, har 'yar doriyar oyoyo!*

A pillar put in place by God, you take off even when you will not make a profit, since some kinds of recompense can only come from God, Kabo, owner of [one who facilitates] welcome and goodbye, including the small addition of 'oyoyo' [ie a welcome as said by children!]

The idea of generosity in the above *kirari* is expressed in the phrase '*a tashi ko ba riba*', 'you take off even when you will not make a profit', and linked to the value of belief, '*don wani sakamakon yana gun Allah*', 'since some kinds of recompense can only come from God'.

Other *kirari*, containing strings of epithetic phrases meant to praise Kabo-air and set it apart from others, include the following extended piece of verbal pyrotechnics:

> *Dangarama dan Jarma, kyawun da ya gaji ubansa, a dade ana kwalfa sai ruwan kogon dutse, marmara gagara ginin gara, gwangwala a hau ki a zame, ki hau mutum ki zauna daidai, tozali gyara ido, tubali tada katanga, ko katangar karfe ce. Kabo-air sun yi nasu, sun yi na rago, kuma sun raka shi da sadaka, karya wurin fadinta daban ne, gaskiya kuwa ko ina a fadeta, shuri shi ke saka, suri shi ke kashe shuka, lissafin Kwabo yana gun talaka, irin na Naira sai mai zakka. Kabo mai tashi da yardar Allah, ya kuma dire da ikon Rabba, Kabo ko da za'a samu kaninka kwakwalwarsa sai ta juya, Kabo mai kabo da adabo, har da yardar Allah!*

Dangarama the son of Jarma! The goodness of a son is to take after his father! To bale out water for a long time can only be done from the water of a cavity in a rock! Laterite is stubbornly opposed to the digging of termites! A stem of a raphia-palm branch, whoever climbs you will slide down, but when you climb one you stay in place! Antimony beautifies the eye! The brick, that straightens the wall, even if it is made of iron! Kabo, they have done their work, and done that of the lazy person and given him alms! There are places where a lie could be told, as for the truth, it could be said anywhere! It is with kicking that weaving is done! It is the ant hill that kills planted seeds! Only the poor count their money in Kobo, counting in Naira is done only by he who has enough money to pay alms. Kabo, one that takes off with the power of God, and also lands with the power of the Lord! Kabo, even if a younger brother to you is to be found, his brain must turn around! Kabo, one who facilitates welcome and goodbye, including the acceptance of God!

Bashir's use of this tradition of *kirari* functions in at least four main ways.

1. He can attribute qualities to the products he advertises (even if they may not be entirely justified):

Sauri babu garaje, tafiya ba da-na-sani, sauka babu gardama
Hurry without haste, journey without regret, safe landing

Tashi ba rugugi, tafiya sarai ba gargada da kwaranti, a kula da kai da duk abinda ka ke so, ka sauka lafiya ba cijewa
Taking off without much noise, smooth journey without bumps and shaking, you are taken care of and provided with whatever you want, you land safely without jerking

2. He can make claims in respect of the product that he need not substantiate:

A tashi ko ba riba
You take off even when you will not make profit

Ba gida ba ko a daji, kabo-air ya wuce dangi!
Not only at home, even abroad Kabo-air is ahead of its kind

Kabo-air sun yi nasu, sun yi na rago, kuma sun raka shi da sadaka
Kabo, they have done their work, and done that of the lazy person, and given him alms!

3. He can make damaging implications about competing products without appearing to be doing so, thereby enabling him to escape being charged with slander, as in referring to other airlines as *karamin tsuntsu*, 'small bird', and *kankamo*, 'spendthrift'.

4. He can also supply facts about the 'products' in a much more interesting way as the example of Kabo-Air has already illustrated.

Clearly, this is far more interesting and effective than simply saying that the plane starts from Maiduguri and stops at Kano and Abuja before arriving in Lagos.

I have discussed the various ways in which Bashir's advertising style puts together the whole gamut of Hausa popular culture genres. He takes aspects of the rhetorical style of Hausa *waka* songs. He paints, in his use of language, the funniest of characters in Hausa stories, *labarai*, and enacts the most common entertaining encounters between them in the tradition of Hausa drama, *wasan kwaikwayo*. He appropriates the cultural values and folk wisdom contained in Hausa proverbs, *karin magana*, and uses the associational tools of Hausa epithetic speech, *kirari*, to attribute them to the products he advertises. He extols the virtues of the products, emphasizing the ways in which they outshine or outperform similar products by using the vilification style of Hausa innuendo, *habaici*, and ridicule, *zambo*, to put down the competition.

Bashir's advertisements are evidence that Hausa verbal art is an ongoing activity that is nourished by the existence of electronic media, notably radio, and commerce. This activity, in which the cultural resources of a wide variety of popular genres are deployed to new purposes and with novel commercial communicative effect, makes the modern something which is both hybridized and localized. The reworking of the familiar in new and engaging ways by the activity of this creative artist demonstrates the process whereby the medium of radio is embedded within a vibrant culture, a medium listened to by many millions of people, every day of the week, every week of the year.

References

Abdullahi, Garba (1992) 'Radio Nigeria Kaduna: an information legacy of the late Sir Ahmadu Bello', *Radio Nigeria Kaduna: 30 Years of Broadcasting to the Nation* (magazine published as part of a 30-year anniversary celebration), 24–5.

Aleshinloye, Alhaji Saka (1992) 'Evolution of BCNN's editorial policy', *Radio Nigeria Kaduna: 30 Years of Broadcasting to the Nation* (magazine published as part of a 30-year anniversary celebration), 12–15.

Berger, Arthur Asa (1992) *Popular Culture Genres: Theories and Texts*, London: Sage Publications.

Biu, Alhaji Ibrahim (1992) 'Birth of the BCNN: reasons and circumstances', *Radio Nigeria Kaduna: 30 Years of Broadcasting to the Nation* (magazine published as part of a 30 year anniversary celebration), 9–10.

Edgar, Frank (1911–13) *Litafi na Tatsuniyoyi na Hausa*, Belfast: W. Erskine Mayne.

Eggerman, Mark (1996) 'BBC International Broadcasting Audience Research', presentation to a BBC English/Hausa planning meeting, January.

Furniss, Graham (1996) *Poetry, Prose and Popular Culture in Hausa*, Edinburgh: Edinburgh University Press.

Kallamu, Dan Baba (1992) 'Rayuwa da ayyukan Alhaji Usman Baba Fategi (Samanja Mazan Fama), musamman a kan shirin "Duniya Budurwar Wawa" da "Samanja Mazan Fama"', unpublished BA dissertation, Bayero University, Kano.

Kofoworola, Ziky O. and Lateef, Y. (1987) *Hausa Performing Arts and Music*, Lagos: Nigeria Magazine.

Last, D. M. (1967) *The Sokoto Caliphate*, London: Longman.

Magaji Wando, Yahaya (1985) 'Wasan kwaikwayo a Gidan Rediyo Nijeriya na Kaduna', unpublished BA dissertation, Ahmadu Bello University, Zaria.

Muhammad, Dalhatu (1979) 'Interaction between the oral and the literate traditions of Hausa poetry', *Harsunan Nijeriya* 9: 85–90.

——— (1980) 'Zumunta tsakanin marubutan wakokin Hausa da makada', *Harsunan Nijeriya* 10: 85–102.

Powe, Edward (1984) 'Hausa combat literature: an exposition and analysis', unpublished PhD thesis, University of Wisconsin.

Skinner, A. Neil (ed.) (1969) *Hausa Tales and Traditions: an English Translation of 'Tatsuniyoyi Na Hausa'*, originally compiled by Frank Edgar, Vol. 1 (1969), London: Frank Cass; Vols 2 & 3 (1977), Madison: University of Wisconsin Press.

Zagga, Umaru (1980) *Jankidi da wakokinsa*, unpublished BA dissertation, Bayero University, Kano.

10
Documenting Radio Culture as Lived Experience*

Reception Studies & the Mobile Machine in Zambia
DEBRA SPITULNIK

The very force and impact ... of any medium changes significantly as it is moved from one context to another (a bar, a theatre, the living room, the bedroom, the beach, a rock concert ...). Each medium is then a mobile term, taking shape as it situates itself – almost always comfortably – within the different roadside rests of our lives. That is, the text is located, not only intertextually, but in a range of apparatuses as well, defined technologically but also by other social relations and activities. One rarely just listens to the radio, watches TV, or even goes to the movies – one is studying, dating, driving somewhere else, partying, etc. (Grossberg 1987: 34)

Widening the frame of reception studies

Over the past decade there has been a radical rethinking of the concepts of 'audience' and 'reception' within media studies.[1] Most significantly, this work has criticized the long-standing assumption that the 'audience' is a unified aggregate

* This chapter is part of a larger project which examines how mass media manufacture national publics and imagined communities of the nation state (Spitulnik, forthcoming). Research was supported by Fulbright-Hays, NSF and Spencer Foundation fellowships, and facilitated by the Institute for African Studies at the University of Zambia during 1988–90. I would like to extend my sincere thanks to these institutions, and to the many Zambians who shared their days, homes and lives with me during that time. Special thanks go to my research assistants Simon Bwalya and Brian Mfula for assistance in documenting radio use and radio sales in the Kasama area. I am also greatly indebted to the SOAS conference organizers Richard Fardon and Graham Furniss, for their perceptive feedback on earlier drafts. Thanks also go to Mansur Abdulkadir, Jean Comaroff, Christopher Davis, Faye Ginsburg, Mark Hobart and Bruce Knauft for their helpful comments on earlier versions of this work.

[1] See for example: Abu-Lughod 1997; Allor 1988; Ang 1996; Caldarola 1992; Fiske 1987; Mankekar 1993a, 1993b; Moores 1993; Morley 1992; Radway 1988; Spitulnik 1993. Much of this research builds on Hall's important theoretical work (1973) which gives an analytical framework for classifying how audiences decode messages differently, based on their social class and ideological positioning.

which receives a fixed message. Scholars have increasingly shifted their attention to the fact that people use mass media, and thus are not passive receivers, but rather are active participants in ongoing communication processes.[2] Part of this de-essentialization of the audience and reanimation of reception has also included a close look at how a single media form itself can be used and interpreted in multiple ways by different individuals.

In line with these recent moves to de-essentialize the audience and reanimate reception, there has been growing attention to the need to study the ways in which 'media are integrated and implicated within [daily life]' (Radway 1988: 366; see also Moores 1993).[3] As Radway and numerous others have argued, it is important to deconstruct and particularize any notion of 'audience' within an ethnographic study of media use, paying attention to the diversity of ways in which people actively construct themselves as media users, consumers and owners.

I propose here that, coupled with this attentiveness to such audience constructions, we also need to attend to two other factors. First, there is the question of how features of the media technology itself enable or inhibit certain kinds of audience engagements. And secondly, there is the possibility that social context is just as much a factor in active audience engagements as is any kind of individual interpretive process.   What I mean here is that there is a danger in active audience research of overstating the role of the individual subject at the expense of social context. Indeed, one of the greatest hazards of conventional reception studies – with their origins in literary criticism, printed texts, the single inter-preting reader and assumptions of a western type of subjectivity – is that they encourage a kind of egocentric (or subject-centric), rather than sociocentric, account of reception practices. From both ethnographic and theoretical stand-points we need to remain aware that the individual interpretive moment of 'decoding' a media message may not be the only – or, indeed, the most significant – aspect of what a particular media form 'means' in a given sociocultural context.

Grossberg's perceptive comments (quoted above) help us to move in this direction, in his more phenomenologically influenced observation that the impact of a media technology changes with both its context and the activities that accompany it. This forcefully suggests how media create social spaces but simul-taneously merge with them. It also draws our attention to the more general question of how communication technologies – as technologies – are integrated with, and impact upon, social practices.[4] Such questions are beginning to be addressed by a growing number of studies which ethnographically document

---

2 Concern with audience diversity and people's active use of mass media is not new; it has been a central focus of empirical media research for over half a century (for further discussion, see Spitulnik 1993).

3 For example, Bausinger argues that media research should turn to 'the culture of the everyday' (1984: 343), understood in a Schutzian phenomenological sense, because both media forms and media uses are completely integral to the way that everyday life is conducted. Morley and Silverstone resonate with this view, maintaining that media research should focus on mass media's 'inscription with the routines of everyday life' (1990: 33). They argue, furthermore, that the meanings of both media texts and media technologies can never be understood in isolation, but rather must be understood as 'emergent properties of contextualized audience practices' (1990: 32).

4 See, for example, the substantial body of work which traces the historical relations between chang-ing modes of communication and changing social institutions, images, and values (e.g. Anderson 1991; McLuhan 1964; McLuhan and Fiore 1967; Meyrowitz 1985; Spigel 1992; Williams 1974).

people's engagements with media technologies as technologies (Manuel 1993; Morley 1992; Silverstone and Hirsch 1992b; Turkle 1984, 1995). These media scholars have begun to problematize the cultural significances of technology, machinery and other physical attributes in their studies of the reception and use of mass media. Morley and Silverstone, for example, propose that interactions with communication technologies are embedded within 'sociotechnical frames' (1990: 51) which include a range of other mechanical apparatuses besides media technologies. In a similar vein, Silverstone and Hirsch (1992a) claim that the meaning of a particular technology is not pre-given but constructed as the technology figures in practices of consumption and becomes embedded in everyday life.

I suggest that, taken together, these lines of research point towards ways of widening the frame of reception studies. We need to understand 'media reception' as a constellation of processes which includes: direct responses to media content; decodings of media messages; phenomenological comportment towards media technologies/appliances; social relations among groups of media users; and the material, economic and cultural conditions of media ownership and use. It is possible to produce different kinds of ethnographies of media audiences, depending on which aspect of this reception constellation is stressed. Simultaneously, the 'audience' may be 'de-essentialized', not only from the perspective of message interpretation, but also from the perspective of styles of use and phenomenological attunement to the medium.

De-essentializing the audience does not mean, however, that analysis degenerates into a running inventory of particulars, that is to say, a series of disparate and unconnected accounts of reception practices. While moving towards documenting the ethnographic particulars that may chip away at notions of the generic homogenous audience, questions of cultural patterns, economic determinants and shared forms of social organization should not be discarded. Within the domain of media studies, the question – does culture (or place) matter? – is especially salient because we live in a context where the prevailing ideas about media hold them to be the same everywhere at all times and for all people.[5]

The current chapter contributes as a corrective to this media imperialism/ globalization view, as it documents the different locally driven engagements that Zambians have with radio technologies.[6] I argue specifically that the local economic and practical conditions of radio listening and radio ownership in large

---

[5] This view is illustrated, for example, in the media imperialism position, which holds that media technologies (like other processes of globalization) have an inherently destructive and homogenizing effect on local cultures (Ginsburg 1991; Sreberny-Mohammadi 1991; Tomlinson 1991).

[6] This discussion stems from 18 months of field research in Zambia, conducted between June 1988 and May 1990. I spent equal amounts of time doing media production and media reception research, with nine months in Lusaka at the Zambia National Broadcasting Corporation (ZNBC) and nine months in the Northern Province town of Kasama and village of Chitimukulu. Research methodology included: participant observation, informal interviews, interviews with questionnaires and guided group discussion in ChiBemba and English; archival data collection; and discourse analysis of radio broadcasting, based on tapes and transcripts of recorded transmissions. Roughly half of the people I worked with were ethnically Bemba, and nearly all spoke the lingua franca ChiBemba. A total of 43 households, consisting of 15 rural and 28 urban families which owned working radios, were studied for their patterns of media use. In addition to these family studies, I had conversations about radio with nearly every person that I met in Zambia. Most of these remarks were recorded in fieldnotes, and I estimate that they represent discussions with approximately 150 individuals in addition to the 43 households interviewed.

measure shape the way that people experience radio in Zambia; and this experience differs quite dramatically from patterns of media use in more affluent societies. Radios are expensive, batteries are expensive and signals are sometimes weak. The functioning radio and radio station cannot be taken for granted. Moreover, radios are valuable property and theft is common. In addition to these differences, I show that a major aspect of radios' material reality in Zambia lies in their mobility: they are portable machines and their sounds drift through social spaces. Following Grossberg's insights, my discussion will illustrate that the mobility of radios is one of the most important culturally-specific aspects of people's reception practices in Zambia. Both the 'meaning' of radio and the experiential aspects of radio culture are often contingent on the portability of the radio as a machine. The 'medium takes shape as it situates itself' – or more accurately, as social actors situate it – within culturally specific encounters and sets of social relations.

The material conditions of listening and modes of audience engagement

Radio is the most widely consumed medium in Zambia, reaching 57 per cent of all national households and 60 per cent of the national population (Tables 10.1 and 10.2). Until 1994, the state-run Radio Zambia – with its three channels, Radio 1, Radio 2 and Radio 4 – was the only domestic radio operation.[7] Since then, three independent radio stations have joined the Zambian airwaves.

Table 10.1 Ownership of media technologies in Zambia, 1991

Own a radio	65	
Own a working radio	57	(of which four need batteries)
Radio broken	8	
Own a TV	17	
Own a VCR	4	

(figures per cent of an estimated 1.1 million national households, adapted from Claypole and Daka 1993: 63)

Table 10.2 Radio listeners in Zambia, 1991

	Listen to radio	Listen to radio often (6–7 days/week)
National	60	25
Urban	74	33
Rural	52	19
Urban men	83	38
Urban women	64	28
Rural men	63	26
Rural women	41	12

(figures per cent of an estimated 8 million national population, adapted from Yoder *et al.* 1996: 193)

---

[7] For more information on Radio Zambia and an overview of broadcasting in the country, see Claypole and Daka (1993), Daloz and Verrier-Frechette (Chapter 13), Mytton (Chapter 12), and Spitulnik (1996, 1998, forthcoming).

Table 10.3 Economic indicators and radio costs in Zambia[a]

| | January 1989 | | August 1998 | |
	Zambia Kwacha	US$ equiv.	Zambia Kwacha	US$ equiv.
Single-band radio, battery only	249	26	52000	27
Two-band radio, battery only	480	50	66000	34
Three-band radio, battery and A/C	582	61	90000	47
Three-band stereo radio dual cassette	4360	454	225000	117
One D-cell battery	6	1	3000	2
Typical monthly radio battery				
expense (4 batteries)	26	3	12000	6
Average radio repair cost	100	10	n/a	n/a
25 kg bag roller meal	41	4	15500	8
(1-2 weeks staple food for a family)				
Average monthly expenditures for urbanites[b]				
Lower class household	400	41	60000	31
Middle class household	1500	156	200000	104
Upper class household	3000	312	500000	312
Typical gross monthly salaries[c]				
Primary school teacher	800	83	130000	68
Nurse	900	94	130000	68
Government office assistant	1000	104	200000	104
State store manager	1500	156	350000	181
Broadcasting manager	2000	208	1066085	554

a 1989 data collected by author. 1998 data collected by Maidstone Mulenga, Pascal Mwelwa and author. Figures are rounded off to whole numbers. January 1989 Zambia Kwacha exchange rate for US$1 = K 9.60. August 1998 exchange rate: US$1 = Zambia K 1925.

b Figures on expenditure vary widely.

c Net salaries are roughly 75% of gross salaries, after deductions for taxes, housing, pension funds and utilities. salaries cited here range by roughly ±10%.

In Zambia, the price of a basic radio is far beyond the reach of most people, unless they make great sacrifices. The simplest radio remains an expensive commodity for an average middle-class family, even one with two salaries. At the time of my research, a standard, single-band radio cost roughly 30 per cent of a primary teacher's gross monthly salary and a two-band radio cost twice that amount (Table 10.3). By comparison, a similar two-band radio costs less than 1 per cent of a teacher's salary in the United States. Typical monthly battery costs, in Zambia, are equivalent to what a large household spends on a 1–2 weeks' supply of staple food.[8] In the current context of overstretched household budgets and decreasing spending power (Ferguson 1999), this means that batteries have to be carefully conserved and that dead batteries may go unreplaced for some time.

---

8 The staple food in Zambia is *nshima*, a dense starchy dough made from mealie meal, a type of maize flour. The grain is milled in two different ways – roller meal (more coarse, less expensive) and breakfast meal (more fine, more expensive) – and is sold in 25-kg or 50-kg bags.

Figure 10.1 The radiogram is the centrepiece of Joseph Kabwe's home. Displayed on top are family photographs and a Prince album. Chiba, Kasama.

Those who can purchase radios tend to be single, middle-class and able to draw upon carefully accumulated savings. Significantly, most owners of radios bought them years ago. Broken radios frequently go unrepaired and unreplaced. Based on their 1991 national survey of radio and television use, Claypole and Daka estimate that 12 per cent of national households own a radio which is unable to receive transmissions (Table 10.1), either because it is broken (8 per cent) or because it is in need of batteries (4 per cent) (Claypole and Daka 1993: 63). While the average radio repair cost – of US$ 10 – may seem modest from a Western perspective, it is prohibitively expensive for most Zambian families (Table 10.3). Furthermore, repair shops often do not stock the correct spare parts to do repairs, and even if they do have them, may refuse service to owners of the simple one-band and two-band radios. Why this is so became clear during field research in 1989, when the owner of Chola Electron Service in Kasama suspended the repair of small radios because new spare parts could more profitably be put into more expensive machines.

> On weekends, Joseph Kabwe, a 26-year-old public sector office worker, sits on the stoop of his one-room home and listens to the radio.[9] Inside the tiny room, his prize

[9] Indented paragraphs are vignettes of radio use, based on ethnographic fieldnotes. They are a combination of direct observational notes and contextualizing remarks about real people in real situations. I use the present tense to convey the sense of habituality (such as typical behaviours and scenes) as well as the senses of immediacy and unfolding ethnographic discovery. In agreement with people's wishes, I use real names instead of pseudonyms.

Figure 10.2 BashiDanny (Robbie Muzhama) listening inside his home. New Town, Kasama.

Figure 10.3 Radio listeners use whatever batteries are available, even if they do not fit inside the machines. A chain of batteries is taped together and wired up to the radio. Kapela village, near Chitimukulu.

possession – a 1960s model radiogram housed in a four-foot long wooden cabinet – takes up an entire wall and one-quarter of the floor space. With twelve batteries it still runs as good as new, but the batteries need to be replaced every month. In January 1989, at the government-controlled price of K 6.47 each (US$0.67), the cost of twelve batteries took up roughly 8 per cent of Joseph's monthly salary. Being single he could afford it; but for others, those twelve batteries could be seen as a 50-kg bag of roller meal, enough to feed a large family for nearly a month.[10] Joseph lives in Chiba, a non-electrified, high-density, low-income neighbourhood in Kasama, the capital city of Zambia's Northern Province. (Figure 10.1)

In non-electrified homes, or in other situations where people are listening to battery-operated radios (such as at markets, on porches or in transit), radio owners are very concerned about conserving battery energy. Claypole and Daka report that 65 per cent of all radio owners use batteries and, of these, nearly one-third report that batteries are not always available (1993: 63).

> It's Sunday at the Muzhama's house. BanaDanny (mother of Danny) and I are chatting and BashiDanny (father of Danny) is sorting beans. The portable radio is right next to him, but it's not on. After a bit, he looks at his watch. It's 18 hours – time for 'News'. He turns on the radio which is already tuned to Radio 2, the English-language channel. BashiDanny doesn't listen very closely, and his wife doesn't listen at all because she doesn't know much English. When the 'News' is over, BashiDanny turns off the radio; he's saving batteries. (Figure 10.2)

Many radio users are compelled to innovate as they rig up their power sources. For example, old car batteries or a long string of nearly exhausted radio batteries can provide a charge strong enough to power a radio for a short time (Figure 10.3). These old batteries can be minimally recharged by placing them in the sun or on the warm coals of a fire.

> We are sitting around the fire on a cool Sunday morning, cooking sweet potatoes for breakfast, in the village of Ndona. Altogether there are seven of us. A man named Edwin comes by, carrying his portable radio in one hand and a bundle of six batteries in the other. The batteries don't fit into the case; he has taped them together and then wired them into the radio. It works just fine, but reception in the area is pretty weak. The 'Kabuusha Taakolelwe Boowa' Bemba advice programme is on, and periodically there are lulls in our conversation and we listen in. The two men who are sitting closest to the radio are paying more attention to the show and, as it ends, Edwin speaks in time with the two broadcasters, who call out the programme's standard closing, 'Buleecha' ('It is dawning'). The 8 hours news follows, and after the opening theme song, the newsreader, as usual, says the national motto – Edwin, without missing a beat, joins in – 'One Zambia, One Nation'.

For those who have electrified homes and radios powered by mains, alternating current, energy conservation is less of an issue. Electricity costs are heavily subsidized by the government and, in many cases, the monthly electricity bill is paid by the employer. While this might imply that radio access is much more regular and

---

[10] Joseph's salary was K1000 per month (US$104). At that time (January 1989), the price of 12 batteries (K6.47 each) was K77.64 total (US$ 8), and the cost of a 50-kg bag of roller meal was K82. Joseph's case is exceptional because most radios are portable and use only four batteries. For such radios, monthly battery expenditure for regular users at this time was K25.88 (US$2.68). The significant point is that even for such users, the proportion of monthly income spent on radio batteries (estimated at 1–3 per cent) is dramatically higher than what obtains among comparable income brackets in the US (estimated at 0.3–0.5 per cent).

inexpensive for people who live in electrified homes, this is not universally the case in Zambia. Economic class is the determining factor. Most urban middle-class households do have electricity, but they cannot afford radios able to run on mains power (Table 10.3). In addition, much radio usage is outdoors, making a battery-operated, portable radio essential. Typically, owners of mains-powered radios belong to upper-class families. Usually their models are upmarket machines with stereo sound and one or two built-in cassette decks.

> The Hamukoma's radio is in the kitchen, and it's almost always on, even if no one is listening. The family spends most of the time in the living room, where the television is. Chilufya tells me that she likes to have some lively music when she's cooking. She's an ob-gyn doctor and her husband, Passmore, is a senior executive for the national mining company where they live in Lusaka. Their little two-and-a-half-year-old daughter, Lweendo, likes to sing the horn part of the 'News' theme song when it comes on. She can also sing all the words to a popular radio song, 'Daddy I love you ... You are my hero'. Passmore's cousin Judy wrote down all the lyrics from the radio and then taught them to Lweendo.

While the radio may be constantly on in such electrified homes, there are certain important moments when a deliberate effort is made to turn it off.

> The radio is almost always on in the sitting room in the Mutales' house in Kasama. It is a four-band radio and it runs off the mains. However, the Mutales don't listen on Friday evenings, or all day Saturday, because they are Seventh Day Adventists. They also turn it off briefly, when they sit down to eat, for long enough to say the mealtime prayer. After the prayer, the radio is turned back on and runs throughout the meal.

Taken together, what these economic factors mean in the contemporary Zambian context is that the typical household with a working radio is urban or peri-urban and has at least one member with a steady wage income. The prevalence of working radios in remote rural areas and among lower income groups has diminished greatly over the last two decades. Yoder *et al.* (1996) report that nearly three-quarters of all urbanites listen to the radio, while only about half of all rural dwellers do so (Table 10.2). Gender identity is also a significant factor in the manner and the degree to which people engage with radio. Men own and control radios much more than women do (Spitulnik forthcoming). They also tune in more frequently. In their 1991 national survey of radio use, Yoder *et al.* found that urban men were 1.3 times more likely to listen to radio than urban women, and that rural men were 1.5 times more likely to listen to radio than rural women (Table 10.2). Consistent with these findings, Claypole and Daka report that the largest proportion of non-listeners is found among rural women (1993: 64). Significantly, many of these 'non-listening' survey respondents describe themselves as being around and hearing radios, but not ever listening in.

As illustrated in the vignettes above, people listen to the radio with varying degrees of attentiveness. BashiDanny listens to 'News' with mixed attention, while his wife and children hardly listen at all. In group settings, radio listening usually alternates with conversation. Often, one or two members of the group (especially the radio owner) listen more intensively than the others. Radio is also used to accompany other activities, as with Chilufya Hamukoma's preference for radio music while cooking. In this sense, radio may be a kind of mood-setter or pleasant background noise, not listened to at all attentively.

These examples also demonstrate how people participate in radio broadcasting – not only by listening, but by speaking with the radio and by speaking like the radio. For example, listeners often take pleasure in voicing a standard radio formula along with the announcer. Standard radio phrases and radio songs, especially those in English, are used for language learning and pronunciation practice, as in the case of two-and-a-half-year-old Lweendo and her cousin. And finally, one finds that children and young teenagers especially enjoy imitating radio voices, radio personalities, and radio programme scenarios (Spitulnik 1996, forthcoming).

Positioning radios around the home

In addition to the specific economic realities of radio ownership and access discussed in the previous section, another highly significant local factor that shapes reception practices in Zambia is the sociality of domestic space. The positioning of radios in and around the home changes frequently during the day, primarily because the sociality of domestic space itself changes over the course of the day. In situations where there are portable radios and batteries people listen outside during daylight. Such listening occurs in an outdoor workspace, under a shade tree, on the stoop of the home, at the market place, or on the road (Figures 10.3–5). If one uses electricity then the radio remains inside, at full volume, so that those outside can hear. While it is extremely difficult to generalize across the whole nation, divergent social settings and diverse socio-economic groups, the tendency is for most daytime social activity and a great deal of domestic labour to take place outdoors; thus the portable radio moves as people move. In most communities – and particularly those at lower socio-economic levels, where the interior home is rarely a space for daytime visiting and entertaining – it is antisocial to remain inside during the day, unless the weather is bad or one is doing indoor domestic work.

In the evenings, however, radios are brought inside the home where it is cooler, safer and more mosquito-free. Especially in middle-class homes, the radio is placed at the centre of the sitting/dining room, from about dinner-time onwards, and (unless there is a television) becomes a focal point of the evening's activities. Finally, at night-time, the radio is moved once again. When the head of the household retires for the evening, he or she secures the radio in the bedroom, where virtually all valuable household property is stored. Nocturnal break-ins are common in urban areas, and electronic goods are the first things to go. The practice in Zambia is to secure these goods (televisions, VCRs, radios, cameras) in the master bedroom, which becomes a kind of psychological, if not actual, fortress and hiding place if thieves visit. The circulation of radios around the home is thus structured, essentially, by sociality and anti-sociality: sharing the radio and hiding the radio. The portability of the small radio works both for it – in terms of its extremely flexible adaptation to different types of social spaces and listening situations, and against it – in terms of the ease with which it can be stolen.

Figure 10.4 Sidney Kambowe tunes the radio outside his home, while younger brother Alex, cousin Ines, and sisters Caroline, Yvonne and Beauty take a break from daily chores. New Town, Kasama.

Figure 10.5 The tunes attract customers and the market stand becomes a hang-out place with the radio-cassette deck. Town centre, Kasama.

Circulating radios beyond the home

The impact and meaning of radio in Zambia is strongly linked to its portable physical form, which equally permits relocation around the home and theft from the home. Radios are carried to the office when presidential press conferences or football matches are to be broadcast, and they are sometimes brought into the field to listen to while farming (Spitulnik forthcoming). Radios are switched on in public spaces, such as bus stops, minibuses, shops, foodstands, bars and markets (Figure 10.5). In many of these public uses, the radio is a split medium: some portable radios are actually radio-cassette decks, which provides a further dimension to the machine's mobility and flexibility.

Not only do radios circulate from home to work but, in some cases, they originate from work and are brought home. Such is the case for countless government workers whose offices are issued radios, for example from the local Ministry of Agriculture office for listening to farming programmes and from the Ministry of Education for listening to the schools broadcasts. These radios are subsequently appropriated by high-ranking employees and are viewed as job perks that signify a good position. Their removal from the workplace is not perceived wholly as pilfering, it is also an act of theft prevention. A radio left overnight in the office may not be there in the morning; so the responsible employee takes the radio home at night for safekeeping; and this shuttling back and forth of the radio results in its temporary or permanent relocation to the employee's home.

The most dramatic circulation of radios occurs when they are carried on long-distance trips (such as 600 miles from the capital city to the grandparents' village) and when they are moved around a community where they have been scarce for some time. Usually these two situations are linked. Radios are extremely rare in Zambian villages, and their presence is nearly always a result of the relocation or visit of an urban wage labourer. Someone who owns a radio and happens to travel to another town or village will invariably take it along, not least because, as many people explained to me, empty homes are the targets for house thefts; and it is simpler to take the radio than to worry over entrusting it to relatives who may remain at the home.[11] In addition, the radio provides entertainment on a long trip and at the final destination.

Once travellers arrive in a rural community, their radios tend to circulate freely among relatives. Thus, in stark contrast to the lack of trust in urban areas which motivates the long-distance hauling of a radio as personal possession, when it arrives in a smaller community the radio to some extent becomes a community possession. An example of this occurred in the medium-sized village of Chitimukulu when a young relative from the Copperbelt showed up for a brief visit.

For weeks there had been no radio sounds coming from the homes of the Chitimukulu village residents, only from the homes of the government employees who had been sent

[11] This nervousness on the part of household heads about entrusting relatives with the security of the home is real and not sheer paranoia. During research, I heard of several cases where heads of households returned from short trips to find that valuable items had been stolen; in one case a relative was suspected of having cooperated and shared the resale profits with the robbers.

to work at the local clinic, post office, school, court or police station. One day, while I pass through kwaTompwe (one of the two villages that comprise Chitimukulu), I hear a radio blaring; it's coming from banakuluLesa's home.[12] It's the morning newscast and I wander over. Her youngest son, who works as a miner in Ndola, has just arrived, she's cooking him a big breakfast; several neighbours are gathered around to hear the radio and see the new visitor. The news is in English, and most people don't seem to be really listening. In a short time the meal is brought out, and the educational broadcasts come on (at 10 hours). The young man turns it off; the schools broadcasts are of no interest. Another young man seated next to me wants to look at the radio, and it is passed over to him. I look on, and notice a long red plastic strip taped along the top of the radio above the frequency band. It is a punch-typed label which reads: EMISS MULENGA.

This is how I learn the name of the radio's owner, the young miner. And this is how I come to track the radio's circulation around Chitimukulu over the next few days. I first see it the following day as I walk by the well at kwaKoni (the other main village of Chitimukulu).

A group of young girls walks up to the well to fetch water; one is carrying a radio, which surprises me, not only because of the scarcity of radios, but because I have never seen a girl carry one. As they get closer I notice the red label EMISS MULENGA. It turns out the girl is a young niece of banakuluLesa. The next day, as I am walking through the most distant edge of kwaTompwe village, I see a group of men listening to a radio: music in ChiBemba. While I greet them and walk by, I look down to the radio on the ground, it's the same three-band Panasonic with the name: EMISS MULENGA. Emiss Mulenga is nowhere to be seen, but his radio is now at his uncle's home. Finally, a few days later on Sunday, I see Emiss with the radio. He and his friend are walking down the path through the government homes carrying it; they have just returned from a long day of visiting in some of the outlying villages. When they see me, they come over and start telling me about how they wish they were in the urban areas so that they could hear the pop music channel, Radio 4. The English language Radio 2 has a few good music programmes on Friday night and during the weekends, but otherwise there has been nothing to listen to out here. Anyway the batteries are finished.

This extended portrayal of a few days in the life of a radio illustrates the true extent of radio's portability and mutability across various social contexts in a rural area. Emiss Mulenga's radio temporarily became a collective asset within his wider kin and friendship networks, but in each instance, as it circulated, it retained his personal mark: the typed red label EMISS MULENGA. In essence, the circulation of the radio was also Emiss's circulation through the village. Moreover, he did not mind passing it around; without his favourite urban station, there was hardly anything he wanted to listen to anyway. A sign of a salaried worker, the radio brought him a degree of status among the rural relatives, which in turn passed on to them when they used the radio in their cohort groups. Significantly, Emiss took the radio (with dying batteries) as he went visiting in the outlying villages. Everyone within the immediate Chitimukulu area had known of his possession within two or three days of his arrival, although he had little contact with his radio after the first day. But it was important he be seen with it in the other villages.

---

[12] Chitimukulu is the home of the paramount chief of the Bemba people. Besides the palace grounds, there are two distinct villages (kwaKoni and kwaTompwe, named after their respective headmen Koni and Tompwe), and between them is an area of government housing for civil servants assigned to Chitimukulu.

Radio as a mobile machine and a 'mobile term' thus has the potential to shape contexts and social relations in manifold ways. The actual portability of radios allows for this circulation in a way impossible for most other mass media.[13] Radios do, however, circulate much like other material possessions, like sunglasses among young men, bracelets among young girls and cooking utensils among neighbouring women. In all these cases, the circulating material good is part of a more general relation of exchange and reciprocity that exists and is constantly renewed between those involved (Appadurai 1986; Mauss 1925). In this sense culture does matter in radio reception practices, because sharing radios fits into other local patterns of creating status and reproducing social ties through exchange relations.

As a final example of the movement of radios, I consider a situation where a radio-cassette recorder was carried by one young man through the various stages of a day-long wedding ceremony which spanned two villages and roughly 10 hours.[14]

We were in Edward village, just outside Mporokoso, one of the small district capitals in the Northern Province. Peter Mutale was getting married, and we had been up half the night participating in the evening preparations and going back and forth between Peter's village and the village of the bride. As we sat around in the morning, waiting for Peter's uncles to prepare him, some of the young revellers from the night before started up again with their *kalindula* music. This morning I had come with my tape-recorder, and got up enough nerve to ask them if I could run the tape.[15] The group consisted of a three-piece band, with five or so cameo vocalists, such as 'DJ Jere' and 'Abena D. Kacasu' (literally 'person of the grain alcohol'). Identifying themselves into the mike, they debated the name of the group: they were either (or both) 'The Mporokoso jive band' or 'The Edward village jazzy band'.

In any case, one young man suddenly came by with a large stereo radio-cassette deck. I was surprised to see such a large machine so far out in the bush, but later noticed the deeply etched owner's name on the bottom of the box: 'GRZ – Ministry of Agriculture'.[16] Peter was the Mporokoso district rural agricultural outreach officer. The carrier of the radio, Bwalya, a young cousin of Peter, asked for a blank cassette tape and started recording along with me. For the next 10 hours Bwalya did not let the radio out of his sight. In fact he seemed to carry it under his right arm, perched on his hip, for nearly the whole time. As far as I know, he recorded nothing more than I had: several wild jamming *kalindula* songs by the Edward village jazzy band (or the Mporokoso jive band) and the more traditional wedding songs sung later on. The *kalindula* songs told of urban adventures and rural sweethearts, unfaithful husbands and the love of beer; Bwalya played them over and over again during the day as we accompanied Peter through the various phases of his wedding ceremony.

Bwalya's first big move occurred as we set off for the bride's village. After Peter and his uncles emerged from the home where he had been prepared for the ceremony, we assembled for the procession. Looking elegant but tired in his black suit, red shirt and white tie, Peter stood waiting with his head bowed. The three uncles, all wearing suit jackets and one with a tie, lined up on both sides of Peter and everyone else assembled behind them. Bwalya – technically out of order, but carrying the prestigious radio-

---

[13] Newspapers and magazines are also portable and do circulate from person to person, but their consumption is usually more individual.

[14] I use the past tense in this ethnographic excerpt because it is an in-depth narrative recounting of a series of events that transpired over several hours.

[15] I was visiting the village, for the first time, with Peter's European boss who had invited his anthropologist friend to come along for the wedding.

[16] GRZ stands for 'Government of Zambia'.

Figure 10.6 The portability of radios and radio-cassette decks allows them to mediate social spaces and to create auditory presences in a vast range of contexts. Here the mobile machine participates in a wedding procession. Edward village, near Mporokoso.

cassette deck – squeezed into the front line, between the rightmost uncle and the tall dry grass on the edge of the path. We were ready to walk out of Edward village, to bring Peter down the road to his bride, Charity. As we entered the main path leaving Edward village, Bwalya turned on the tape-player. It was one of the *kalindula* songs. After about two minutes, the elder uncle asked him to turn it off. It was time to start singing the wedding songs. Realizing that his musical selection was not appropriate, Bwalya started to record the wedding processional, a loud and wavering chorus of voices singing of the lucky groom and his happy family.

As we approached the bride's village, the singing subsided. We entered the village's main path in silence, but Bwalya soon turned on the machine, this time playing the loud wedding processional that we had just been singing. Again Bwalya's ritual intervention was tolerated for only a few minutes – no doubt it served to display the recording technology of the groom as we approached – but again the elder uncle requested that the machine be turned off. Charity, in full-length wedding gown with white veil, gloves and heels, was then brought to meet Peter and his escorts, and together they were marched up a small path to meet her senior relatives. By now a self-designated attendant, Bwalya again squeezed into the front line of the wedding party, this time between the maid of honour (also in a formal white wedding gown) and the tall dry grass on the edge of the path [Figure 10.6]. All the uncles were now on Peter's left side; Charity stood to his right, next to her attendant and Bwalya with the silent radio-cassette deck. Within moments this arrangement was broken up. After walking up the aisle to the doorstep of the bride's family's house, the bride, her bridesmaid and Bwalya the musical escort stepped aside so that the groom could stand alone with his closest kin. For the first time, a female relative stood with Peter, along with the three uncles. They were then addressed by Charity's father's sister and her three most senior male relatives.

While only half the story – Bwalya continued to stay on the periphery, waiting for further chances to play the tape, and later ended up socializing with the younger people who were excluded from the indoor rites – this lengthy recounting provides yet another view of the mobility of the radio machine. In this case what was valued was not the radio as such, but the cassette-recorder, or just the box itself – a prestige commodity in a remote rural area. The mobile machine circulated throughout the course of the wedding ceremony, but it was always held by one individual. As with Emiss Mulenga's radio, however, it circulated as both communal and individual property. Displayed prominently in the arms of Bwalya, who marched in the front line with the groom, the machine represented the groom's wedding party, the groom (who had been issued the machine as part of his prestigious government job) and, of course, Bwalya himself.

During much of the procession the machine was actually silent and thus occupied the position of 'carried ritual object', somewhat analogous to the family staff carried by Peter or the flowers carried by Peter's senior aunt. As a tape-recorder, the machine also came to occupy a whole new role, namely, the voice (or re-voicing) of the groom's wedding party. The radio-cassette deck was not only incorporated into the ritual as a commodity, but as an active participant – at least for those few brief moments when Bwalya was allowed to play it. In this mixed media village wedding, with a bride and groom employed as civil servants in the small town nearby, the active use of the radio was met by a certain level of toleration, amusement and tension. The senior relatives still had ultimate control and dominion over the proceedings, but Bwalya was able to interject and adopt his musical contributions within limits.

With these examples of the mobility of the radio machine and also its mobilization, we can now revisit Grossberg's observation that the force of a mass medium changes with its context and the activities that accompany its use. Rather than ascribing all this potential simply to the flexibility of the medium (in Grossberg's words its 'taking shape as it situates itself' (1987: 34)), we need also to interject a sense of the agency and interconnections of the particular radio users. These extended ethnographic examples indicate that individual and group mobilization (such as use, placement and circulation) of the radio machine is an essential part of radio culture. Radio users, sharers, carriers and deniers play off the significance of radio-as-prestige commodity, within a wider set of social relations involving kinship obligations, gender relations, generational differences, socio-economic status, urban-rural tensions and so on. Whether one is 'studying, dating, driving somewhere else, partying' (Grossberg 1987: 34), going to the well, or accompanying a cousin in a wedding procession, the mobilized radio enters into these social relations, and indexes the person who has actively chosen to carry or share it.

Conclusion

I have argued that the practical and economic conditions of radio listening and radio ownership are part of the broader problem of the sociocultural meanings of radio. The consequence of this view for questions of 'audience' and 'reception' is that the consumption and use of a mass medium such as radio does not strictly revolve around people's interactions with media content. The notions of 'audience' and 'reception' – if limited to the sender/receiver dyad and the individual inter-pretive moment of decoding messages – neither exhaust nor encompass the range of relations that people have with radio. This does not mean that these notions should be discarded, but rather that they should be expanded or supplemented by the study of other activities and domains of experience which structure media meanings and use. In Zambia, the consumption of radio includes the culturally-specific ways that people attune themselves to (or attenuate themselves from) the radio machine, its technology, its portability, its commodity status and the fact that it produces unique sounds which can travel through communities.

These facts are dramatic illustrations that radio technology in Zambia only occasionally has that 'relative invisibility in use' which is claimed of it within Western societies, where the functioning media apparatus is taken for granted and is generally part of the background of a given social situation (Morley and Silverstone 1990: 36). While there are instances in Zambia where media technol-ogy has been 'absorbed' and 'naturalized' in everyday life (Bausinger 1984), there are infinitely more situations in which radios are far from invisible, where the radio as machine, as commodity, as urban transplant, and as portable or borrowed object is foregrounded and becomes even more important than the sounds emanating from it. In Zambia, people are acutely conscious of radio's physicality and its commodity status, like the ease of its theft, the weakness of its batteries and its potential for display in a social situation.

Related to this, an important minor point needs to be made about radio and the construction of social space. By contrast again with what has been claimed for radio and television in Western societies, radio in Zambia is not strictly, or even primarily, a 'domestic' technology (Morley and Silverstone 1990). Radios circulate far beyond the home and enter into a variety of social relations and social situations beyond the same-residence family.

Most Zambians have not experienced that same kind of increased interioriza-tion of social life and location of leisure time within the home that has occurred in Western cultures since the advent of broadcasting (Morley and Silverstone 1990; Spigel 1992). With dramatic rates of urbanization and the emergence of a highly economically stratified society in Zambia, interior social life has increased for middle- and upper-class sectors of the population. But there are two crucial differences. First, these 'interior families' are comparatively fluid extended families, not nuclear families. Secondly, such leisurely moments at home are rarely an occasion when all family members are relaxing together around the radio.[17] Quite often, the male head of the household is absent from the scene; his leisure time is frequently spent outside the home. And, in many cases, the female head of the household also is not present, or only partly present; instead she is busy working in the home or conversing with other adult women such as neighbours or visitors.

In fact the claim about radio's domesticity is even overstated in the Western case. Car radios and portable boom boxes are the best examples of the mobile

---

[17] A more convincing case can be made for television and video because of their fixed position in the home, and because of the greater appeal of television programmes and videos to all family members.

machine in US culture, and it may be the case that these are now the primary modes of radio listening in the US. Scenes analogous to Emiss's circulating radio, or Bwalya's manoeuvring for attention and 'airplay', can be found in a wide range of contexts – including the American use of blaring car radios and boom boxes during urban commuting, street cruising and picnics – to achieve prestige and attract attention. At least three things are the same in these vastly different social contexts: the radio is portable, it has a commodity status which is correlated with the prestige of the owner/user, and it has a presence and an ability to create social spaces. In these three senses, the radio exhibits the exact opposite of 'invisibility in use'. The culturally specific differences between the Zambian cases and their US counterparts outstrip the similarities, however, as they involve different sets of variables such as the social identities of users/listeners (kin networks versus youth networks), whose attention is being attracted (members of the community versus peer groups and potential sexual partners), and the specific way that prestige is created (simply by indicating ownership versus demonstrating the sheer volume of the radio machine or that its owner is fully attuned to the very latest music trends).

I would like to suggest, along these lines, that more comparative research should be done to determine, on the one hand, the extent to which local culture matters in the integration of media within daily life and, on the other hand, the extent to which particular media technologies have inherent properties that predispose them to certain kinds of uses and interpretations regardless of locale. I would also like to suggest that, in some instances, it is not possible to make an absolute determination one way or the other.

As we widen the frame of reception studies to include the whole of culture, documenting radio culture as lived experience becomes all the more challenging. The idealized picture of the single interpreting subject and the radio as hearth (with the attentive family audience clustered around it) may exist in the minds of many media producers, public policy planners, and those who use the nostalgic 'Radio Days' image as a reference point for audience practices. But, rather than being consumed by an attentive family, the radio more often plays on within a complex nexus of social relations and activities in which numerous things are happening simultaneously – other media, other sounds, children, visitors, activities like baking buns and pounding maize and so on. Radio culture is integrated within the textures of daily life, and as such is shaped by local constraints and preoccupations. From an anthropological perspective, to determine precisely where radio culture ends and where the rest of daily life takes over may pose an insoluble, and ultimately, uninteresting question. It may be more a matter of accepting, in Hebdige's terms, that 'we are in a field without fences' (1988: 81). The effort to document radio culture at this early point in scholarship should take the opportunity to wander in this field and welcome the unboundedness of its subject.

References

Abu-Lughod, Lila (1997) 'The interpretation of culture(s) after television', *Representations* 59: 109–34.

Allor, Michael (1988) 'Relocating the site of the audience', *Critical Studies in Mass Communication* 5: 217–33.

Anderson, Benedict (1991 [1983]) *Imagined Communities: Reflections on the Origin and Spread of Nationalism*, London: Verso.

Ang, Ien (1996) *Living Room Wars: Rethinking Media Audiences for a Postmodern World*, London and New York: Routledge.

Appadurai, Arjun (1986) 'Introduction: commodities and the politics of value', in A. Appadurai (ed.) *The Social Life of Things: Commodities in Cultural Perspective*, Cambridge: Cambridge University Press, 3–63.

Bausinger, Hermann (1984) 'Media, technology and daily life', *Media, Culture and Society* 6: 43–51.

Caldarola, Victor J. (1992) 'Reading the television text in outer Indonesia', *Howard Journal of Communication* 4(1/2): 28–49.

Claypole, Andrew and Daka, Given (1993) 'Zambia', in Graham Mytton (ed.) *Global Audiences: Research in Worldwide Broadcasting*, London: John Libbey, 59–70.

Ferguson, James (1999) *Expectations of Modernity: Myths and Meanings of Urban Life on the Zambian Copperbelt*, Berkeley and Los Angeles: University of California Press.

Fiske, John (1987) *Television Culture*, London: Methuen.

Ginsburg, Faye (1991) 'Indigenous media: Faustian contract or global village?' *Cultural Anthropology* 6(1): 92–112.

Grossberg, Lawrence (1987) 'The in-difference of television', *Screen* 28(2): 28–45.

Hall, Stuart (1973) 'Encoding and decoding in the television discourse', *Stencilled Occasional Papers* 7 (Media Series), Centre for Contemporary Cultural Studies, University of Birmingham.

Hebdige, Dick (1988) *Hiding in the Light: On Images and Things*, London: Comedia.

Mankekar, Purnima (1993a) 'National texts and gendered lives: an ethnography of television viewers in India', *American Ethnologist* 20(3): 543–63.

—— (1993b) 'Television tales and a woman's rage: a nationalist recasting of Draupadi's disrobing', *Public Culture* 5(3): 469–92.

Manuel, Peter (1993) *Cassette Culture: Popular Music and Technology in North India*, Chicago: University of Chicago Press.

Mauss, Marcel (1967 [1925]) *The Gift: Forms and Functions of Exchange in Archaic Societies*, New York and London: Norton.

McLuhan, Marshall (1994 [1964]) *Understanding Media: the Extensions of Man*, Cambridge, MA: MIT Press.

McLuhan, Marshall and Fiore, Quentin (1996 [1967]) *The Medium is the Massage*, San Francisco: Hardwired.

Meyrowitz, Joshua (1985) *No Sense of Place: The Impact of Electronic Media on Social Behaviour*, Oxford: Oxford University Press.

Moores, Shaun (1993) *Interpreting Audiences: the Ethnography of Media Consumption*, London: Sage.

Morley, David (1992) *Television Audiences and Cultural Studies*, London: Routledge.

Morley, David and Silverstone, Roger (1990) 'Domestic communication: technologies and meanings', *Media, Culture, and Society* 12(1): 31–55.

Radway, Janice (1988) 'Reception study: ethnography and the problems of dispersed audiences and nomadic subjects', *Cultural Studies* 2(3): 359–76.

Silverstone, Roger and Hirsch, Eric (1992a) 'Introduction' in Roger Silverstone and Eric Hirsch (eds) *Consuming Technologies: Media and Information in Domestic Spaces*, London & New York: Routledge, pp. 1–11.

—— (eds) (1992b) *Consuming Technologies: Media and Information in Domestic Spaces*, London and New York: Routledge.

Spigel, Lynn (1992) *Make Room for TV: Television and the Family Ideal in Postwar America*, Chicago: University of Chicago Press.

Spitulnik, Debra (1993) 'Anthropology and mass media', *Annual Review of Anthropology* 22: 293–315.

—— (1996) 'The social circulation of media discourse and the mediation of communities', *Journal of Linguistic Anthropology* 6(2): 161–87.

—— (1998) 'Mediating unity and diversity: the production of language ideologies in Zambian broadcasting', in B. Schieffelin, K. Woolard and P. Kroskity (eds), *Language Ideologies: Practice and Theory*, Oxford: Oxford University Press.

—— (forthcoming) *Producing National Publics: Audience Constructions and the Electronic Media in*

Zambia, Durham, NC: Duke University Press.

Sreberny-Mohammadi, Annabelle (1991) 'The local and the global in international communications', in J. Curran and Michael Gurevitch (eds) *Mass Media and Society*, pp. 118–38. London: Edward Arnold.

Tomlinson, John (1991) *Cultural Imperialism*, London & New York: Routledge.

Turkle, Sherry (1984) *The Second Self: Computers and the Human Spirit*, New York: Simon and Schuster.

———— (1995) *Life on the Screen: Identity in the Age of the Internet*, New York: Simon and Schuster.

Williams, Raymond (1974) *Television: Technology, and Cultural Form*, London: Fontana.

Yoder, P. Stanley, Hornik, Robert and Chirwa, Ben C. (1996) 'Evaluating the program effects of a radio drama about AIDS in Zambia', *Studies in Family Planning* 27(4): 188–203.

III
Radio, Conflict
& Political Transition

11
The Future
of Community Radio in Africa

The Case of Southern Africa
AIDA OPOKU-MENSAH

The meaning of community radio

The phrase 'community radio' implies a two-way process: one which entails the exchange of views from various perspectives, and the adaptation of media for use by communities in the light of them. In an ideal world, community radio would allow members of a community to gain access to information, education and entertainment. In its purest sense, community radio is a medium in which the community participates – as planners, producers and performers – and it is a means of expression of the community rather than for the community (Berrigan 1979). In short, ideally it represents an alternative means of expression for the otherwise silenced majority. Until recently, media policy has not emphasized this two-way process. Instead it has focused on the use of the media of mass communication to send messages from capital cities to the periphery; feedback from the communities that live there has been correspondingly limited.

The key words in community radio are 'access' and 'participation', but they can come to mean many different things depending on local circumstances. In India, increasing women's access to radio often means no more than that women will be permitted to listen to the radio set. The crucial issue is not whether people have access to a radio station to express their opinions or personal messages, nor even whether some local people participate on a paid or volunteer basis in radio programming. What really matters is the institutional structure of the radio station. Who is in control? Is it democratically managed? Is there a mechanism to make it accountable to those it serves (O'Connor 1990)? This chapter explores these issues.

Community radio: participation and ownership

A community radio station, like any other community media, must encourage community participation. Community participation may be defined as the educational and empowering process in which people – in partnership with those able to assist them – identify problems and needs, so that they increasingly assume responsibility to plan, manage, control and assess the collective actions that are proved necessary.

In a community radio station, people choose what problems they should pay attention to and how they want to solve them; typically the producers and the listeners are interchangeable. The people, guided by trained journalists, produce their own programmes. What is broadcast is the people's, rather than the journalists', agendas. The medium of community radio allows agendas to be set by the people rather than by media professionals. It may be that the people wholly or partly own a community radio station themselves through a cooperative enterprise. The cooperative movement in Zambia has been involved in relatively successful businesses, on behalf of both producers and consumers. Provided the people have the will to run such cooperatives they can run media cooperatives, such as community radio broadcasting stations and community newspapers, with equal success. Unlike community radio stations established by the government, which normally become local mouthpieces of the administration and the ruling party, once established such cooperative radio stations have few political strings attached to them (Kasoma 1990).

The history of community radio in Africa

Although community radio as we know it today has had a chequered history in Africa, the concept has always been recognized in one form or another; for instance in the guise of rural radio (radio clubs) and/or radio forums, concepts which originated in Canada. Rural radio has existed for 30 years and came to be known as the voice of the peasants/people. Through radio forums, groups of villagers or farmers met in each other's homes in order to listen to broadcasts, study a pamphlet and discuss particular problems with a view to cooperative action in solving them. In 1964, with UNESCO and Canadian aid, 40 villages were involved in an experiment that improved the take-up of the scheme. The system was subsequently adopted widely, and eventually involved some 400 groups in Ghana, Zambia, Malawi and Nigeria. Radio listening clubs are another step in the participatory direction. These involve club members expressing views concerning their problems which are recorded and then made into broadcast programmes.

Rural radio has been dismissed by some critics who allege it does not adequately represent the voices of the people: it is government-controlled, lacks resources to ensure its continued existence, and has no real political commitment behind it. However, the crisis of rural radio and farm radio forums lies equally in the overall crisis that the African continent faces: that of a stagnating resource base.

Perhaps Africa's first real community radio was the Homa Bay Community Radio Station established in the western part of Kenya in May 1982. This station was not only an experiment in decentralization of structures and programming but also an effort to gain experience in the utilization of low-cost technology for broadcasting. The Homa Bay project was an initiative by the Kenyan government and UNESCO; however, in 1984, the Kenyan government closed it down. Another initiative was the establishment of three rural broadcasting stations as part of a policy to decentralize rural development in Liberia. Although these examples were attempts to decentralize broadcasting and to make it more people-centred, various pressures made it impossible for them to survive, and they failed to create the social transformation that African societies needed for modernization in the development process.

Early development communications theorists believed that mere exposure to radio messages was enough to cause social changes that would lead to development. This belief led to the launching of numerous radio-for-development projects. In the earlier farm forum programmes, development messages were primarily sent 'down' from the government agricultural department, or the extension agent, to the rural people. Only the most limited feedback from farmers was invited; messages were often too prescriptive, complex and technical to be understood. These early schemes clearly revealed the limitations of 'top-down' government campaigns designed to foster development (Fisher 1990).

This history, of relatively ineffective initiatives, demonstrates the need for interactive community radio projects to encourage grassroots development in Africa. The opening-up of the airwaves offers opportunities for the introduction of just such interactive projects, able to serve the majority of the people.

The justifications for community-led radio are as follows:

1. Given the large numbers of different local languages in African countries and communities, only community-level stations are able to ensure that people are able both to hear broadcasts and, more importantly, to understand them.
2. Community-led radio encourages media education, which the majority of citizens in Africa lack. Most Africans have been starved of information; in the contemporary information society, community radio can help create an information culture.
3. Community-led radio enhances political emancipation and creates a platform for debate, exchange of ideas and reactions to plans and projects. It can accommodate people's ideas, and satisfy their spiritual and psychological well-being, much better than any other form of broadcasting.
4. With globalization of information and the advent of satellite communications, community radio can both offer communities a cheap but vital way of protecting their language and heritage, and serve as a means to standardize a local language.

Community radio for development and democracy

That there exists a need to expand community radio in the interests of development and democracy in Africa seems self-evident. However, the questions that urgently arise are: what kind of development or democracy? And who is to define the types of development or democracy that are to be sought?

Used strategically, community radio may accelerate or catalyze social transformation. Handled properly, community radio can emancipate people politically by providing them with information on the political life of their country. An example of a community radio strengthening democracy was given at a recent broadcasting seminar held in Zambia. In Los Baños in the Philippines, the governor of the district goes on air at a community radio station one day a week to answer questions that listeners raise by letters and telephone calls to the station. The government is thus held accountable locally through the community radio station (Kasoma 1997: 55).

The future of community radio: the case of southern Africa

Since the opening-up of the airwaves in some countries in southern Africa there has been great concern about people's access to communication, and to broadcasting in particular. Community radio or broadcasting is a very popular idea in this part of the world. However, broadcast liberalization policies have largely ignored the existence of community broadcasting. Most new acts concerned with broadcasting have broken the monopoly of state-owned and/or controlled broadcasting entities and allowed 'independent', usually commercial, broadcasters to establish their predominantly urban-based operations. However, not all have effectively encouraged community radio. Of those that have made steps in this direction, South Africa has introduced a three tier broadcasting system – public, commercial and community; and Namibia's ground-breaking liberalization of broadcasting granted autonomy, initially to the national broadcasting corporation, and allowed the establishment of private television and radio stations, especially community stations. Many other countries have simply developed a mix of state and commercial radio.

Strictly speaking, the community radio broadcasting landscape in this region is limited to South Africa, which has approximately 82 such stations. Community radio is still a new concept, and what it means remains subject to debate which is often inconsistent. In South Africa, community radio stations belong to 'communities'; in Mozambique and Zambia, they are owned and operated by the Roman Catholic church (although in Mozambique there are also government-owned community radio stations). In Namibia, Katatura Community Radio was the brainchild of, among others, the Council of Churches, NANGOF (the umbrella body for NGOs) and the Legal Assistance Centre, which, as recognized representatives of the community, initially formed the management committee. In Zambia, a commercial and independent radio station, Radio Phoenix, identifies itself as a 'community' station catering for the needs of the people it serves, and so does the Roman Catholic station Radio Icengelo (see Daloz and Verrier-Frechette, Chapter 13). How communities gain access to, and become involved in, the running of the stations is quite variable. Underlying principles – concerning who controls a station, how democratic management is assured, and what if any mechanisms make managers and broadcasters accountable to those they serve – still need to be worked out everywhere, even in South Africa.

Francis Kasoma (Professor of Journalism and Mass Communications in the University of Zambia) contends that there are various, viable forms of community radio ownership in Africa and mentions that FAO is about to set up a community radio station in Luapula Province in Zambia (Kasoma 1997). A feasibility study for the project has already been conducted to establish the distribution of radio ownership and the listening patterns of the people in the province. The possibility of establishing a mobile community radio station is also being considered. If this system is implemented it would use an outside broadcasting (OB) vehicle fitted with a transmitter and studio equipment. Antennae would be erected in each district, and the OB vehicle would simply be plugged into the relevant antenna in order for programmes to be broadcast in a particular district. After some weeks or months, the mobile broadcast station would move on to the next district. An NGO community radio station has also been earmarked for Solwezi in the Northwestern Province.

The community media movement in southern Africa

Liberalization of broadcasting in many countries in southern Africa has generated enormous interest from many groups, particularly from the NGO sectors. However, there is debate whether NGOs should be initiating community radio stations themselves, or whether they would not do better to stimulate local communities to own their own stations.

A movement is emerging in the southern Africa region aimed at enhancing awareness of community media issues, and in particular of community radio. For instance, the COMNESA is made up of organizations such as MISA, IPS, KCOMMNET, Panos Southern Africa, the National Community Radio Forum, South Africa, AMARC Africa, and EcoNews Africa, Kenya. These organizations are committed to stimulating debate on community radio through research, work-shops and seminars that bring policy-makers and other groups in civil society together.

Panos Southern Africa, for instance, has organized two major seminars in Zimbabwe and Zambia on broadcasting in general, with particular emphases on the emergence of community radio in these countries and the regulatory process. In April 1997, Panos brought together policy-makers and media practitioners to discuss current national broadcasting policy issues and its impact on Zambian society. Specific objectives of the seminar were:

• to bring broadcasters, development workers and MPs together to debate the state of broadcasting policy in Zambia;
• to stimulate debate about the role of broadcasting for democracy and development;
• to sensitize Zambian members of parliament to developments in community and grassroots broadcasting in neighbouring countries.

Participants included representatives from the ruling party, MMD, and the National Party as well as from ZAMWA, ZNBC, *The Times of Zambia* newspaper, CPU, PANA, ZUJ, Icengelo (a Roman Catholic radio station), Radio Christian Voice and Radio Phoenix. In discussing a regulatory framework participants made the following eight recommendations (Panos 1997: 75):

Community radio
1. That government puts in place a deliberate policy for the establishment of community-owned radio stations in Zambia.

Regulator
2. That there shall be an independent regulator who shall be answerable to an independent board of governors whose appointment and dismissal shall be ratified by parliament.

Tenure for regulator and independent board
3. That the board should be funded for an initial period of three years from parliament. Thereafter the board is expected to be self-sustaining through radio and television licensing.
4. That the tenure for the regulator and the board shall be for not more than five years.

Regulation of procedures of the board
5. That the board shall regulate its own procedures.

Requirements of the regulator
6. That the regulator should be a suitably and professionally qualified Zambian.
7. That, in effecting the legislation, the functions of licensing broadcasting may be relegated to the Communications Authority.

Jurisdiction
8. That the regulator should:
   (i)   issue, withdraw, amend, revoke, prescribe penalties and enforce conditions,
   (ii) inspect and approve installations,
   (iii) appoint, hire and fire staff,
   (iv) be responsible for preparing the regulatory report to the board for presentation to parliament.

Based on the case studies and examples of community radio in South Africa, MPs and NGOs were undoubtedly convinced of the need for similar stations in Zambia. All the MPs talked about the establishment of community radio stations in their constituencies; some, however, continued to see community radio as a tool to advance their own goals, and one MP even mentioned that if he could have a station in his constituency, it would help him during his campaign for re-election. When participants reminded him that such a station should be people-driven he retorted, 'I am the people'.

MPs' comments included:

'This seminar was an eye opener on the impact of broadcasting and development as well as the legal conflict in the acts of law today.'
'It provided for a wider understanding on the need for the establishment of community radio.'
'I didn't realize how important community radio is until after attending this seminar.'
'I now understand that there can be regional/community and national broadcasting stations owned and financed by the communities themselves.'
'It broadened my knowledge about technological changes and the usefulness of alternative broadcasting, like community radio.'
'By explaining the wider aspects of broadcasting – which includes frequency, allocation, funding etc – I now understand that broadcasting can be possible even at the community level.'

Financing community radio

The revenue potential of an established and well-run station is quite good; however, reaching the point at which a station is well-established and has a solid advertising clientele takes time. During the intervening months, the station should be expected to operate at a loss. Taking this into account, it might be argued that potential owners and operators of stations be evaluated according to their ability to sustain an operating loss for a period of at least one year. Moreover, granting too many licences may itself inhibit the growth of the broadcasting industry.

In practice there are two schools of thought: one believes that community radio stations should be set up as business enterprises by private individuals who will use the necessary means to make them sustainable. The second argues that community radio stations are for the poor in society, and they are therefore unlikely to make commercial profits. The second argument is most often advanced by NGOs which feel that, for the time being, community radio stations should be financed through donor support and/or through a financial mechanism embedded in national regulatory frameworks.

Against the NGOs' arguments, it has to be noted how often stations are revealed to be unviable commercially, and therefore collapse when their sponsors decide to pull out. Kasoma feels the solution lies in community radio stations being

> established either by co-operatives or as public enterprises by government. However, since government radio stations and all government media for that matter tend to be propaganda organs rather than utilities for people's free expression, this author strongly recommends that Zambia takes the path of establishing co-operatives or privately-owned community radio stations. NGOs can initiate some of the stations but the local community should be prepared to take them over as co-operative ventures so that their sustainability is assured. (Kasoma 1997: 54)

The immediate future

The concept of community radio in southern Africa is only now beginning to take shape, and there are many hurdles to surmount if it is to become a permanent feature of the broadcasting landscape. One major hurdle is direct or indirect political interference. Community radio represents a decentralization of the power which has been jealously guarded in the hands of governments. Governments in the region still have overwhelming power and hold one of the keys to the future of community radio in the region.

Whilst the community radio movement in South Africa has lobbied for effective policies that can enhance this sector, for several reasons this proactive approach is still relatively new in many countries in the southern African region. South Africa's unique history ironically created the conditions whereby, in 1993–4, there was enormous sensitivity to the control of communications once the general elections were held. Out of the political struggle came the struggle for equitable access to broadcasting channels for the previously disadvantaged

Africans and the creation of an Independent Broadcasting Authority (see Minnie, Chapter 12). This situation is totally different from that in other countries where regulatory authorities lack the credibility and independence they need to carry out their responsibilities.

Zambia, for instance, created the CA but how it will oversee and regulate the broadcasting sector remains unclear. To date the CA does not even have equipment to monitor stations. Moreover, it is seen as an appendage of the government, supervised by the Ministry of Communications and Transport. Broadcasting licences are given by the Minister of Information and Broadcasting and not by the CA.

A member of the ruling SWAPO party heads the Namibia Communications Committee (NCC) whose commissioners are appointed by the Minister of Information and Broadcasting. For example, a year after it had gone on air, Katatura Community Radio (KCR) found it was being drowned out by test broadcasts from a new commercial radio station, Radio 100. KCR complained to the NCC, only to be told that, because 'the International Telecommunications Union's frequency allocation plan for Namibia made provision for a limited number of frequencies', KCR would have to move to a different frequency. The ITU denied that it could allocate frequencies within a country, a task that in Namibia is entrusted to the NCC through the NCC Act. Following an outcry, the NCC allowed KCR to stay put at 106.2 Mhz and ordered Radio 100 to move to a different frequency, 100MHz. It turned out that Kalahari Holdings, the company owned by the ruling political party, holds a majority shareholding in Radio 100, now known as Radio Energy. The new station was competing for the same township youth market KCR had cornered since going on air in 1995.

Zimbabwe, Mozambique and Malawi are still struggling with the creation of independent regulatory structures that can effectively regulate the broadcasting sector.

Another burning issue is how community radio stations will be financed. Indications so far suggest that many stations in South Africa are struggling to survive. No doubt, their presence has made a tremendous contribution in the short term, but it remains to be seen whether, in the longer term, they will be able to survive in the commercial world. The donor community is eager to support the establishment of community radio stations, on the grounds that such initiatives strengthen pluralism and represent the tenets of good governance. However, the self-same donors are equally keen to support initiatives that have a future and will be sustainable.

For now, the future of community radio stations in southern African can be assured through either government policies or willing donors. However, without a progressive political outlook – allied to a communications policy that reflects that outlook – and a vibrant civil society that can make it work, community radio stations will become yet another fashionable concept that will soon die a natural death.

References

Berrigan, Frances (1979) *Community Communications: The Role of Community Media in Development*, Reports and Papers on Mass Communication, no. 90, UNESCO, May.

Fisher, Harold (1990) 'Community radio as a tool for development', *Media Development* 4: 19–24.

Kasoma, Francis P. (1990) 'Media ownership: key to participatory development communication', *Media Asia: an Asian Mass Communication Quarterly* 17(2): 79–82.

——— (1997) 'Community broadcasting in Zambia: prospects and potential', in Panos Institute Southern Africa (ed.) *Broadcasting and Society. Forum on Broadcasting in Zambia*, pp. 51–7. Panos: Lusaka.

O'Connor, Alan (1990) 'Radio is fundamental to democracy', *Media Development* 4: 3–4.

Panos Institute Southern Africa (ed.) (1997) *Broadcasting and Society. Forum on Broadcasting in Zambia*, Panos: Lusaka.

12
The Growth of Independent Broadcasting in South Africa

Lessons for Africa?
JEANETTE MINNIE

Although this chapter[1] is a personal account of the growth of independent broadcasting in South Africa, the political and sociological issues I address may have interesting ramifications for the rest of Africa, and indeed for other parts of the world. The South African experience raises (at least) two crucial, interrelated questions: what are we to understand by 'independent broadcasting' and how should we act on this understanding?

'Independent broadcasting' is often thought about in terms of either/or distinctions: either private or commercial, either public or community-based. As Aida Opoku-Mensah rightly notes in Chapter 11 broad policy distinctions do have to be drawn in these terms. However, in practice distinctions tend to be more nuanced: for instance, a public broadcaster may also be independent. This is what we have been trying to achieve since the early 1990s in South Africa; and we have made some progress despite the present danger of backsliding.

As a context, I shall give a brief historical background to the growth of independent broadcasting in South Africa. The Campaign for Open Media (COM) – not accidentally an abbreviation of comrade – of which I was the coordinator, was established in the early 1990s. COM was, unapologetically, the outcome of a creolized hotchpotch of ideas. Our overriding concern, however, was less with ideological purity than with how to wrest political control of the SABC from the old National Party apartheid regime before the first, historic, non-racial and democratic elections in 1994. If we failed in this, the SABC, which at that time was virtually a monopoly broadcaster, could have jeopardized free and fair elections.

As it became clear that Apartheid really was going to end, our main worry was that the SABC, which had always been the propaganda voice of Apartheid,

---

[1] This chapter is a transcript of a recorded presentation. It was lightly edited to produce a written text and revised by the author. A brief résumé of some of the ensuing debate has been appended.

would be exploited by the old regime as an election tool in the 1994 elections. So COM put together a very powerful coalition called the Campaign for Independent Broadcasting (CIB). More than 30 different organizations were involved, ranging from political parties and liberation movements (such as the ANC and the AZAPO), to some of the liberal parties, and we even tried to gain the support of the far right wing. It had to be made abundantly clear that the CIB was not about party politics but about the independence of the public or state broadcaster from political or state control. The CIB included national trade union federations, such as COSATU and NACTU, a number of journalists' organizations and cultural associations, and even some sports bodies. The CIB held consultative conferences and seminars over a number of months, discussing what sort of broadcasting we wanted for the new South Africa. The consensus was that it should be the people's. In other words, we wanted a form of broadcasting which would not be controlled by the ruling party or unduly influenced by other political parties: the people, with all their different cultural and political persuasions and language affiliations, would nominate members for an independent board of the SABC. Fine as a principle, but how was this ideal to be put into practice?

At the same time, we realized that those nominated for the board would need to bring with them varied professional expertise and knowledge. Some of them would need to know something about finance, broadcasting or journalism, technology and engineering. We would also need people who were interested in culture and art, who were knowledgeable about languages and possibly issues of ethnicity, as well as science and education. To fit this bill, we had to decide upon criteria which the nominees would satisfy as a collectivity, and we were aware that this would not be an easy task.

Next, we had to decide who would actually appoint these board members after they had been publicly nominated. Since we wanted neither the government nor any political parties to do this, we decided that there should be an independent selection panel of the 'wise and wonderful'. In other words, people with integrity whom the public trusted, people who rose above party politics, such as Archbishop Desmond Tutu.

Once this proposal had been put together and elaborated, we had to try sell it to the old regime: this was far easier said than done. A few members of the coalition were elected as representatives of the CIB, and they met four times with members of the old National Party. It soon became clear to the government that, if it approved our plan, it would lose political control over the public broadcaster in the greatest election contest that it had ever faced. As a result, it quickly showed us the door, and we had to come up with another strategy. We decided to go straight to the ANC, which was an affiliate member of the CIB at the time. The ANC, like all the political parties affiliated to the CIB, had not been allowed to sit on the CIB's steering committee. In keeping with our principles, we did not want the CIB to be controlled by any political party. We felt that it would be expedient at this point, however, to ask the ANC as a member organization of the CIB to become more directly involved, since it was already involved in bilateral negotiations with the government. By now it was early 1992, and we hoped that the ANC could persuade the regime to agree as quickly as possible to the establishment of an independent board of control for the SABC. It was emphasized that the ANC would be working on a mandate from the CIB and not vice versa; and the ANC agreed to this because it shared the views and endorsed the principles of independent broadcasting held by the CIB.

Over a period of six months, our main negotiator was Joel Netshitenzhe, who is now the Director of Communications in President Mandela's office. Together with representatives of the ANC, he held talks with the former Minister of Home Affairs and other National Party representatives to try to negotiate a deal. An agreement was finally reached, but with a number of compromises: the appointment of an independent selection panel of the 'wise and wonderful' was not approved, and instead it was decided that a panel of judges and magistrates would fulfil this function. We were not very happy with this because, in the past, judges and magistrates had been appointed by the regime. But it was the best deal that could be brokered and, in the end, quite a fine independent judicial panel was chosen.

Immediately this agreement was concluded, however, huge controversy broke out because De Klerk, the former state president, broke his word by refusing to accept all the persons who had been appointed by the independent judicial panel after an extensive process of public hearings to consider the shortlisted nominees. The agreement that the ANC had come to with De Klerk, on behalf of the CIB, was entirely extralegal; essentially it was a political deal. The ANC representatives and the former government had agreed that De Klerk, as state president, would have to accept the appointments of the independent judicial panel. They had agreed that if he had problems with one or two names, he could raise these with Mandela as the ANC's leader, and presumably they would seek a negotiated solution. In law, however, De Klerk had the right as state president to appoint the board of the SABC himself. Ignoring the spirit of the agreement, De Klerk refused to accept seven particular nominees, including the chair and deputy chairperson, as appointed by the independent judicial panel.

His action threw the new SABC board into a crisis of credibility, and threatened the entire negotiated process with collapse. At this critical moment, the SABC defied De Klerk by refusing to appoint the chairperson he wanted; they elected instead someone from their own ranks, managing in this way to reinstate public confidence in themselves. The CIB tried to persuade them, as an act of further defiance, unilaterally to extend their numbers by including all the seven nominees rejected by De Klerk. But the new board of the SABC would not agree to go so far.

Once the first politically independent board had been formed, the CIB had next to decide how to gain formal legal standing for it. After much discussion, it was agreed that an Independent Broadcasting Authority (IBA) should be established which would license all broadcasters in the country, including the SABC. The IBA would in no way be connected to the ruling party or other political parties, and although it would be statutory, its members would again be publicly nominated. Originally, it was hoped that the nominees for the IBA would be appointed by an independent panel of the 'wise and wonderful'.

By this time, the new government had come to power, and the ANC started almost immediately to pull in the reins. They claimed that since they represented the people, they could have a say in who appointed statutory bodies. The ANC remains implacable on the issue, and in some ways they are right: why would it be wrong for parliament to have a say if, after all, they are the people's representatives? Yet it does seem that the ANC has somewhat reneged on the ideal they originally supported: that of an IBA completely separate from the influence of the ruling party and other political parties. At present, parliament appoints both the counsellors of the IBA, who have been publicly nominated, and the members of the board of the SABC. This is why people from the CIB, who originally campaigned for total independence, are worried both that parliament monopolizes such appointments and that the extent of its control over broadcasting is gradually increasing.

The behaviour of some of the IBA's counsellors in 1997 has seriously threatened the concept of independent control: they unwisely misappropriated public funds in South Africa, which led to a scandal and forced the resignation of five of them in public disgrace. Two of the counsellors were cleared and have already been reappointed, but they accepted collective responsibility for the other three who certainly will not be reappointed. The problem has been compounded by the print media virtually calling for the IBA to be closed down. In advocating this, print journalists have failed to understand the issues of independent regulation of broadcasting. Because South African broadcasting is not technologically advanced, the airwaves remain a scarce resource, and there have to be mechanisms to decide who has access to this resource and on what terms. In turning a justified attack on particular abuses into an attack on the IBA as such, print journalists are damaging the institution which guarantees the freedom and the independence of the broadcast media in South Africa. In this respect they are failing to understand fundamental issues concerning the relationship between media and democracy in the new South Africa.

This situation has been exploited by the Minister of Broadcasting, who resents the fact that he does not have the same policy control over the IBA that he enjoys over the regulatory authority (SATRA), which issues telecommunication, but not broadcasting, licences. For a long time, he has been advocating that SATRA should merge with the IBA, which will give him effective policy control over both, however much he may claim in theory that he will not interfere with the content of broadcasting. Divorcing these issues is at best naive, because it is obvious that issues of access to frequencies, the independence of broadcasters and freedom of expression are interrelated. To his credit, the minister could have used the recent scandal at the IBA as an excuse to have it closed down, but he did not do so. Instead, he called for public renomination of representatives and has, thus, allowed the IBA to remain in existence. But his efforts to bring the IBA under his control is decidedly a move away from the ANC's earlier commitment to independent and nonstate control of broadcasting in South Africa.

Those who campaigned through the CIB are understandably upset about the regrettable behaviour of some people at the IBA. The developing situation in South Africa will need to be watched carefully to see whether it will be possible to retain a genuine notion of independent broadcasting. The SABC is in a serious financial crisis at the moment because, unlike the rest of Africa, the new South African government does not as a rule fund the SABC. The SABC derives its income primarily from advertising (about 80 per cent) and from licence fees (about 20 per cent). As a radical democrat from the CIB, I insist that it is the public duty of the government to finance the SABC as a broadcaster independent of state control, in just the same way that it is responsible for supplying education, health, roads or welfare. The severity of the financial crisis at the SABC leaves the government no practical alternative to making some funds available to it. The government has not yet agreed to do so, but has promised to reassess the situation. Understandably, government ministers may be more preoccupied with meeting immediate primary needs – such as housing, health and education – than with public broadcasting. My point, however, is that freedom of information is also a vital need in a democracy.

To conclude, I would like to come back to the point about dichotomies from which I started. When considering the independence of broadcasting, we should not see public broadcasting as necessarily belonging to the government. Public broadcasting does not have to become a toy of the ruling party. It is possible for it to be politically independent. Independent broadcasting does not mean only privatized broadcasting. These struggles are not just South African but have relevance elsewhere in Africa where public broadcasters struggle to obtain a measure of political independence from their governments. The South African example raises the whole question of the financial survival of public broadcasting in Africa. There is no necessity to make an exclusive choice between traditional forms of broadcasting ownership: a mixture of private, public and community ownership is desirable.

At a time when so many important changes are occurring in Africa, I find it sad when my African brothers' and sisters' anger at being dominated by political tyrants for the last 30 or more years expresses itself through their media's rejection of a valuable public asset, such as state broadcasting. I understand their reaction, but if Africans are rebelling against their leaders because they want their freedom and dignity as communities and individuals, then they should not throw out the baby (of public broadcasting) with the dirty bathwater (of its past abuse). Instead, we should all be struggling to find the means to turn state broadcasting into independent public broadcasting in the true democratic sense: that is to say, broadcasting in the interests of the broad public.

Discussion

As a Senegalese public broadcaster himself, Ibrahima Sané fully supported Jeanette Minnie's position. At the very least, public broadcasting is always there. There seems to be a spectrum: at one end is Radio Suisse Internationale, an associative public broadcaster funded by the state but able to determine independently what it broadcasts. At the other end of the spectrum is the SABC. Somehow African countries must find a compromise between these positions, perhaps on the lines of the BBC's charter. Graham Mytton, from the BBC World Service, agreed but added that having a charter is only a first step. The SABC, as well as MBC in Malawi and GBC in Ghana, possessed charters which were virtually BBC clones. The way in which a charter will be interpreted depends on who controls the interpretation. SABC was a mouthpiece of the apartheid state; this has changed, and it would be sad if South Africans did not recognize the fact both for themselves and as a precedent for the rest of Africa.

Two further questions were raised by the same speakers. The first concerned Channel Africa, South Africa's international broadcaster, and its demise as a service to Central and East Africa.

Jeanette Minnie responded that the Freedom of Expression Institute (FXI), a successor organization to COM and the CIB, of which she was the immediate past executive director, advocated a role for Channel Africa. There were two problems in persuading the government: previously, Channel Africa had been used to promote arguments in favour of Apartheid, and at present, the government did not feel it had a duty to provide news to the rest of Africa. Channel Africa did have a role to play in breaking South Africa's erstwhile isolation, but this was not an argument that had yet persuaded the government to divert resources to it.

A second question concerned the criteria for choosing the 'wise and wonderful' as counsellors to an IBA. They seemed to have been preponderantly white. Jeanette Minnie clarified that the CIB's proposal had been that the independent selection panels for both the board of the SABC and the council of the IBA should consist of the 'wise and wonderful', and not the actual boards of these organizations. The boards had to consist of professionals and persons who represented particular public interest groups, such as women, labour, rural constituencies and other previously disadvantaged groups. The independent judicial panel which selected the members of the new board of the SABC, as well as the multi-party panel which had appointed the counsellors of the IBA, consisted predominantly of black South Africans. The new board of the SABC was also dominated by black South Africans. White South Africans, however, dominated the first IBA council. This system of calling for public nominations, and interviewing nominees in public, provided real transparency in relation to the persons finally appointed. The public was enabled to judge whether political agendas were involved or whether unacceptable criteria, such as race, played a role. Given the domination of black persons on the selection panels, this was very unlikely in the case of the council of the IBA. Although no system was foolproof, a transparent nomination and selection process had to be much better than a system where governments unilaterally appointed boards behind closed doors.

13

Is Radio Pluralism
an Instrument of Political Change?

Insights from Zambia
JEAN-PASCAL DALOZ &
KATHERINE VERRIER-FRECHETTE

Radio is rightly acknowledged as the crucial medium of mass communication in Sub-Saharan Africa: both more widespread than television and more accessible than newspapers. Its omnipresence in everyday life, whether in rural or urban settings, explains its strategic importance as a means of communication. Debates among social scientists about the significance of radio in Africa have taken place against a background of different paradigms and shifting concerns. If moderniza-tion theorists once endowed radio with a capacity to induce rapid transition from 'tradition' to 'modernity', adherents of the dependency approach have subsequently insisted we pay close attention to just whose message is heard (usefully summarized in West and Fair 1993). Even more recently, there have been attempts to displace analysis towards the micro-level, considering the part played by radio in the defini-tion of national communities (Spitulnik 1994). Recurrent in these analyses is a confidence in the potential of radio to act as an instrument of 'social engineering', capable of shaping listeners' knowledge, opinions or even behaviour. Historically, it has indeed been the case that radio has played a major role at least so far as overt propaganda is concerned.[1] It was an essential vector for nationalist ideologies in the 1960s; and African leaders relied on radio both for political mobilization and for their own glorification, often in the form of personality cults. How critical are the stakes at play in control of radio stations is well illustrated by their being early targets of national coup attempts.[2] At a continental level, the 'shortwave battle'

---

[1] Even before independence, when broadcasting stations were entirely under colonial control, radio contributed to the development of educated Africans' political consciousness. See for instance, Tudesq (1983).

[2] For example, on the occasion of the attempted Zambian coup in 1990, Lt Luchembe took control of the ZNBC radio station to announce that he had successfully seized power. This news, broadcast and heard by every Zambian, had a tremendous impact on the population; a majority of the people came out of their houses to celebrate the end of Kaunda by dancing in the streets. Similar illustra-tions can be found in the recent political history of numerous Sub-Saharan African countries.

waged between various international and regional radio stations throughout the cold war period provides further illustration of the political importance of radio broadcasting.

Recent national conferences in Francophone Africa have reached entire national populations due to being broadcast over the radio. In Niger, transmission of the whole of their national conference allowed the populace access to the detailed unfolding of events. Africans listened raptly to live revelations and scandals concerning political personalities.[3] In societies where oral communication remains predominant, radio is more than a mere tool of communication and information, it is a fundamental instrument of power: commented upon, reinterpreted, and reinforced by *radio trottoir* (pavement radio, the Francophone Africa expression for the lively rumour mill of the streets).

Recent 'democratization processes' in some Sub-Saharan African countries have undeniably led to enhanced freedom of speech. However, this has not been uniform. While newspapers have proliferated, attempts to establish opposition radio stations have often encountered governmental resistance. This suggests that opposition voiced on radio continues to seem more threatening to political regimes than does dissent in the nascent print forms which are accessible to a smaller proportion of the population. For instance, in an attempt to silence opposition, the Congolese government did not hesitate to bulldoze a new broadcasting station. The limitations frequently imposed on independent radio stations are testimony to fears of their potential political impact.

Nevertheless, a new and freer attitude towards criticism and non-official discourse is expected of new regimes that wish to claim they are following a democratic path. Freedom of communication is a measure of the reality of political liberalization used by both political scientists and some international agencies. Radio, and the media more generally, are perceived to be core constituents of the enabling environment of democratization that needs to be created in Sub-Saharan Africa. Although ending of the state's monopoly over information is fairly recent – even in some old democracies, such as France – this ideology is now globally triumphant, and seen as a necessary part of the extension and entrenchment of democracy.

Although Zambia has often been cited as one of the few success stories for democratization south of the Sahara, there are numerous indications that political change remains superficial, and these lead some researchers to adopt a degree of scepticism towards its new regime. Beyond new ideological trends (such as the rhetorics emphasizing political and economic liberalization, the rule of law and human rights), we suspect that the nature of leadership and the politics of legitimization may transpire to be hardly different in the new Zambia of the Third Republic from what prevailed under the former regime of Kenneth Kaunda.[4] This chapter examines the question of radio pluralism within this context of ambiguous change. More particularly, we shall investigate the implications of the creation of Radio Phoenix, an ambitious station launched in Lusaka in March 1996. Does a

---

[3] However, transmission of the debates was predominantly in French, which excluded listeners not fluent in this language. Brief summaries were provided in local languages at the end of every daily session.

[4] For more on the political evolution of Zambia, see Bratton (1994) and Daloz and Chileshe (1996).

new radio station necessarily create a new locus of political contestation? Does it allow more space for dissent to be voiced? Does it have a specifiable impact on the pluralism of the politic system? With respect to the progress of Zambian political liberalization, we shall question two related issues: the emergence of a potential new forum to express political views, and its consequences – if any – for the transformation of Zambian political culture.

The limited contribution of Radio Phoenix to the development of a debating arena

Africanist political anthropology has produced various reflections on the relationship between speech and power. Avoiding the excessive cultural relativism of some of this literature, we can nevertheless generalize some of the norms and codes regulating access to speech. A speaker is expected to show responsibility by weighing up each of his sentences. Leaders, as spokesmen of a community, are especially supposed to choose their words carefully, as their words indirectly bind their followers. Even if debate is often encouraged at an initial stage, seniors generally have the final say in order to reflect a consensus. In other words, the expression of divergent points of view is concluded by an authoritative statement in the name of unity.

Single-party regimes, as well as state control over the media, have sometimes been interpreted as expressions of these norms. In Zambia, the ZNBC used its monopoly of radio and television information to cover – in obsessive detail – every decision, action, slightest doing or declaration of the president. As Kaunda strengthened his grip on the political system, he became increasingly reluctant to tolerate opposition, and largely deprived his people of any opportunity to express their views on Zambian policies or decision-making. Some authors have emphasized the importance of derision as one of the few means of resistance available in such authoritarian circumstances. However, it is notable that governments tend to tolerate this kind of satirical behaviour with a certain equanimity, which suggests that they see in it an outlet for, as much as an expression of, social *dé-dramatisation*.[5] It may well be less dangerous for a regime to tolerate this kind of safety valve than to countenance the creation of an official space within which adversarial voices and discontent may be articulated.

New issues arise with the advent of media pluralism as part of the democratization process. Ethnic and regional rivalries may have had less dramatic consequences in Zambia than in other parts of the sub-continent but, in the absence of rules and regulations about what is and is not acceptable, there remains a danger of the media being used to promote particularistic, even extremist, viewpoints.[6] The previous authoritarian regime controlled centrifugal tendencies through a judicious mixture of patronage, cooptation and the careful use of coercion; but

---

[5] For a critical appraisal of writings on derision and caricature as mechanisms of resistance, see Daloz (1996).

[6] We are thinking particularly of the extreme case of Radio-télévision libre des mille-collines in Rwanda (on which, see Carver, Chapter 14).

such tendencies quickly reappeared with political liberalization and electoral competition.

At a more general level, the impact of mass media may differ in settings which do not entirely share the characteristics of mass societies: atomization of individuals, weakening of communal structures and homogenization of social behaviour. The impact of media pluralism is not inevitably positive. Recent developments in the media sector in Sub-Saharan Africa have included both the good and the bad: interesting, serious investigative journalism, on the one hand, and the misuse of facts and the fabrication of scandals, on the other. The evolution of *The Post*, one of the newer newspapers in Zambia, is testimony to the attractions of going down-market and adopting a gutter-press style in order to promote sales. After playing a major role at the beginning of the political liberalization process by opposing the Kaunda system, and supporting Frederick Chiluba's MMD, *The Post* turned itself into a vocal adversary of the new regime, systematically attacking and even insulting major political leaders.[7]

If, by contrast, Radio Phoenix's management and journalists have aimed to provide only serious and well-attested information, the station has also sought to avoid political controversy. The time it dedicates to news coverage is limited: three news bulletins, one press review (broadcast twice) and a single recap of headlines are spread throughout the day and amount to only about an hour-and-a-half in all. Radio Phoenix's main priority is to entertain; hence the prominence it gives to music. Some time is given over to approved community awareness issues, such as education and health information, vaccination programmes, prevention of AIDS, or the 'Keep Lusaka tidy' campaign. But, having been granted a broadcasting licence and officially inaugurated by President Chiluba himself, it appears that the station has endeavoured to maintain a consensual treatment of national politics. So far as polemical topics are concerned, it seems to have exercised a policy of self-censorship. Political events have been presented cautiously, as if an implicit understanding had been reached with the current regime.[8]

The so-called freedom of speech enjoyed by Radio Phoenix is in reality quite limited. The station, located at the top of one of Lusaka's highest buildings, is under constant surveillance. Paying a first visit to the radio team in July 1996, one of us was surprised to encounter one armed soldier at the door of the elevator and another guarding the broadcasting studio. Officially they were there to deter criminal activity, but we suspected their real purpose was to remove any unwanted visitors. Other constraints are less overt. Because Radio Phoenix is privately

---

7 *The Post's* investigative journalism began promisingly by uncovering some genuine scandals, but the newspaper rapidly deteriorated into a sensationalist tabloid. For a nuanced analysis of the positive and negative aspects of the contemporary Zambian press, see Kasoma (1996).

8 Although uncorroborated, one of us was told in April 1997 that Mr Hickey, the general manager of Hickey Studio and main shareholder in Radio Phoenix, was granted a broadcasting licence because of his personal links with President Chiluba's MMD. According to our recent interviews, the threat of having this licence rescinded seems to preoccupy the radio's staff and management. The Foundation for Democratic Process's *Final Election Monitoring Report* shares our sense: '[Radio Phoenix] does appear to have some bias towards state-owned media in its "What the papers say" programme". It tends to quote them more than the independent press, such as *The Post*. In a situation where the state has declared the war on *The Post*, it can only be assumed that this is due to their fear of possible reprisals from the state.' (1996: 36)

owned it relies, like any other commercial radio, on advertising revenues to ensure its financial survival and, eventually, some profits. One wonders how far the independence of the station is practically limited by its need to please its major client. Considering how closely intertwined are the Zambian political elite and local business community, upsetting the advertisers is tantamount to upsetting the government. Add to this the desire to maintain political neutrality in the hope of attracting the widest possible audience, and the constraints on Radio Phoenix's political involvement are numerous.

For all these reasons, the contribution of Radio Phoenix to democratic debate has been restrained. Although the newsroom staff of Radio Phoenix decided to oppose the Media Council Bill proposed by the government in order to curb the diffusion of false information,[9] we have found no instance of the radio presenting open criticisms of the MMD's policies, or acting as an independent watchdog. Since the official radio station (ZNBC) apparently remains under strict governmental control, opposition leaders, compared with ruling party members, are undoubtedly at a disadvantage when it comes to disseminating their views. As a project, democratization of the airwaves remains far from completion.

Contribution to the formation of a new political culture?

Notwithstanding these limitations, does Radio Phoenix have important indirect impacts on the medium-term transformation of Zambians' attitudes towards the political system? This is not to suggest, like the modernization theorists criticized earlier (p.180), that the creation of new radio stations necessarily has positive effects on democratization, but that it is worth exploring empirically whether people's perceptions of political relationships might be changed by the media. Radio Phoenix's dynamic image contrasts with the surrounding disillusionment noticeable in the country. Its energy appears to be an important vehicle for the introduction of western conceptions and values; Radio Phoenix deliberately promotes itself as the symbol of modernity in Zambia.

In the political sphere, this promotion of modernity materializes through an emphasis on citizens' awareness programmes. Social and political issues are presented to listeners, stressing themes of accountability, representation or good governance. During the election campaign of 1996, two radio shows were dedicated to political information: 'Quest for Democracy' and 'What the People Say'. Both were presented weekly. 'Quest for Democracy' consisted of interviews with political personalities and other prominent members of society carried out by Mumba Kapumpa, a well-known lawyer. The audience was invited to phone the studio and pose questions to the guests directly. Technically speaking, presentation of the programme was slightly amateur; however the interviews conducted on various governmental matters were generally well-researched and carefully prepared. The second programme, 'What the People Say', aimed to give a voice to randomly chosen people in the street – the 'common man' as we were told by Radio Phoenix staff – to discover their views on political concerns and various issues affecting Zambia's future.

[9] Mostly with reference to *The Post*'s exaggerated coverage.

What might be the potential virtues of such programmes in terms of political socialization and enlightenment? Certainly, the ambition to empower citizens appears to be in tune with current stresses on individual civic rights and responsibilities. However, 'Quest for Democracy' was jointly sponsored by USAID and Southern University, which raises queries about what financial interest Radio Phoenix had in such ventures. The station has revealed a remarkable capacity to respond to western priorities and preoccupations by tapping into the resources of international agencies, and it is therefore prone to promoting whatever conceptions happen to be in vogue with them. Although this type of programme sets out to inform the population, it may also affect their perceptions more diffusely through its terms of presentation. However, the question of neutrality remains troubling. We have already mentioned the bias that may be imparted to programmes, without journalists realizing the fact, from the agendas of the concerned donors. More worryingly, we were told that representatives of the MMD ruling party had actually been in attendance on journalists during 'What the People Say' street interviews. While these two programmes are a positive development, in so far as they have broadened the scope of political debate, any indirect effects they may have had on citizens' awareness remain to be proven.

From an even wider perspective, it remains to be seen whether Radio Phoenix has set in train any more subtle sociocultural processes of mutation. Our impression is that this radio station certainly serves as a window between the rest of the world and Zambia. The Zambian political transition has been accompanied by a key debate concerning the relationship between the country and foreign powers, especially western ones. According to the advocates of change, Zambia was 'like an island' under Kaunda, obsessed by the idea of its national self-sufficiency. But for critics of the new regime, the Third Republic is simply neocolonialism by another name, opening up the country's borders to capitalist interest.[10] The extreme importance that many Zambians attach to Radio Phoenix must be analysed with this controversy in mind. Recent research into the image of the station reveals a strong sense of pride amounting to fervour for what Radio Phoenix represents. In the eyes of many the media epitomize access to modernity: they, and especially Radio Phoenix, allow listeners to partake vicariously in the dynamics of a global world, sharing – in apparent simultaneity – the fantasy of a lifestyle shared with people from the developed countries.[11] Radio Phoenix's initiatives – to create a fan club at the top of the tower, to assure that its trendy DJs get the latest hits,[12] and to recruit young and promising staff – are all part of this sense of constructing an unprecedented international undertaking.

All this raises the controversial question of the permeability of societies to exogenous cultural patterns. Rather than subscribing to the fears of acculturation

---

[10] For a detailed account of this topic, see Daloz (1997a).

[11] This hypothesis is developed in Daloz (1997b).

[12] Interviews carried out in April 1997 suggested that the choice of music was a delicate issue: because the station had yet to target a specific audience, it did not want to put off potential listeners by broadcasting only youth music and thereby becoming identified as a station for teenagers. Ms Pemba, Radio Phoenix's general manager, expressed concern that too much American music was broadcast at the expense of a local sound. One of the DJs stressed the need to set up an efficient infrastructure to produce and market Zambian music which is, according to him, perfectly able to be modern by fusing a commercial beat with a Zambian sound.

theorists, who foresee western cultural domination, we prefer to understand contemporary Zambian developments through the paradigm of limited effects, on the assumption that receiving cultures retain their capacity to reinterpret external messages. Such reinterpretation occurs at two levels: the station – as an intermediary – has the capacity to transform these messages, and so does the audience itself. If, as in the case of the 'Quest for Democracy', the radio staff was in no position to dictate what its listeners should think, the programme may nevertheless have played a role in putting questions on the agenda and indicating the terms in which they might be discussed. In this way, there may have been some contribution to the reform of social and political fields.

Regardless of analytical perspective, there is no denying that the establishment of radio stations creates a new arena of competition, both nationally and internationally. Presently, Radio Phoenix's broadcasting radius extends to 120 kilometres around Lusaka, but a more powerful transmitter is being set up with the aim of reaching not just Livingstone, close to Victoria Falls, but also the Copperbelt region and even the southern Democratic Republic of Congo (including Lubumbashi). As a result, major international broadcasting companies, such as the BBC, RFI, VOA and the SABC, are competing for opportunities to have their programmes broadcast on Radio Phoenix's transmitter. In addition to programming, at stake are international agreements on technical cooperation as well as overseas training sessions for journalists. Behind such contests over cultural spheres of influence lie the strategic geopolitical interests of the international powers.

Conclusion

Radio Phoenix was founded as recently as 1996, so it would be premature to reach conclusions about its impact, especially when the Zambian political situation remains so fluid. Radio Phoenix has the potential both to enlarge the arena of debate within Zambian public culture and to assist the reformulation of Zambian political culture. Assessment of its success involves issues of practice and theory. In practice, we have sounded a note of scepticism: it is not yet evident that the media practices of the Third Republic will transpire to be very different from the Kaunda regime that preceded it. Radio liberalization may have more complex, indirect effects; however, assessment of these requires us to resolve a series of epistemological questions about the sort of knowledge that radio produces. Is the radio medium capable of inducing transformations in social and political consciousness in itself? Or do changes in broadcasting culture only reflect the changes that have already occurred in the broader society? Or, if we must resolve the claims of both these arguments, how are we to do so?

References

Bratton, M. (1994) 'Economic crisis and political realignment in Zambia', in J. A. Widner (ed.) *Economic Change and Political Liberalization in Sub-Saharan Africa*, Baltimore: Johns Hopkins University Press.
Daloz, Jean-Pascal (1996) 'Les ambivalences dans la caricature des dirigeants politiques: illustrations africaines', *Mots*, No. 48, Paris: Presses de Science Po, September.

—————— (1997a) ' "Can we eat Democracy?" Perceptions de la "democratisation" zambienne dans un quartier populaire de Lusaka', in Jean-Pascal Daloz and P. Quantin (eds) *Transitions democratiques africaines: dynamiques et contraintes*, Paris: Karthala.

—————— (1997b) 'Le temps mondial en tant que representation et ressource politique au sud du Sahara', in Z. Laidi (ed.) *Le temps mondial*, Brussels: Editions Complexe.

Daloz, Jean Pascal and J. D. Chileshe (eds) (1996) *La Zambie contemporaine*, Paris: Karthala.

Foundation for Democratic Process (1996) *Final Election Monitoring Report*, Lusaka: FODEP (November).

Kasoma, F. P. (1996) 'Les médias dans les années 1990', in Jean-Pascal Daloz and J. D. Chileshe (eds) *La Zambie contemporaine*, Paris: Karthala.

Spitulnik, Debra (1994) 'Radio cycles and recyclings in Zambia: public words, popular critiques, and national communities', *Passages* 8: 10, 12, 14–16.

Tudesq, Andre-Jean (1983) *La radio en Afrique noire*, Paris: Pedone.

West, H. G. and Fair, J. E. (1993) 'Development, communication and popular resistance in Africa: an examination of the struggle over tradition and modernity through media', *African Studies Review* 36 (1): 91–114.

14
Broadcasting
& Political Transition

Rwanda & Beyond
RICHARD CARVER

In the transition from autocracy to democracy, radio plays a crucial role. This may be a truism, but in Africa no other mass medium has remotely the reach and accessibility of radio. If citizens are to make an informed and active choice in electing their political representatives – in other words, if democracy is to be more than a mere formality – then they must have accurate information about the characters and programmes of the political parties and leaders, as well as about their record in government.

There is legitimate and extensive debate about what constitutes a democratic political system and how appropriate a western-style multiparty system is in the African context. Yet whatever the answers to these questions, it is axiomatic that effective democratic participation depends upon a free flow of information so that the populace is able to make knowledgeable choices.

It is in this context that this chapter looks at the role of the radio in the Rwandan genocide. Almost every study of recent Rwanda has been at pains to emphasize what is unique and exceptional in the events that led to the genocide in 1994. In order to understand Rwanda, such an approach is clearly essential. But if the purpose is a more normative one, if it seeks to draw lessons and develop standards which can be applied elsewhere, then an analysis of Rwanda must stress the elements which are common to other situations. I argue that an important way of approaching the genocide is to see it as the final, awful consequence of a failed political transition. One aspect of this was the failure to liberalize broadcasting, which had direct consequences for the political and ethnic manipulation of the radio in the period leading up to the genocide.

Rwanda

Even before the outside world recognized the enormity of events in April 1994 –

and before the word genocide was employed to describe them – the role of the radio was already being highlighted. The part played by Radio-Télévision Libre des Mille Collines (RTLM) was widely reported, although seldom analysed. In part this reflected the narcissism of the western media, which took their own supposedly boundless influence for granted. If broadcasting could cause genocide, this only underlined the media's own influence for good or for evil. (In fact, the role of the international media in the Rwanda crisis was far from exemplary. The Joint Evaluation of Emergency Assistance to Rwanda concluded that 'inadequate and inaccurate reporting by international media on the genocide itself contributed to international indifference and inaction' (*Joint Evaluation of Emergency Assistance to Rwanda* 1996: 66.) According to the evaluation, the international media chose not to report on evidence of plans for the genocide. The emphasis of the coverage also tended to skew relief operations.)

RTLM was a nominally private radio station, owned by a number of prominent figures within the political establishment, which began broadcasting in July 1993. It was the first and only privately-owned radio station (other than the illegal Radio Muhabura, voice of the Rwandan Patriotic Front (RPF) rebels). When the RPF launched its insurrection in 1990, the state-owned Radio Rwanda had been the main vehicle for government propaganda. However, in April 1992 a transitional government was formed and the information portfolio passed to an opposition politician. Hutu extremist groups immediately began to complain about undue leftwing influences on Radio Rwanda and RTLM was born.

Foreign journalists immediately stressed RTLM's role in the genocide:

> Much of the responsibility for the genocide in Rwanda can be blamed on the media. Many people have heard of Radio des Mille Collines, which began broadcasting a steady stream of racist, anti-Tutsi invective in September 1993.

> ... it made sure that a large audience in Rwanda heard speeches by the likes of Leon Mugesera, who called on supporters of the Hutu regime to 'dump the Tutsi in the Nyabarongo river'.

> Radio des Mille Collines' shrill appeal for genocide on Rwandan airwaves accelerated as the apocalypse approached ... these calls became more intense as the bloodthirsty gangs carried out their sinister task. (Broadbent 1995)

One bizarre account even suggested that the massacres were carried out by militia members with radios in hand:

> Hutus could be seen listening attentively to every broadcast. ... They held their cheap radios in one hand and machetes in the other, ready to start killing once the order had been given. (Chilaizya 1995)

A much more serious case is presented by, for example, the human rights group African Rights:

> For the most part these journalists did not wield machetes or fire guns. Some of them did not even directly incite people to kill. But they all assisted in creating a climate of extremism and hysteria in which ordinary people could easily be influenced to become killers. (African Rights 1995: 160)

The United Nations Special Rapporteur on Rwanda, Professor René Degni-Ségui, reported on the campaign of 'incitement to ethnic hatred and violence orchestrated by the media belonging to the Government, or close to it, such as Radio

Rwanda, and above all Radio Télévision Libre des Mille Collines' (UN Doc. E/CN.4/1995/7, 28 June 1994, para. 26). He took the media's role as evidence of the pre-planned nature of the genocide.

These accounts were all more or less contemporary and all stressed the influence of the media on the *génocidaires*. A similar approach was taken in later more substantial studies (such as Chrétien 1995a). However, all these accounts had important methodological weaknesses, as follows.

First, they made little or no distinction between what was broadcast before 6 April 1994 and what was broadcast after. A close study of RTLM transcripts show that at the time of the Kigali plane crash which triggered the genocide, the radio's tone changed dramatically. Before 6 April RTLM was heavily suffused with general, implicit propaganda against the rebels of the RPF and – by implication but never explicitly – against the Tutsi population as a whole. The station's output was snappy, streetwise and entertaining – indeed, it was the preferred listening of the RPF guerrillas themselves, rather than their own dour and worthy Radio Muhabura. On 6 April, RTLM took on an entirely different role. It acted as a direct organizing centre, sending militias to particular locations and broadcasting names, descriptions and car number plates of those fleeing the genocide.[1] Yet some studies only quote from post-6 April broadcasts, implying that this was the character of RTLM broadcasts throughout (Chrétien 1995b).

Such accounts made no attempt to assess how the RTLM broadcasts influenced behaviour. There was a tendency to stress the accounts of participants, without regard to how self-serving these might be. Militia members who faced a potential indictment for murder would be inclined to pass the responsibility to any other agency, such as RTLM. Most commentary on Rwandan hate radio has worked on the simple assumption that since RTLM broadcast propaganda for genocide and genocide did indeed occur, there must be a causal relationship between the two. This is the same argument, in essence, as that propounded by those who argue that pornography is a prime cause of sexual deviancy or that film and television violence has led to an increase in violent crime. A detailed examination of these two propositions has shown that even where linkages can be established between media representations and social reality the causal relationship is obscure and almost impossible to establish with certainty. It might be argued that in the case of genocide the academic niceties of proving cause and effect should be dispensed with. Clearly the threat of genocide poses an urgency of response which will not allow for years or even months of academic reflection. But it does not remove the onus of proof from those who wish to impose bans on the media.

A third, and related, point is that an overemphasis on the role of the radio in inciting the genocide seems to be related to a particular interpretation of its nature which was prevalent in journalistic accounts at the time but which has little serious credibility. The notion that people could be incited to acts of extreme violence merely by listening to the radio is only tenable if it is accepted that RTLM propaganda unlocked profound or even primordial hatreds. Yet all the

---

[1] All these points and much else in this chapter are drawn from Linda Kirschke (1996). This is by far the best documented and most thoughtful account of the role of the media in the Rwandan genocide.

evidence is that the genocide was a meticulously planned and well-organized affair, with the Hutu extremist militias acting under strict orders according to a prearranged strategy. The apparatus of militias, hit squads, arms caches and death lists was put in place in the months before April 1994. In other words, the radio may have produced propaganda for the genocide but it did not incite it.

These three points have enormous practical implications. It is clear, for example, that after 6 April foreign governments not only had the right to intervene to jam RTLM broadcasts, they had an obligation to do so if they were able, under the Genocide Convention. This was because RTLM was engaged in transmitting orders for genocidal acts to be carried out. However, it is not useful to backdate that obligation retrospectively to the pre-6 April period. This is precisely what happened in relation to Burundi. Many critics of the weak international response to the Rwanda crisis drew the conclusion that expressions of hatred in the Burundian media should lead to bannings. The United Nations Human Rights Commission passed a resolution to that effect in April 1996, avoiding the rather thornier problem of how to marginalize the extremist militias, and the government banned a number of newspapers.

The problem of hate speech is a permanently vexing one for defenders of freedom of expression. At a certain point, exercise of free speech begins to impinge on the rights of others – for example, freedom from discrimination – and these rights need to weighed against each other. After its stirring defence of freedom of expression in Article 19, ICCPR continues in Article 20:

1. Any propaganda for war shall be prohibited by law.
2. Any advocacy of national, racial or religious hatred that constitutes incitement to discrimination, hostility or violence shall be prohibited by law.

In practice the interpretation of these words has been far from straightforward. The difficulty lies in the phrase 'that constitutes incitement'. What is to be prohibited is not mere advocacy of unacceptable and dangerous views, but advocacy which may incite others to action.

This balancing of rights is difficult even in circumstances when the hatred is being vocalized by minority groups with only limited power to carry out their threats, such as European racist groups. One of the clearest examples of such propaganda comes from South Africa. Radio Pretoria and other far-right radio stations broadcast illegally in 1993 and 1994. They defied somewhat half-hearted attempts by the Ministry of Home Affairs to close them by deploying armed and uniformed members of the neo-Nazi Afrikaner *Weerstandbeweging* (Afrikaner Resistance Movement). This was in contrast to unlicensed community radio stations, such as Bush Radio on the Cape Flats which was closed down after a few hours on the air. The climax of the Radio Pretoria saga came in March 1994 when the station used its broadcasts to organize fascist commandos in defence of the 'homeland' government of Lucas Mangope in Bophutatswana, which was threatened with a popular insurrection. The fascists were roundly defeated and the Mangope regime was overthrown.

In 1992 and 1993 the state-owned media in Zaire incited hatred against Kasaians and Balubas. Radio and television broadcasts accused people from Kasai Province of monopolizing the country's jobs and wealth. Half a million Kasaians were expelled from Shaba, many of whom later died in camps for the displaced.

In the case of Rwanda, as in Zaire, hate propaganda emanated from a powerful quasi-state radio station. One argument against banning such broadcasts is that allowing expressions of hatred to remain publicly visible is a means of early warning. In Rwanda, the broadcasts of RTLM and Radio Rwanda were an extremely important source of early warning, one which was utilized by both an international non-governmental Commission of Inquiry (*Report of the International Commission of Investigation on Human Rights Violations in Rwanda Since October 1, 1990*, March 1993) and the United Nations Special Rapporteur Bacre Waly Ndiaye. The latter stated in his August 1993 report that incitement to racial hatred had been noted on several occasions, for example through Radio Rwanda. The contents of news programmes in the Rwandan media differed substantially depending on whether the listener was receiving the French version or the version in Kinyarwanda (UN Doc. E/CN.4/1994/7/Add.1, 11 August 1993, paras 56–8).

In his recommendations Ndiaye suggested that a radio link be set up in order to inform the population about the violence which had taken place. The aim of this would be to stop delays in information as well as failures and manipulation of communication (UN Doc. E/CN.4/1994/7/Add.1, 11 August 1993, para. 66). The Rapporteur also suggested that a national reconciliation campaign should be organized in order to stop the 'incitement to hatred'. The campaign should begin with a public commitment to reconciliation on the part of the authorities, broadcast in both French and Kinyarwanda. The campaign should be followed by a series of public education programmes about human rights (UN Doc. E/CN.4/1994/7/Add.1, 11 August 1993, para. 68). However, Ndiaye noted the practical problems in implementing these recommendations: 'The Minister for Information is also attempting to effect reforms, but his powers are limited and his action too often thwarted' (UN Doc. E/CN.4/1994/7/Add.1, 11 August 1993, para. 69).

This final observation also raises a pragmatic problem with the call for banning: namely, the assumption that limitations on freedom of expression will be applied impartially across the board. The reality is that governments are most often inclined to exercise their censorship powers on behalf of the powerful and often oppressive voices in society and seldom on behalf of the weak and vulnerable. The problem in Rwanda was that it was a section of the government that was disseminating divisive propaganda, through Radio Rwanda and RTLM, the only independent licensed station. The issue was not that there was too much freedom of expression; rather, any alternative voices were excluded from the airwaves.

Re-examination of the Rwandan genocide has been a frenzied retrospective search for the moments when the course of history might have been diverted. Yet the probability is that in late 1993 and early 1994 nothing short of concerted international action could have prevented the genocide. The massacres would have taken place with or without the RTLM broadcasts.

However, there is a value in reflecting upon how it happened that the extremist Hutu faction acquired a virtual monopoly of the airwaves, first through Radio Rwanda and later RTLM. The situation which gave rise to this was far from unique. Rwanda was a failed transition to democracy. The government introduced a multiparty system reluctantly, under western donor pressure, without carrying out thorough institutional reform. The broadcasting system was one of the institutions which was left unreconstructed (as in almost every other transitional democracy in Africa). Hence Radio Rwanda continued under direct government control. The absence of an independent and transparent licensing system allowed RTLM on the air, as a scarcely disguised voice of the most extreme faction within the government. Root-and-branch reform of broadcasting at an early stage in the transition could have prevented the RTLM phenomenon (although not the genocide itself).

Broadcasting and political transition

For most of the post-colonial period in most African countries, the structure of broadcasting was the same. Newly independent governments inherited from the colonial power a monopoly state-owned national radio station. Formal guarantees of the structural or editorial independence of the state broadcaster were minimal or non-existent, because the colonial models had the same defects. Some state broadcasters were simply departments within a government ministry. Those that had a formal statutory identity usually had their boards of management directly appointed by the government. State broadcasters were dedicated to the tasks of 'nation-building' or 'development'. In their political coverage they were shameless propagandists for the government. In most instances there was no legal political opposition and thus no obligation on the radio station to reflect a range of political viewpoints. The nature of this propaganda role differed little whatever the ideological complexion of the government. For example, the Rhodesian Broadcasting Corporation, which had broadcast incessant propaganda against the country's nationalist movements, made an easy transition into the Zimbabwe Broadcasting Corporation (ZBC), doing the same job in defence of the new order.

From the late 1980s popular movements for democratic reform began to combine with external pressure for good governance in many African countries. In many instances the private print media played an important role in breaking the state monopoly of dissemination of information (see Carver 1991). In one or two instances, Mali being a particular case in point, private radio stations also played that role (Institut Panos 1993 Vol. II: 3–35). In many cases the process of democratization was structurally flawed. Minimal constitutional changes permitted the emergence of opposition parties, but this was not accompanied by thorough institutional reform. Highly centralized presidential control over government continued in many cases, while the single-party model of rule by party bosses persisted at a local level. Several years after their democratic transition, Kenya, for example, where the old party continued in power, and Zambia, where the opposition took control, both exhibit similar lack of accountability and abuse of human rights.

One of the institutions which generally evaded reform was the state broadcaster. In only one instance, South Africa, was the question of who controlled the broadcasting station put on the table as part of the transition process (see Minnie, Chapter 12). It is scarcely surprising that this provided the most progressive and thorough reform of broadcasting, with control of the South African Broadcasting Corporation (SABC) emphatically removed from government control and responsibility for the issuing of broadcasting licences assigned to an independent authority.

Even in some later democratic transitions where the constitutional entrenchment of fundamental rights was much stronger, such as Malawi, the question of broadcasting was avoided. The result has been that in most instances the structure of public broadcasting has remained unreformed even after the change to a multiparty system.

Both the indigenous democratic movement and western donor governments generally failed to understand the importance of public broadcasting. Early pressure on broadcasting reform focused almost exclusively on opening the airwaves to private broadcasters (probably because it was driven largely by the political agenda of the United States, where public broadcasting is historically marginal). Yet the economics of African broadcasting mean that for the foreseeable future the only national stations will be ones that are not run for profit. Private investors will be largely in the urban FM music stations, where advertising revenue will be most plentiful. There is some evidence that good private stations ginger up the public sector – this seems to have been the case in Uganda, for example (Maja-Pearce 1995a) – but this seems fairly marginal. In any case, procedures for allocating private broadcasting licences are almost invariably not transparent and the range of candidates is often limited to those with personal, political or financial links to government. Hence the emergence of a private sector has seldom resulted in genuine pluralism.

Transitional elections are an important moment in the development of broadcasting, both because the radio has a major influence on the outcome and because election coverage may be the first opportunity (sometimes under international scrutiny) for radio journalists to practise their trade in a relatively professional and impartial manner. A properly supervised election, presided over by an independent authority such as an electoral commission, will be conducted in the media according to a set of formal and predetermined rules. These will govern both direct access broadcasts by political parties and, if the electoral commission is doing its job properly, general news coverage by the state broadcasting station.

In practice the quality of election reporting in the state media has varied enormously. On the one hand, the state broadcast media in Kenya were spectacularly biased in favour of the ruling party in transitional elections in 1992 and again in the second multiparty elections in 1997 (Kenya Human Rights Commission and Article 19 1998). The same was true, for example, in Cameroon, where the theme music for election programmes consisted of praise songs to President Paul Biya (Conscience Africaine and Article 19 1997). On the other hand, in Malawi and Mozambique in 1994 broadcasters in some measure imbibed the new standards of fairness of impartiality. However, even where elections have resulted in a significant improvement in the professional standards of broadcast journalism, it is doubtful whether this has been sustained without entrenched institutional reform. In Malawi, the democratic government's failure to amend the law governing the state broadcaster has meant a slide back into the old ways since the positive experience of the 1994 election.

Most African governments continue to argue the need to retain control of broadcasting as an instrument of national development. Indeed, governments like to use the emergence of the private sector as an argument in favour of retaining their own direct control over the state broadcaster. According to the Zambian Deputy Minister of Information:

> The government ought to have a mouthpiece to explain government policy to the people. Under the Constitution the public have a right to information and therefore the government is obliged to provide information. If all the media are privately owned, they are not obliged to propagate government's views. (Maja-Pearce 1995b: 120)

However, the trend in international jurisprudence is to stress the obligation on governments to guarantee pluralism of the media as part of their responsibilities under Article 19 of the International Covenant on Civil and Political Rights and corresponding regional treaties such as Article 9 of the African Charter on Human and Peoples' Rights. Important recent decisions of national courts point in the same direction.

Governments argue that they must maintain a continuing share of media ownership as a means of promoting development. Yet debate within the United Nations increasingly stresses the central role of fundamental civil and political rights, including the right to freedom of expression, in realizing the right to development: 'The exercise of the various rights to participate may be as crucial in ensuring satisfaction of the right to food as of the right to take part in public affairs' (UN Doc. E/CN.4/1488, para. 98).

In two UN studies carried out in the early 1980s, a number of rights were seen as crucial to participation in the development process (UN Docs. E/CN.4/1421 and E/CN.4/1488):

> The right to hold opinions and the right to freedom of expression: these rights were seen to include the rights to know, to seek out and be given information, to impart information and to discuss issues of common importance. They were considered to be infringed when information is deliberately withheld or when false or distorted information is disseminated and when individuals or groups are silenced by intimidation or punishment, denied access to channels of communication or denied the opportunity to participate freely in public discussions (UN Doc. E/CN.4/1488, para. 100).

> The right to freedom of information: this right was considered to be of central importance to the promotion of the right to development and was understood to be based on the right of individuals and groups to have full details of relevant legislative and executive decisions. The right was seen to be severely tested by various actions including physical violence and intimidation, repressive legislation, censorship, bureaucratic obstruction, judicial obstruction and parliamentary privilege. Less visible obstacles to the right were seen to include economic and social constraints, de facto monopolies, narrow definitions of what constitutes news, what should be published and what issues should be debated, and entrenched cultural attitudes (UN Doc. E/CN.4/1488, para. 101).

> The right to take part in the conduct of public affairs: this right was considered to be an essential element to the realization of the right to development. It was noted that 'the existence of formal mechanisms for participation does not necessarily provide any guarantee of genuine popular participation' (UN Doc. E/CN.4/1488, para. 108).

In summary, participation in development depends upon pluralism – not only in high politics but in society as a whole – and government openness. In practical terms, this establishes a set of priorities in the media field which are rather different from those chosen by most African governments, with their continued insistence on control of the national radio station.

The key policy reform which most transitions to multiparty rule have failed to realize is the transformation of state broadcasters into independent publicly funded broadcasters. This can be achieved by ensuring the independence of the governing board from government interference, as well as by entrenching editorial independence. The establishment of an independent licensing authority working in a transparent fashion according to predetermined criteria is the other urgent priority. This would not only ensure fairness in the allocation of private commercial broadcasting licences, but also facilitate popular participation through the development of community radio. The South African transition uniquely achieved both these fundamental reforms and even entrenched the independence of the regulatory authority in the constitution.

Conclusion

The UN Special Rapporteur on Summary and Arbitrary Executions saw reform rather than bannings as the way to address the problem of hate media in Rwanda:

> A reform of the role and structure of the media should be envisaged. Journalists have already begun to study this question and have adopted a code of ethics. They should be provided with training opportunities, in order to enhance their professionalism and eliminate any lingering partisan tendencies. (UN Doc. E/CN.4/1994/7/Add.1, 11 August 1993, para. 69)

Is it fanciful to imagine that a Radio Rwanda on the public service model and an independent licensing authority could have made any difference to the course of events? This would not have stopped the genocide, certainly, since that had far deeper causes than pernicious radio programmes. However, as part of a wider reform of the institutions of autocracy increased radio pluralism might have had important effects in developing a more tolerant popular culture.

These are the might-have-beens of history which can never be known. It is fairly certain that other countries which fail to reform their broadcasting systems will not pay such a heavy price as Rwanda. However, radio plays such a central role in African political life that, without such reform, African countries will fail to make a full transition to democracy.

References

African Rights (1995) Rwanda: Death, Despair and Defiance, London: African Rights (revised edn).
Broadbent, Ed (1995) 'Media, even in the West, is partly to blame for the Rwandan Massacres', The Gazette (Montreal), 3 May.
Carver, Richard (1991) Truth from Below: the Emergent Press in Africa, London: Article 19.
Carver, Richard and Naughton, Ann (eds) (1995) Who Rules the Airwaves: Broadcasting in Africa, London: Article 19 and Index on Censorship.

Chilaizya, Joe (1995) 'Africa – media fuels ethnic strife – not only in Rwanda', *Inter-Press Service*, 12 May.

Chrétien, Jean-Pierre (1995a) *Rwanda: les médias du génocide*, Paris: Editions Karthala.

—— (1995b) *Media and Propaganda in Preparation for and During the Rwandan Genocide*, Reporters sans Frontières/CNRS/UNESCO.

Conscience Africaine and Article 19 (1997) *Premier rapport d'observation de la radio nationale*, Yaoundé, October.

Institut Panos (1993) *Le pluralisme radiophonique en Afrique de l'ouest*, Paris: L'Harmattan.

Joint Evaluation of Emergency Assistance to Rwanda (1996) *The International Response to Conflict and Genocide: Lessons from the Rwanda Experience*, Synthesis Report, Copenhagen.

Kenya Human Rights Commission and Article 19 (1998) *Media Censorship in a Plural Context: A Report on the Kenya Broadcasting Corporation*, Nairobi.

Kirschke, Linda (1996) *Broadcasting Genocide: Censorship, Propaganda and State-Sponsored Violence in Rwanda, 1990–1994*, London: Article 19.

Maja-Pearce, Adewale (1995a) 'Uganda', in Richard Carver and Ann Naughton (eds) *Who Rules the Airwaves: Broadcasting in Africa*, London: Article 19 and Index on Censorship.

—— (1995b) 'Zambia', in Richard Carver and Ann Naughton (eds) *Who Rules the Airwaves: Broadcasting in Africa*, London: Article 19 and Index on Censorship.

Report of the International Commission of Investigation on Human Rights Violations in Rwanda Since October 1, 1990, March 1993.

15
The Multiple Voices
of Sudanese Airspace

WENDY JAMES

The relationship between the output of radio stations and their listeners takes many forms. One of the factors influencing this relationship is the wider context of contact and circulation; what geographical distances or political boundaries separate the people on the ground, what kinds of communication link them? Are there roads, telephones, newspapers, computers and e-mail? Another factor bearing on the listener/radio relationship is the political situation: at its starkest, is there peace or is there war? In many parts of north-east Africa there has been a combination of factors giving radio a crucial role in recent political and social history. There are enormous distances and often real difficulty in overland travel, a great lack of infrastructure and of both ordinary and electronic communications, added to recurring conditions of war, mostly patterns of civil war exacerbated by crossborder population movement and intrigue. While the increasing availability and use of radio over the last two decades has been, in a sense, to introduce global technology and ideas to the peoples of the region, and certainly to bring the region within the horizons of global interests, the effects of radio on the whole have tended to intensify the ways in which people imagine local loyalties and local hostilities.

In this chapter, I offer a case study from the Sudan, illustrating and commenting on some of the uses of radio in the shaping of warfare and its moral rhetoric.[1] Although I concentrate on examples of radio output rather than on the listening communities as such, I am conscious of the question of understanding the impact on listeners, and the need for more research in this area (bearing in mind the

[1] Versions of this chapter have been given to the Centre for African Studies in the University of Leiden, and also to the Department of Anthropology in the University of Kent. On each occasion there were thoughtful contributions to the discussion which have helped me clarify the argument and presentation of the chapter, while making me conscious of how much further research needs to be done on the reception of radio broadcasts, especially in war zones.

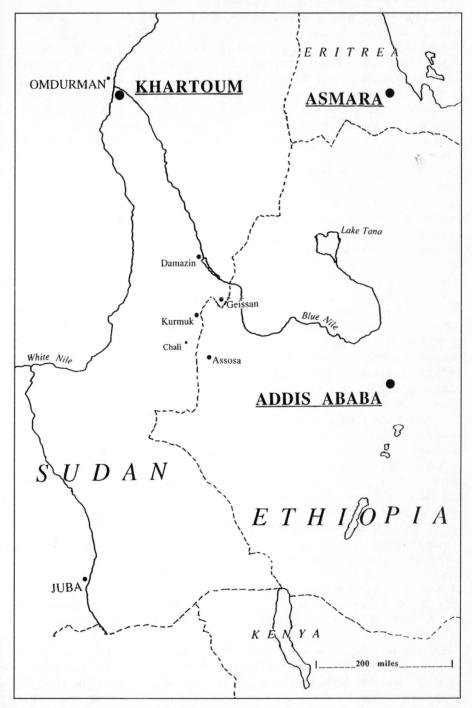

Figure 15.1 Radio and the war in Sudan

interesting way in which Steven Feierman has integrated radio into his discussions of peasant intellectuals in Tanzania; Feierman 1990: 251–3, 257, 259). The civil war in the Sudan began in mid-1955, a few months before independence. I spent some time in Khartoum during the 1960s, when there was just one national radio station, using standard Arabic and English with a sprinkling of cultural programmes in southern languages. I do not believe that radio played a significant part in this 'first' civil war, except by maintaining a kind of silence about what was going on. As my first radio quotation below indicates, there was a certain resentment in political circles in the south that local languages were being used on the radio at that time simply to stem disaffection; these languages apparently disappeared from the national radio when peace came. Occasionally there were brief news reports of 'rebels' being dealt with here and there, but in the absence of an 'opposition' radio the national broadcasters scarcely acknowledged that there was a civil war going on. One relied on foreign radio stations for political news about the country one was living in. I remember sitting listening to the BBC World Service during the urban riots of 1964, and hearing that 'We have no news of the situation in the Sudan; Khartoum is cut off; the radio is silent and the airport closed'.

In 1972 the Addis Ababa Agreement secured a decade of peace, and towards the end of this period I had the opportunity of living in Juba, then the capital of the semi-autonomous Southern Region which had been established by the agreement. It was during the decade of relative peace that radio stations had begun to multiply in the Sudan, as in other parts of Africa. As the transistor set became so widely available, the role of radio in disseminating information, education, culture and mild official propaganda became tremendously significant. I used to listen to Radio Juba, partly supported by the Sudan Council of Churches. This station used English, standard and Sudanese colloquial Arabic, and offered a wide range of cultural broadcasting in the languages and musical traditions of the southern peoples. It also ventured, I think for the first time, to use the street dialect of Juba on radio. This is a very local form of colloquial Arabic, influenced partly by its roots as a lingua franca in the military and trading history of the Nile valley, and partly by its contact with African languages. Together with its close relative Ki-Nubi in Uganda, Juba Arabic was on the point of becoming a creole, that is, the mother-tongue of a rising generation of children. It occupied a special slot in the programming of Radio Juba, being used for a regular series of mini-soap dramas on topical problems concerning life in Juba. Plots and characters were sharp and funny, the moral advice discreet but clear on such questions as how to balance love and money in town, whether to take the child to the witchdoctor or the hospital, how to be streetwise but sensible. The programmers, whom I met and talked to, were addressing their own people and building a kind of moral community in town.

The Southern Region was abolished in 1983, and civil war broke out afresh. Within a fairly short time, radio had begun to play a significant role in raising consciousness and stimulating opinion across the south of the country, including the regions tributary to the former southern capital of Juba. This was not the voice of the old Radio Juba, however, which remained fairly apolitical in tone, but the new station established in 1985 by the Sudan People's Liberation Movement/Army

(SPLM/SPLA). It became popular listening not only in the south but also across the northern Sudan, and it provoked the national radio station into acknowledging the war and contesting the claims of the rebels. In what follows, I illustrate how the homely tone of the old southern broadcasts, initially carried over into the early programmes of SPLA radio, was gradually transformed into a harsher political style as the war escalated. I consider in particular the use of radio in the struggle over the town of Kurmuk, right on the margins of the northern Sudan and the border with Ethiopia. The town was taken twice in the late 1980s, and then again in January 1997. As of mid-1999, the SPLA still holds it, as a partner in the National Democratic Alliance grouping of opposition forces. In the course of the war, the various voices of Sudanese airspace have spoken less and less to local communities on the ground, wooing their support, but more and more to each other, and to the international world – the agencies, embassies and diasporas from where the crucial support (for either side) now comes. Public radio has been of crucial strategic and political importance at key points in recent years, for example in reporting the defection of senior figures from one side to another, or interviewing prisoners of war after an engagement which the other side claims not to have happened, etc. It is important to remember that people are not restricted to listening to only one station: in the bush and in the refugee camps throughout the 1980s and 1990s they were regularly monitoring both rebel and government radio voices, as well as foreign stations. Radio was also, and is still, an important means of helping those in exile stay in tune with what is going on inside the country.

The Sudan is a large geographical space and inhabited by local communities speaking a wide range of languages belonging to several major language families, though Arabic is the main national lingua franca and colloquial dialects of it are spoken and understood very widely. English is also fairly well understood. National politics has always included the problem of the relative status of English and Arabic, and this is reflected in the history of radio, along with the status of the major African languages of the country. In addition to this given complexity of voices in the country, the internal history of political division and sociocultural strife has intensified the edge of language competition. In the development of the present war, radio has played a very important role, not only in representing the political situation but in helping create and shape it. Politics is played with the radio as a key medium. It has entered into Sudanese political life; and brought the wider population including the vast majority who have no access to newspapers, telephone, etc, into a changing and complex internal debate on the politics and morality of the war. I became aware of this during a series of visits to the region from the late 1980s and have since discovered the overwhelming amount of interesting material in the BBC *Summary of World Broadcasts*. Carrying a selection of broadcasts from across the world, translated where necessary into English, this publication is a wonderful archive for social and historical study.

The first years of Radio SPLA

Under the patronage of the Ethiopian leader Mengistu, the SPLM/A took over the former facilities of Radio Voice of the Gospel which had operated from Addis

Ababa. From 1985, Radio SPLA was on the air for a few hours each day, opening with a volley of firearms and triumphant military music. The station regularly used standard and colloquial Sudanese Arabic and English, along with the local southern Arabic dialect. They came to broadcast also in a number of African languages from the south (including Bari, Latuka, Nuer, Dinka, Shilluk) and from time to time in a variety of others.

There was a reasonable and homely explanatory tone to much of the early political propaganda on Radio SPLA, especially when using the vernacular languages. These often referred to local proverbs and the wisdom of the grandfathers, using the idiom of kinship in addressing the listeners. Here for example are translated excerpts from a broadcast in the southern language of Bari, spoken predominantly around the former regional capital of Juba, on 16 June 1987:[2]

> There are many other languages on standby which will be heard on Radio SPLA as soon as we acquire facilities for them. Many people in the past thought that national languages like Bari, Latuka, Shilluk and Nuer were broadcast to convince people to join the SPLA, because they would think that as the SPLA broadcasts their languages, it is the best organisation for the country. But, brothers and sisters, I wish to tell you that we have been on the air for two years and those years we have spoken the truth, we have sung our songs, we have discussed our own traditional cultures and we have told our own folktales, which remind us of our origins. The second important thing is that we must realise that oppression does not simply mean being used as a child to do any kind of job such as 'Give me water, get me fire, take this stool of mine' and so on and so forth. But really, that is not oppression at all. Real oppression is being denied the right to speak your own language ...
>
> The Khartoum government does not want and is not willing to hear our languages on the national radio. In the past, many people tried hard to introduce national languages on the national radio but failed. They were told that the introduction of such languages would demand a high consumption of diesel and petrol [to run generators] and that there was not enough money. But that was not the reason. They just did not want us to speak our own languages. Moreover, they wanted us to forget our own languages and speak only one language.
>
> Now, brothers and sisters, if you look at the languages spoken on the Radio Omdurman you will find that only one language, Arabic, is used. If by accident English comes into it it will only be for a short time before the radio returns to Arabic. All songs are sung in this one language, television and other things are dominated by it. Our languages have disappeared from the national media. It is only their children on the television: our children cannot be seen on television. We are forced to see the images of their children on television because they are our gods in Sudan.
>
> But it is our pleasure to tell you that the time has come. The purpose of starting up Radio SPLA was for all Sudanese people to know that a radio has been started for all of them. Radio SPLA was established so that it can broadcast various national languages, including English and Arabic, because the languages can be heard in many countries. But it is also important for our national languages to be spoken on the radio so that the Sudanese people can hear what is going on in their country, so that they can know their own suffering, so that they can sing their own songs and express themselves better in languages they know better. Therefore the SPLA-SPLM high command started Radio SPLA so that Sudanese people can understand their problems and act accordingly. That is why till now Radio SPLA has not changed its broadcast.
>
> Some time back, Radio Juba and Radio Omdurman claimed they wanted to broadcast

---

[2] This and all subsequent radio quotations, except where indicated otherwise, are taken from the relevant volume of the BBC's *Summary of World Broadcasts* Middle Eastern Series. See bibliography.

in the Latuka, Nuer and Bari languages, as they did in the Anyanya I war [in the 1950s and 1960s]. During the Anyanya I war, when the rebels were about to defeat the enemy, the Khartoum government tried to introduce various languages just to confuse the people and prevent them from joining the Anyanya. Now that they are fighting the SPLA, they are trying the same thing. They are hoping that when the SPLA has been defeated, those languages will be abolished, and they will be abolished, and they will give the reason that there is not enough fuel [that is for electricity generators, WJ].

But the national languages on Radio SPLA have come to stay and we shall broadcast more languages. When we take over the government in Khartoum, people will speak in their own languages on radio and television and they will write in their own languages and speak freely in their own languages. This will enable the outside world to know that Sudan is composed of many tribes. (ME/8597 A/5–6, 18 June 1987)

Along with the songs and music there were political broadcasts in a number of vernaculars. In the early days, even while threatening and justifying violence, these often maintained the person-to-person tone of the peacetime cultural broadcasts. There was an apologetic and gentle touch even in the speeches of guerrilla commanders; for example, another Bari-language broadcast (28 April 1987) pleaded with the citizens of Juba, explaining why they should leave the town:

Announcer: We now present a commentary by James Wani Igga [alternately member of the SPLM-SPLA high command and zonal commander for central Equatoria] on the war which is hotting up in Equatoria region.

[Igga: voice] I comment today on the fighting in progress around Juba. Greetings to you all, people of the same womb, greetings to all the skies over the land of the Bari. We have been advising you since last year to leave the town. Some of you followed our advice and moved your families out of Juba, but others have not yet done so. I now appeal to you most sincerely to respond immediately, because SPLA soldiers are already operating in Juba, the town which the Arabs want to take from us by force. If any of you is hit by a stray bullet, do not blame the SPLA. We have washed our hands, because war is war, and even the innocent can be struck down because bullets are blind.

It is not our intention to kill the innocent – our own people – but the Arabs, the oppressors who do not want to give us breathing space. I would like to remind you again not to forget the 1965 incident in which the Arabs killed several thousands of our people. People died like fish in poisoned water. People were burnt in their own houses like bricks.

Now you, the Bari community, what are you waiting for? Even in the olden days a whistle was blown as an appeal to the people to reorganise themselves. The Arabs now claim that we are hunting down innocent civilians. This is a big lie. How could we hunt down our own people for whom we are fighting? The SPLA wants to rescue you from the talons of the vulture, from the claws of the hyena which is oppressing the people. We have suffered for nearly thirty years. Why should you give way now? Haven't you heard the saying of our grandfathers that achieving freedom is not like getting a plateful of peanut butter? Remember that even that butter is the result of hard work both on the farm and at home. If you don't sweat to tend your peanuts you will not get the butter.

We will not let the Arabs take our land during our lifetime. We shall not allow it. Now that SPLA soldiers are in Juba, I appeal to you to treat them well. They are your own flesh and blood. Give them everything they need. We are grateful for the way the Mundari people received the SPLA when they arrived. We were only surprised to see a few of them running away to Juba after having been deceived by people like Makelele Nyajok [Juba military commander] and Gajuk Wurnyang Lupaya [Equatoria administration affairs commissioner sacked on 9 February 1987]. This upset us very much. It is very painful to see people for whom we are fighting running away from us. But this happened because the country has been spoiled. Since time immemorial, what Bari or Mundari has ever been a friend of an Arab?

It is surprising to see you today being given weapons to fight your brothers. Will this not enrage our grandfathers, who may punish us in one way or another? Which Equatorians are now claiming to be friendly to the Arabs? Who started the first civil war in Equatoria? Was it not the Equatorians? The Equatorians fought alone for seven years until 1962 when they were joined by their brothers in Bahr al-Ghazal and Upper Nile. At that time we only fought with traditional weapons. How about now when we have plenty of weapons? Is this the right time for us to eat one another like fishes? Perhaps some of you are angry, because after fighting the civil war you were not rewarded at all. We know all this and that is why we are fighting for justice. What kind of man is it who burns his house down because he has seen a snake in it?

I wish to inform you that I am about to come to Juba as a member of the SPLM-SPLA high command. I hope to meet some of you. I appeal to my fellow SPLA soldiers to observe discipline. If any of them takes somebody's property, even if it is a needle, he will be severely punished. I am sure the SPLA soldiers will treat you well because they are your own children, your own people. With this, let me end here until we meet again. (ME/8556 A/4–5, 1 May 1987)

Even the programmes in Arabic and English seemed to be devoted, in the first few years, to the general political education of local listeners. Then came the more bold and direct military use of the radio: appealing, for example, to national army soldiers in garrisons which were about to be attacked, suggesting they defect; and to local citizens to leave such garrison towns, and get out of the way of SPLA operations. There was information and counter-information; an eye witness reported on government radio that John Garang had been shot dead, with all kinds of gory details; it was only an SPLA broadcast some months later with the voice of Garang himself that nailed that misinformation. What is described in the BBC *Summary of World Broadcasts* as an anti-SPLA radio began to be heard inter-mittently, without any station signal, associating itself with the views of the government, and what had become its allied militia known as Anyanya II. This station later became officially recognized as based in the capital and was labelled National Unity radio. Both sides increasingly claimed to represent the truth, not only about battle casualties and captured tanks, but about moral, ideological and religious truth.

Through the radio, ordinary listeners gain an exciting and glamorous picture of the struggle; the names of commanders, of battalions and units – Fire, Eagle, Bee, Za'alan ('Anger'), Bright Star, etc. Later, several names revive memories and glories of the past – New Funj, New Cush. By this time, we might ask who are the listeners: the 'moral community' imagined by the programmers (and their backers) of one side, or the other, or both sides? One clue is again the use of language; certainly the SPLA radio used both ordinary Sudanese colloquial and the southern or Juba Arabic (common as a lingua franca in the SPLA as in all other military organizations of Sudanese history where a large proportion of soldiers have always been from the peripheries of the Nile valley). I do not have precise information but I think it very likely that the National Unity radio was also, by this time, sometimes using southern Arabic. Both also regularly used English. The listeners are certainly no longer a local community in the normal sense. Those in Juba were (and still are) under a government garrison and under siege; elsewhere, many were displaced, internally or over the border into refugee camps in neighbouring countries. The radio was not used so much for entertainment, but for information. It was also, surely, a means of locating oneself politically, sensing who one was and what one's friends were up to in between the warring rhetorics of one side or another. Certainly those with radios listened, and listen, to more than one station. Different versions of a battle or a political event were and are positively sought by switching channels. Listeners come to detect and to discount the conventions of emphasis, style and oratory on both sides.

Radio was becoming important in the Sudanese struggle in other ways too. As well as in the actual military campaigns, there was widespread use of two-way radios in the basic logistical organization of the combatants on both sides. Careful intelligence was devoted to tracking the other side's communications. While travelling in an agency Landrover at one time I tuned in myself, by accident, to what seemed to be a Sudanese government forces frequency. Even UN and other international agencies were totally dependent on radio links. Even OXFAM (based in Khartoum) was dependent on their own radio communications by the mid-1980s, and when the government later wanted to ban their use of radio (on the grounds that they might be in touch with the SPLA), they pulled out of the country temporarily. In at least two cases with which I am familiar from the early 1990s, there seems little doubt that government monitoring of UN radio communications led directly to the bombing of places where refugees were reported to be on the move.

It is no wonder that as the SPLA consolidated its position in the late 1980s during the prime ministership of Sadiq el Mahdi, the use of its radio became even more confident; its proclamations provoked counter-broadcasts by the national station and the armed forces radio. National and guerrilla leaders, between whom ordinary communications like the telephone were not normally available, were using the radio to attack each other (no doubt covertly also indicating a bargaining position). Following the coup of 1989, when the present regime of Omer el-Beshir came to power with the support of the National Islamic Front, the political use of public radio became even more aggressive.

Kurmuk: a small place on the edge of the cold war

To illustrate the shifting kaleidoscope of Sudanese broadcast voices over the last decade, I would like to take as a case study the ways in which radio played a part in the recent history of Kurmuk. It happens to be a town I know from earlier. It is in a very interesting position, in hilly territory right on the frontier with Ethiopia (in fact there is an Ethiopian Kurmuk). It happens to be the most southerly town in the northern Sudanese province of the Blue Nile, bordering the Upper Nile and overlooking the vast southern plains. Its vulnerability to infiltration or attack, either from the south or from the Ethiopian side, is matched only by the very important symbolic significance it has acquired, as a result of the war, to both southern and northern Sudanese and to any future government in Khartoum.

Kurmuk is set right on the border: in fact it is a double town, straddling the stream bed which constitutes the frontier. Although it had originally been established in 1910 as a border post to stamp out smuggling and slave-trading, and had been bombed by the Italians in the early 1940s, in times of peace people used to cross to and fro without difficulty. On my first visit to the Sudanese Kurmuk in 1965–6, a couple of friendly policemen invited me over with them for an afternoon's shopping and a drink in the twin town on the other side. At that time the 'old' Sudanese civil war was felt to be very far away in the remote south. During the period of the socialist state in Ethiopia (1974–91) which came to be dominated by Haile Mariam Mengistu, however, the pleasant wooded stream linking the two Kurmuks became the frontier of the cold war. As I have already mentioned, Mengistu lent support to the SPLA, and partly because of this the almost unknown town of Kurmuk suddenly became famous. During his regime it was taken twice by the southern-based rebels, and once again a few years later. On all three occasions, Ethiopia was accused of playing a direct role in the attacks, and while this could be contested, there is no doubt of the significance of the background support available from time to time on that side of the border.

The commonest approach of anthropologists, aid workers and journalists to the changes affecting frontier regions has been to focus on displaced communities as such, and the story of their sufferings (see, for example, Allen 1996; James 1997). An alternative analytic focus, however, would be to look at the key strategic points of local power and significance within the frontier zone, the small towns over which regimes, guerrillas and local elites strive to establish control and use to extend their resources and reputation further. A small border town which remains almost unknown during times of stability can become a very precise object of political and military desire. As a result, one set of inhabitants may flee, to be replaced by another; it may mean many different things to different people, and to the rhetoric of different warring parties. There is no normal continuity in the history of such a place, or even in its language, and no normal social reality; stories from and about such a place may offer different and contradictory perspectives, especially when carried over the airwaves to communities otherwise *incommunicado*.

The SPLA had acquired a base in the Assosa area by about 1985 and began to infiltrate the Kurmuk district. Counter-insurgency operations against the local civilians (including the villages of the Uduk-speaking people where I had previously carried out anthropological fieldwork) were begun in 1986. By early 1987 large-scale burning of villages led to the flight of the population over to the Assosa district in Ethiopia where a camp was set up. From this point on, there was no local community to speak of in Kurmuk town, and precious little in the rural areas of the district. Even most of the merchants had already left for the northern cities. By the time the SPLA mounted an attack on Kurmuk in late 1987, partly from the Ethiopian side, it was virtually empty of civilians. Radio broadcasts and print journalists have continued, up to the present, to appeal to the people of Kurmuk as though they were still there; over the heads of this imaginary community, however, the real target of many programmes referring to Kurmuk became the international political audience.

The first attack on Kurmuk was part of the general 1987–8 advance and consolidation of the SPLA against Prime Minister Sadiq el-Mahdi's 'democratic' regime in Khartoum. The ground had already been prepared after counter-insurgency measures taken by the army. Akira Okazaki has told me of the surprise, excitement and fear with which the Gamk people of the Ingessana Hills, well to the north of Kurmuk, received radio appeals in their own language from the SPLA at this time. The following quotation from Radio SPLA in late April 1987, when there had already been military clashes and mass destruction of villages in the district by the government forces, does include reference to the local population, though by standards of the early days it is a rather formulaic one.

> The Deputy Chairman and Deputy C-in-C of the SPLM/SPLA, Lt-Col Carabino Kuany Bol, met chiefs and elders of Kurmuk district in his HQ in southern Blue Nile. Welcoming the chiefs and elders, [he] told them that the people of Kurmuk district and southern Blue Nile in general should not worry about their security, adding that the SPLA is in southern Blue Nile to protect the citizens against Sadiq's repressive army. He explained to the chiefs and elders the historical background of the formation of the SPLM/SPLA which, he said, is to fight against oppression, exploitation and other social injustice perpetuated again the Sudanese masses by the successive ruling cliques in Khartoum [...] The chiefs and elders of Kurmuk expressed their happiness and appreciation for the warm welcome accorded to them by the SPLA soldiers. They expressed their anger about atrocities committed by Sadiq's soldiers against the local population in Kurmuk, which includes the massacre of innocent civilians including women and children and raping of their wives and daughters [...] (ME/8556 A/5, 1 May 1987)

Radio SPLA's account of the eventual surprise capture of the town (16 November) was graphic, and claimed a video recording to prove their claims:

> The overall commander of SPLA forces in southern Blue Nile, Cdr Salva Kiir Mayar Dit [last two names phonetic] has released the details of the capture of the enemy garrison of Kurmuk and the quantity of the armaments captured from the fleeing enemy troops. Speaking to a Radio SPLA correspondent in the liberated town of Kurmuk, Cdr Salva Kiir Mayar Dit said that over 300 soldiers of Sadiq al-Mahdi were killed and the following armaments captured: [...] Correspondent says that further stock-taking is still taking place in Kurmuk and the other small garrisons captured after Kurmuk.
>
> It is to be recalled that five days before the start of Kurmuk operation, Sadiq al-Mahdi publicly said over Radio Omdurman that if the SPLA captures Kurmuk, he would resign. Commenting on this statement, the official SPLM/SPLA spokesman has said that Sadiq should honour his word and resign instead of giving lame excuses that there was foreign intervention.
>
> The spokesman pointed out that the whole battle of Kurmuk was taped on video by the SPLA. Press and Sudanese journalists are welcome to see for themselves the truth, adding that [as heard] as in all other battles, the SPLA has no foreign troops, nor foreign fire support. And on principle, it would not ever accept foreign intervention on its side.
>
> In this connection, the spokesman pointed out that the only country ever to give the SPLA tanks and Howitzer 122-mm artillery is the Sudan itself. The tanks, artillery, anti-aircraft guns and anti-tank weapons captured in Pibor, Jokau and Kurmuk alone are sufficient to give Damazin a good pounding. And when this happens, Sadiq al-Mahdi will point a finger outside the Sudan, said the spokesman. The spokesman revealed that there were about 1,100 troops of Sadiq al-Mahdi in Kurmuk, commanded by two colonels and a lieutenant-colonel. Amongst these, 300 were killed and several others were wounded.
>
> The spokesman went on to say that the commander of Sadiq al-Mahdi's troops, who had earlier prided himself with the title of 'hero of Daju' [a tribe in Western Sudan [sic][3]],

---

[3] I believe this reference must be to a government search-and-destroy campaign which had gone south of Kurmuk to the Daja or Daju valley earlier in the year, and has nothing to do with the western Sudan.

fled at 0900 hours Sudan local time with remnants of his soldiers, most of whom died of thirst and some, who have been in hiding are now reporting themselves in Kurmuk (ME/0003 A/6, 18 November 1987)

The government-supported Sudan News Agency reported (in English) a different angle (19 November):

Rebel troops captured by the armed forces just before the rebels' attack on Kurmuk town recently revealed that Ethiopian and Cuban troops had effectively contributed to the attack, the daily *Al-Usbu* published today. The daily said the captured rebels unmasked that the offensive had been prepared long beforehand by transporting groups of the rebel troops by Ethiopian planes to Assusu region and then by the Ethiopian military trucks to (?Doal) and Khawr al-Gana regions which were evacuated from the citizens [as received] as preparation for bombarding the Sudanese border town of Kurmuk.

The rebels affirmed that all the artilleries used for shelling the town of Kurmuk were Ethiopian, adding that the Ethiopian militants had been (?rectifying) the range of the artilleries during the shelling. They unveiled that the total number of the forces [which] attacked Kurmuk was about 15,000 forming five brigades, three of them consisting of rebels and the other two Cuban and Ethiopian.

The rebels who were captured before the attack said they infiltrated into the town for carrying out sabotage acts that could hinder the armed forces from defending the town during the attack, the daily said. (ME/0005 A/3, 20 November 1987)

The SPLA radio may have been intercepting military intelligence communications of the other side for some time, and began to relay for public consumption what they had learned, to back up their own versions of the truth. For example they reported in English (26 November):

The former commander of Sadiq al-Mahdi's forces in Kurmuk has admitted in a message to the Damazin commander, intercepted by SPLA mobile communication unit in Kurmuk, that the number of soldiers killed in Kurmuk was 330, 66 wounded and seven surrendered to the SPLA. He also admitted the losses of tanks, APCs and Howitzer artilleries to the SPLA. In another development, Radio SPLA has learnt that Sadiq's commander of 14th brigade in Damazin, after the capture of Kurmuk by SPLA forces on 12th November 1987, rounded up the southerners, Ingessena and any other black men inside Damazin. Most of these people were believed to have been killed in cold blood as a measure of revenge. (ME/0012 A/4, 28 November 1987)

They also claimed that interviews on the Armed Forces radio were forged (26 November, in English):

Yesterday evening the so called Armed Forces Programme, Omdurman radio played a forged interview with an alleged SPLA soldier captured in Kurmuk. In that interview, the man alleged that there were nearly a company of Ethiopian army and a company of Cubans that attacked Kurmuk with the SPLA troops. In response to these allegations, the official spokesman for the SPLA High Command said that the Khartoum's [as heard] allegations were false, intentionally done to divert the Sudanese masses' attention and to deceive the soldiers who have been ordered to recapture Kurmuk that there will not be resistance in capturing Kurmuk. If the Khartoum army were capable of capturing SPLA soldiers, why did they leave behind their wounded and all their heavy guns, said the spokesman. The spokesman made it clear to the Khartoum soldiers coming to attack Kurmuk that they are being deceived into their deaths, adding that the SPLA is armed to the teeth to defend Kurmuk and the Khartoum troops will find this out if they venture to come, says the spokesman. (ME/0012 A/4, 28 November 1987)

The Khartoum government mounted a high-profile campaign, again partly over the airwaves, though of course in Arabic, to raise support across the Middle East for the retaking of Kurmuk and its neighbouring border town of Geissan. These were represented as cities of the Arab homeland. The retaking took place just about a month later, after (as claimed by the SPLA) the rebels had decided to leave with their captured equipment and loot. The military and government presence was re-established, but I do not believe that the former town population returned in any strength. Many merchants remained in the north, and the local rural population (including the Uduk) remained for the next couple of years in the refugee camp across the border.

At this interesting point, the stakes were raised again between the guerrilla and national radios over the question of vernacular languages. Using the Latuka language, Radio SPLA commented as follows on Khartoum's proposal to introduce more broadcasts of its own in southern languages:

> Listeners, before ending this commentary, I would like to tell you that reliable sources in Khartoum say that Sadiq al-Mahdi's government has reached a decision on introducing some of the Sudanese languages on Radio Omdurman, as is the case with Radio SPLA. We don't know what these chosen announcers will tell the people in southern Sudan. As I told you before, during the 17 years' war, that is Anyanya I, the then government did introduce southern languages on the national radio Omdurman, only to discourage those trying to join the Anyanya movement and to tell lies to the innocent Sudanese people. Now the same Sadiq al-Mahdi is trying again to use the cards he played in the early 1960s, that is introducing some of the Sudanese languages to the national radio and having some of the traditional dances on the television, such as Latuka dancers, Dinka, Zande, etc. In fact we don't know what has happened and you should also think of what might have happened to you. Perhaps you now have culture. In those days the Khartoum government used to say that you were people without culture and therefore appearing on television was useless. Since they are now introducing these languages, you people should get together and consider why they are being introduced at this time. Certainly you will find that they want you to forget all about the SPLA-SPLM movement [...] (ME/0012 A/5, 28 November 1987)

Over the next two years tension increased between Khartoum and Addis Ababa; after the coup of Omer el-Beshir in mid-1989 the former stepped up its general support of the gathering forces opposed to the Mengistu regime. For example it opened a refugee camp inside the Kurmuk district (at Yabus) for Oromo refugees, and allowed at least the relief wing of the Oromo Liberation Front (OLF) to move southwards through Kurmuk to reach it. In mid-1989 the SPLA sacked this camp, and later in that year took Kurmuk itself again.

The tone of radio broadcasts on each side became much harsher, the moral stakes were raised, and the appeals were clearly addressed to the Middle East, to international embassies and politicians in exile. The Republic of Sudan Radio, Omdurman, broadcast in Arabic as follows on 28 October 1989:

> In the name of God, the Compassionate, the Merciful. A statement from the General Command: [Koranic verse omitted].
> (1) We have been following the course of events in the southern Blue Nile area, specifically in the Kurmuk area, where the outlaws, using various names, strove to create a state of panic among the citizens and to kill innocent people without abiding by the cease-fire or respecting the simplest human principles of the citizens in this area.

(2) The outlaws carried out numerous acts of aggression in the area which affected peaceful villages, where they killed, pillaged and took innocent citizens prisoners. Their aggression extended to an attack on our garrisons and mobile convoys, in addition to planting a large quantity of mines with the aim of impeding the movement of our forces.

(3) In spite of all that, our forces are still adhering to the ceasefire declared by the state and they are administering their outposts through the usual administrative movements. Despite this, the outlaws tried to prevent the movement of our forces with the aim of inflicting the heaviest losses in their ranks and of preventing supplies from reaching our outer garrisons.

(4) The area has witnessed ferocious battles in the past few days, in which your forces in Kurmuk and other positions defied death. They inflicted heavy losses upon the aggressors in lives and equipment. Our forces also sacrificed a number of martyrs.

(5) The General Command wishes to assure you that your armed forces will not give up an inch of the soil of this homeland, and that they fight aggressors and throw back their plot at their own throats, and that they will safeguard the unity of this soil and its territorial integrity and security against any sinful aggressor, and they will score victory after victory.

God is the greatest. Glory be to Sudan. In the name of God, the Compassionate, the Merciful. Victory cometh but from God. God is the most powerful and the wisest. God has spoken the truth. (ME/0600 A/6, 30 October 1989)

Radio SPLA offered the following in English on 29 October, with fewer moral embellishments but more conviction in conveying the facts of battle:

The SPLA high command today issues two strong warnings.

Warning Number 1: The SPLA COS, Cdr William Nyuan Bany, who is also the commander of the New Funj forces in Blue Nile, today issued a strong warning to the force of Col Muhammad Ali al-Haji not to attempt to advance to Surkum. The SPLA COS said such an attempt would definitely lead to total destruction of Col Muhammad's force to an extent even worse than suffered by Lt-Col Sayid Jamal al-Din. Cdr William Nyuan Bany said SPLA sources in Damazin have reported details of Col Muhammad Ali Al-Hahi's forces, including the number and types of combat vehicles and artillery pieces. These weapons will not help.

As a colleague and a patriot, Commander Nyuan Bany strongly warns and advises Col Muhammed Ali al-Haji not to commit innocent soldiers to sure and unnecessary death. Why should these soldiers die for [rank as heard] Brig Umar al-Bashir, who aborted peace on 30 June and who will soon be driven out by the wrath of the Sudanese people? Cdr William Nyuan Bany also appealed to the men, NCOs and officers of Col Muhammad Ali al-Haji's force to refuse the illegal order if they are forced to advance. We congratulate you for returning back to Dondoro [phonetic] when you met the remnants of Lt-Col Sayyid Jamal al-Din's force.

In a related development, reliable SPLA sources in Damazin have sent to SPLA high command the full details of the battle of Surkum. The so-called Aman al-Kurmuk force was 347 men, NCOs and officers. Of these, 226, or 65 per cent, were killed with their bodies left on the battlefield. Another 84, or 24 per cent, are unaccounted for, or some deserted to SPLA forces. Others were captured in the Funj villages. The remaining 35, or 11 per cent, reached Dondoro, including the commander, Lt-Col Sayyid Jamal al-Din [all figures as heard]. From these true casualty figures coming from Damazin itself, it is obvious that the battle of Surkum was a major defeat and disaster for Umar al-Bashir's junta. For what reason did these innocent 226 soldiers die? (ME/0602 A/7, 1 November 1989)

And on 31 October there was a direct appeal to youths from across the northern Sudan to join the cause:

The official spokesman of the SPLA today disclosed to Radio SPLA that various groups of youth from northern Sudan have written to the SPLM-SPLA Chairman and C-in-C requesting military training and armaments, and to be informed where they can join the SPLA to get the training and armament. The spokesman said: The C-in-C appreciates the stand of those youth, and he has directed them to find their way to join SPLA forces of New Funj in southern Blue Nile, or the forces of New Cush in southern Kordofan. The youth of Jazirah, Blue Nile and White Nile can join either the forces of New Funj or those of New Cush, according to their convenience. The youth of western Sudan are to join the forces of New Cush. Those in Khartoum are to find their ways to southern Kordofan or southern Blue Nile. Sympathetic military and police personnel are to help and facilitate the movement of those coming to join the SPLA. (ME/0603 A/7, 2 November 1989)

Local people in the Sudan of course can often understand radio stations in other parts of the Middle East, as well as the BBC and US stations. It is interesting that a series of broadcasts across the Middle East took up the Sudan government's suggestion that Israel was behind the second taking of Kurmuk. It was generally known that the old rival Ethiopia was already being challenged by its own internal armed opposition and was politically weak, while the Cubans, Russians, and so on, were on the way out.

It was at this time that the SPLA finally ousted the government garrison at Chali, centre of the former Uduk homeland (something it had not achieved in the 1987 advance). I was sitting in a hotel room in Nairobi, on sabbatical leave but unable to get to the field, having tuned in as usual in mid-afternoon to Radio SPLA when I suddenly heard a speech in the Uduk language. I do not believe this very small minority language had reached the airwaves any time before this occasion, nor has it done so since. The occasion was the victory celebration of the liberation of Chali. An officer originally from the district spoke in brief formulaic sentences, followed by a simultaneous translation into southern Arabic. But where were the listeners, the community whose morale and gladness was to be raised by this liberation of a small homeland? They were all elsewhere: almost all in fact across the border in the Assosa refugee camp. It took an almost total displacement and an enforced exile for them (and for me) to hear of their 'freedom', in their own language, over the airwaves (courtesy of the politics of the cold war, a global context which, however, was about to be completely transformed).

The town of Kurmuk was again held only for a brief period; as international government rhetoric was stepped up, the retaking of Kurmuk coincided with a series of advances towards Assosa by anti-Mengistu forces on the other side of the border. The SPLA retreated southwards in January 1990. The refugee population at the camp near Assosa had to leave, some returning to Kurmuk but the majority, including virtually all the Uduk, fleeing far to the south, and into a much extended exile (where they still are).

Post-cold war: Kurmuk on the front line again

Radio SPLA had to close down in 1991, when with the fall of Mengistu it lost its former Ethiopian backing. There were relatively good relations between the Sudanese and Ethiopian governments for a period. Kurmuk was no longer facing potential hostility across the border. However, its character as a Sudan government garrison town facing the internal war zone was stepped up. The town in fact played a key role in the processes whereby Sudanese government forces in 1992 were able to push back the SPLA and rebuild their position in the south, with some background support from the new Ethiopian regime. Sudanese consulates were established across the border in Assosa and Gambela.

By late 1995, however, the newly cooperative diplomatic relations between the Sudan and Ethiopia were damaged again by a series of high-level events. Kurmuk had to reorient itself to the politics of the international frontier. The consulates in Assosa and Gambela were closed (much to the relief of the refugees). The Sudanese political opposition became more effective, and the SPLA was able to reconstruct its strength. In early 1997 it took Kurmuk again, for the third time. A new opposition radio began to operate from Asmara, in Eritrea. This is in the name of the National Democratic Alliance (NDA), a new grouping of forces which includes the SPLA and now controls substantial parts of the northern, as well as the southern, Sudan. It is appealing over the heads of the military government to the ordinary Sudanese people of the north, just as the SPLA battalions did in approaching particular garrison towns in the south. And now one of the voices one hears on the NDA radio, alongside the southerners, is that of former prime minister Sadiq el-Mahdi, against whom the struggle was once directed. He himself has now fled the country and is asking for the people to rise up against their government. The current tone of radio broadcasts is more professional and sophisticated than before, less personal and more often in English or the kind of modern standard Arabic which can be understood across the Middle East. On both sides, NDA and government, one has the feeling that broadcasts are addressed not so much to the ordinary population, but to the international global players in Cairo, Baghdad, Tel Aviv, Washington, etc. I am not in a position to know whether, or to what extent, African languages are being used on either side's broadcasting, but if they are, this is no longer reflected in the *Summary of World Broadcasts*, and I suspect they no longer have the political role they once did.

By early 1997, international interest was certainly high. The first report quoted in the BBC World Service summaries was in Arabic from the Egyptian Middle East News Agency (MENA):

Khartoum, 13 January: MENA's Khartoum correspondent has learned that the large scale offensive launched by the Sudanese opposition forces from Ethiopian territory against the towns of Kurmuk and Qaysan on Sunday [12 January] has resulted in the seizure of huge areas of the Blue Nile Province, in south-eastern Sudan. The correspondent added that many people were killed and others had to flee to Ethiopia.

Sources close to the military operations east of Sudan noted that the losses were inflicted due to a lack of Sudanese forces on the Sudanese-Ethiopian border in the face of the attacks and heavy bombardment. The sources added that the attackers exploited the deployment of the government forces in the eastern border area with Eritrea; these areas have been used as staging points by the opposition forces [...] (ME/2816 MED/14–15, 14 January 1997)

Republic of Sudan Radio, Omdurman, reported in Arabic on the same day:

The presidency of the republic issued a statement in the early hours of this morning declaring a mobilisation and alert of the official and popular bodies in the country to stand united in order to protect the faith and the country and deter the enemies of peace and humanity. The following is the text of the statement:

A statement from the presidency of the republic: [...] Our great people has been following the conspiracies being hatched against the country by the forces of injustice and arrogance, who are plotting conspiracies and intrigues. Some neighbouring countries are preparing for this role.

Sudan has always been patient and is trying to be wise in dealing with the matter in order to achieve good neighbourly relations and to abide by international agreements. Despite our great efforts to contain the situation, the forces of injustice and arrogance went ahead with the aggression. The forces of the enemies from Ethiopia have moved towards our eastern border in Kurmuk and Qaysan.

To this blatant aggression and unjust hostility there must be decisive and deterrent measures in order to protect our land and honour, preserve the dignity of the country and its citizens and repel the plots of the enemies and opportunists who have targeted our country's civilised orientation and our people's Islam and tolerance in this great month [Ramadan], the month of victories and triumphs.

By doing this we want to turn the attention of the African, Arab and Islamic world and international public opinion to the conspiracy which has begun against our country.

Therefore, the presidency of the republic declares a general mobilisation and alert of official and popular bodies so that they stand united in order to protect the faith and the country and deter the enemies of peace and humanity. God is great and honour is for Sudan. (ME/2816 MED/15, 14 January 1989)

Ethiopian Radio, in Amharic (the same day, 13 January), immediately refuted the accusation of aggression and criticized the *jihad* (holy war) talk of Khartoum:

A Foreign Ministry spokesman this evening said that the Sudanese accusation levelled against Ethiopia today, saying that Ethiopia had attacked two Sudanese border towns, was a typical false accusation.

The Sudanese government's complaint, soon after the Sudan People's Liberation Front announcement yesterday that it had liberated two Sudanese towns from the hands of the Sudanese government soldiers, was that Ethiopian forces had attacked its towns. This is an incitement to *jihad* and a ploy that makes others scapegoats for its internal problems.

The spokesman, who talked to the Ethiopian News Agency on the phone, said that Ethiopia had nothing whatsoever to do with the attack. The spokesman who said that the *jihad* called for by a Sudanese diplomat in Mogadishu recently was part of this familiar behaviour noted that an official statement would be issued very soon. (ME/2817 MED/15, 15 January 1997)

The next day, Sudan's national radio reported the government's call for an emergency meeting of the UN Security Council to examine its complaint against Ethiopia's aggression. Hassan Turabi, Speaker of the Sudanese National Assembly (and charismatic inspiration of the National Islamic Front, NIF) was also reported in the BBC summaries as speaking on 14 January, in fact on Radio Monte Carlo (Middle East), from Paris, in Arabic. In this broadcast he directly challenged Ethiopia over the airwaves, threatening to give arms to the refugee opponents of Ethiopia and Eritrea:

In an interview with Radio Monte Carlo, Dr Hasan al-Turabi, Speaker of the Sudanese National Assembly, admitted that the Sudan's People's Liberation Movement [SPLM] under John Garang had occupied several towns in the Blue Nile area with Ethiopia's help.

Turabi says that Sudan would help the Ethiopian and Eritrean opposition, which has taken refuge in Sudan, by giving them weapons in response to the assistance Ethiopia and Eritrea were offering to the Sudanese opposition. (ME/2817 MED/13, 15 January 1997)

Meanwhile the new NDA opposition radio from Asmara noted that some Sudanese airforce officers were refusing to carry out bombing raids in the southern Blue Nile. They repeated their call for a popular uprising, *intifadah*, in Khartoum, to exterminate the nefarious regime of the NIF. They also broadcast, in early February, an appeal for aid to be sent to the war-hit east, where they claimed 600,000 people were in a catastrophic situation as a result of the actions of government troops and bombing raids. This broadcast was in Arabic, while Sudan television was appealing for aid for those displaced by the 'Ethiopian aggression' in English. Turabi, back in the Sudan and near the eastern war zone, again raised the political temperature by blaming this aggression on the 'minority Tigrays' in Ethiopia. This provocative claim was made in the context of an address to Islamic worshippers in the threatened town of Damazin, to the north of Kurmuk. Broadcast on the national radio station, it included a call for *jihad*, holy war against the infidel. Let me finish with a final quote from this broadcast, in Arabic on 8 February 1997:

> The speaker of the National Assembly, Dr Hassan Abdullah al-Turabi, has stressed that international laws guarantee Sudan the right to deter aggression and repulse enemies.
> Dr Turabi said in a press statement that the minority Tigrays in power in Ethiopia should have been wiser, considering the fact that the Sudan hosted thousands of Ethiopian opposition. He however said that Sudan had no desire for this option since it would have fatal consequences for Africa.
> Concerning the initiative of Shaykh Zayid Bin Sultan Al Nuhayyan [president of the UAE] to reconcile Sudanese [political] forces, Dr Turabi stressed that Sudan would reveal the truth of the situation and prove that the minority Tigrays were guilty of the crime of aggression.
> The speaker of the National Assembly made the remarks while addressing worshippers at Damazin town [in the Blue Nile State, near the border with Ethiopia], yesterday morning. He stressed that the aggression was instigated by arrogant powers who did not care about what happens between neighbours. He called all people of Sudan to *jihad* and (?to support) the *mujahidin*, saying that the National Salvation [Revolution] brought religion into public life, and revived the tradition of *jihad*. He said past regimes had lost the Islamic *shari'ah*, prostrated themselves before foreign powers and humiliated the homeland. (ME/2840 MED/10, 11 February 1997)

We have come a long way from the homely proverbs of the mid-1980s vernacular broadcasts. What are local communities, whether in the north or south, to make of appeals like Turabi's? What are displaced people, in camps or shanty towns, to make of it? There is no word in Bari, or Latuka, for *jihad*. For a large proportion of the Sudanese people, including ordinary Muslims, broadcasts like this must seem designed not so much to court their individual support in a political struggle as to inspire a fear that hostility is being organized and directed against them on a collective basis.

As of early 1999, the SPLA are still in Kurmuk, and there is no prospect of a military counter-move. The combined forces of the NDA have been able to hold not only Kurmuk and Geissan but other parts of the eastern Sudan. The ironies of the current situation in Kurmuk were reflected in an article by the well known politician-in-exile and journalist Bona Malwal, who visited Kurmuk in mid-August 1997. He was a guest specifically of Commander Malik Agar, originally from the Gamk people of the Ingessana Hills just to the north of this region. Malwal reports:

> I was pleasantly surprised to discover the determination of the people in and around Kurmuk to remain free of Khartoum's administrative stranglehold ... Kurmuk has been captured and overrun by the SPLA in the past ... Back in 1987 ... the government in Khartoum whipped up a racial hysteria claiming that black African hordes from the South had overrun a Northern Arab town. Observers could have been forgiven for accepting such hysteria until they found out the truth about the people of Kurmuk. The people of Southern Blue Nile are very much a black African people and are definitely non-Arab. (Malwal 1997: 8)

He explains that while many are Muslims, they do not accept the policies of the present NIF regime. The regime had recently constructed a new and elegant regional headquarters at Kurmuk, where everything had been inscribed with Koranic verses. The SPLA had secularized everything in the building, which now flies the SPLA/M flag, and are rebuilding the civil administration. Malwal reports that the northern merchants (*jallaba*) who used to dominate the market have all gone, but that a steady stream of refugees is entering the town from the north, from the NIF-controlled areas. Meanwhile, there are many thousands of internally displaced, as well as those who have crossed the frontier again to seek asylum in the Assosa district (Malwal 1997: 9).

It seems unlikely that the various displaced rural communities are really of much interest in themselves to any radio station these days. Many in them must feel in some way that they still belong to places like Kurmuk and its district, and even that places like Kurmuk belong to them. In some cases at least, the refugee communities have more access to modern facilities, including transistor radios, than they ever had before, and are avid monitors of the multiple voices of the air. But these voices are rarely now addressed to the rural, the displaced and the marginal. The shouting goes on above their heads, even when it refers to the places that used to belong to them.

References

Allen, Tim (ed.) (1996) *In Search of Cool Ground: War, Flight and Homecoming in Northeast Africa*, London and Trenton, NJ: James Currey and Africa World Press. (For specific information on the war in the Blue Nile and its aftermath for the Uduk people, see Wendy James's contribution to this volume, 'Uduk Resettlement: Dreams and Realities', 182–202.)

BBC, *Summary of World Broadcasts: Middle East series*, 1985–present.

Feierman, Steven (1990) *Peasant Intellectuals: Anthropology and History in Tanzania*, Madison, Wisconsin: University of Wisconsin Press.

James, Wendy (1997) 'The names of fear: history, memory and the ethnography of feeling among Uduk refugees', *Journal of the Royal Anthropological Institute* NS 3(2): 115–31.

Malwal, Bona (1997) 'In Kurmuk the thoughts are all about defeating the NIF regime', *Sudan Democratic Gazette* VIII, 88 (September): 8–9.

16
Local Radio
Conflict Moderation

The Case of Sierra Leone
PAUL RICHARDS

Introduction

During the cold war the African airwaves were alive with shortwave broadcasts subsidized by the contending super-powers and their allies. Since then African conflict has changed and, with it, the role of radio broadcasting. This chapter focuses on local broadcasting. Sometimes local broadcasting is a problem. For instance, it became a tool of factional violence in Rwanda (see Carver, Chapter 14). My chapter alludes to the possibility of a constructive role for local broadcasting. I focus in particular on local radio in Sierra Leone, drawing attention not so much to its role in facilitating inter-factional dialogue (an issue pursued elsewhere, cf. Richards 1997) but in helping sustain a rudimentary framework of shared values and social commitments in circumstances of otherwise near complete social collapse and extreme political violence.

New political violence in Africa

The Cold War inflicted several messy proxy wars on Africa. Post-cold war armed conflict remains a fact of life in several African countries. There is consensus neither about how these conflicts are best explained nor about how they might be resolved.

Most commentators are agreed, however, that the Clausewitzian notion of war as a clearcut struggle between broadly equivalent competing parties has to be modified or abandoned. Intense controversy surrounds an alternative: the neo-Malthusian idea that continuing conflict is an unthinking response to population pressure and resource competition. A third (cultural) ontology of war is central to my argument below that certain forms of (forcible) social exclusion foster a secular sectarianism, and that crossing the boundary between sect and society becomes a flashpoint for violence and its escalation.

The conflicts in Algeria and Sierra Leone are both instances of the kind of violent dynamic I have in mind. For violence to be mitigated social norms have to re-converge. But how can this happen when terror ends all forms of social interaction between the enclaved perpetrators of violence and a wider civil society? Local radio (as my case study will suggest) may keep alive some transactional possibilities even where the gulf of terror appears unbridgeably wide.

Radio and reconstruction

International agencies are currently quite keen on radio as a tool to promote good governance and post-conflict recovery. The British government aid programme supports a number of radio soap operas broadcast over World Service frequencies, one in particular – 'New home, new life' – aimed at war-torn communities in Afghanistan. The French-based Fondation Hirondelle established a radio station in the Central African Lakes region to counter earlier uses of the medium to stir up ethnic hatred in Rwanda, and opened Star Radio in Monrovia in 1997 to provide neutral national election coverage (the only other national radio station in Liberia, owned by Charles Taylor, was blatant in its support of Taylor's presidential election campaign).

Without intending to devalue such efforts, my interest in this chapter lies elsewhere. I have two basic kinds of question. How is local radio broadcasting used in African war zones when it is not didactic or propagandistic? And what part if any might such broadcasting play in dispelling the kind of violent enclavization witnessed in conflicts such as the civil wars in Algeria and Sierra Leone?

Requests in time of war

My chapter is built around a case study of a small locally-owned commercial FM station broadcasting to the central Sierra Leonean town of Bo and surrounding districts, and is particularly concerned with understanding its output and impact during and after the attack on Bo by units of the rebel RUF/SL begun on 27 December 1994, and in subsequent local peace-making efforts in 1996–7.

What is interesting about Kiss 104 FM Bo is that, unlike its Liberian counterpart, it is not owned by one of the contending parties to the conflict. Its rationale, as a commercial station, is to make money for its owners and, within the scope of the limited freedom enjoyed by the media in Sierra Leone at the time, it was prepared to open its airwaves to anyone prepared to pay. Its main business was to play requests for a small fee. The entry price of a handful of Leones was all that was necessary to secure a song and the reading out of a short message of dedication.

These requests and dedications often reflected local attitudes to the war. Some songs were chosen to preach peace and reconciliation. Other messages came from the rebel side of the conflict, expressing concern with the morale of isolated fighters in the bush. How much of this material made it on to the airwaves is unclear since, fearing army retribution, broadcasters seem to have weeded out those too obviously stemming from rebel sources. But I present an instance of one such message below.

Kiss FM Bo also accepted other more large-scale patronage, notably support from VOA to re-broadcast its news (replacing the more popular BBC World Service bulletins), and in 1996 was prepared to sell airtime to local groups with ideas about mediating between civilians, the army and the rebel groups in and around Bo.

To understand the (admittedly very fragmentary) observations concerning local broadcasting in a war zone sketched below, we have first to pay attention to the general dynamic of the Sierra Leonean conflict. I make no apology for devoting considerable space to unfolding this story, for otherwise it is impossible to understand the ways in which the gaps opened up between contending social worlds and value systems that broadcasting continues to bridge.

War in Sierra Leone

Civil war began in Sierra Leone on 23 March 1991 with the crossborder incursion into Kailahun and Pujehun Districts of two small contingents from an armed dissident organization calling itself the Revolutionary United Front (RUF/SL). Led by Foday Saybana Sankoh, a charismatic former Sierra Leone army corporal cashiered and jailed for participation in a coup plot against the All Party Congress (APC) president, Siaka Stevens, in the 1970s and later trained in guerrilla warfare in Libya, the RUF/SL claimed to have launched a military campaign to free Sierra Leone from the tyranny of one-party rule by the APC.

Imitating the movement's backer, the Liberian warlord Charles Taylor, and probably using Taylor's French-supplied satellite phone link in Gbarnga, Sankoh soon phoned the BBC Africa Service in London to explain RUF aims. Interviewed by Robin White he proclaimed an ambition to reach Freetown to deliver a free and fair multiparty election. He denied presidential ambitions.

At the time the national broadcasting service, SLBS, hardly reached beyond the Freetown area. BBC Africa Service broadcasts were the main means through which provincial citizens followed events in their own country. Whereas Charles Taylor proved himself a master of broadcast misinformation over BBC, Sankoh – his apparent protégé – was largely ignored by Sierra Leonean listeners. They widely assumed the so-called RUF/SL was no more than a small crossborder destabilization effort undertaken at Taylor's behest and intended to hit at Sierra Leone for supporting the largely Nigerian-dominated peacekeeping forces opposed to Taylor's interest in Liberia.

Sankoh claimed support among the Mende-speaking populations of the border region, and even to be fighting in the interests of the recently revived Sierra Leone People's Party (SLPP), once the main party reflecting the Mende political interest in Sierra Leone. Radio listeners in Bo dismissed this claim as nonsense. 'The man speaks English with a Temne accent,' they said, 'let him invade his own part of the country'. Indeed it later transpired that Sankoh was a Temne from Tonkolili District in northern Sierra Leone.

The composition of Sankoh's force, and whether indeed at that stage Sankoh was its leader, or spokesman for a collective leadership, are still matters of controversy. Some of the prime movers in the rebellion were secondary-school-level unemployed youth radicalized by street life in Freetown and contact with student Green Book study clubs. Others were frustrated young men driven into economic exile in Liberia, some with an ambiguous border-zone national background. Yet others seem to have been hardened cadres of Taylor's militia, perhaps psychopaths Taylor was glad to be rid of. Clearly some RUF/SL commanders were all too familiar with the use of atrocity as a tool of social control.

The initial campaign was a pincer movement intended to control the diamond-rich central and eastern portion of Sierra Leone before the RUF/SL gathered recruits to march on Freetown. The RUF/SL planned to make Bo, the second city of Sierra Leone and provincial capital of southern Sierra Leone, its provisional headquarters while training a 'people's army' of recruits press-ganged into service from the ramshackle schools and sweated-labour diamond mining camps of the border region.

The campaign failed for a number of reasons. Liberian-style atrocity put much of the civilian population to flight, including many of the young people the RUF/SL saw as its natural constituency. The RUF/SL garnered very little popular support in the border region, except among the wildest and most deracinated 'sand-sand' boys working (often clandestine) forest alluvial diamond mines in conditions of great hardship for corrupt officials of the one-party state. The key strategic army base at Daru was strongly defended with the help of a contingent of well-armed Guinean soldiers fighting under the terms of a mutual defence pact negotiated by Stevens and Sekou Touré. Daru, key to the border-zone communications, never capitulated, and as a result the main towns of the south and east – Bo and Kenema – remained in government hands throughout the war, despite periodic infiltration and surprise attack. Conditions changed along the Liberian side of the border with the emergence in 1992 of a strongly anti-Taylor militia, the United Liberation Movement for Democracy in Liberia (ULIMO). ULIMO was instrumental in driving out the RUF/SL from Pujehun District, and some ULIMO recruits later worked with the Sierra Leone government army as 'special forces'. Finally, a coup in April 1992, partly led by young officers from the war front with family connections in the Liberian border zone, ushered in the National Provisional Ruling Council to end APC one-party rule. The NPRC originally intimated to the RUF/SL leadership the possibility of a power-sharing agreement to end the war, but capital city interests behind a personable young Krio chairman, Valentine Strasser, prevailed upon the new regime to go it alone and crush the rebel force.

The NPRC vastly enlarged the army, recruiting from among the street drop-outs the RUF/SL had intended as the backbone of its planned 'people's army'. Others of these young recruits were under-age irregulars whose parents and patrons were butchered by the RUF/SL in the 1991 border zone invasion. These 'border guard' under-age irregulars became some of the most effective fighting forces ranged against the RUF/SL.

It is estimated that the great majority of RUF/SL forces were also children or young teenagers. Most RUF/SL combatants were made by capture. That few ever succeeded in leaving the movement has to be explained first by the traumatization of capture, equivalent to the kind of initiation experience through which so-called secret societies in the region break the child's attachment to the immediate family and turn him or her into a youthful citizen loyal to a wider social group, and second by the unwise actions of government troops in summarily executing rebel captives (first documented by Amnesty International (1992) but a feature of the war to this day). Civilian lynching of rebels and rebel suspects has also been a regular occurrence (for photographic evidence see a picture published in the London *Observer*, 10 May 1998).

Rebel captives, marked on their bodies with RUF/SL tattoos or scars, soon realized that escape was a death warrant. Many became dedicated hard-core combatants fiercely loyal to a movement which initially 'stole' them from their home communities. Fifteen-year-old fought fifteen-year-old using the same forest-zone ambush tactics, and the war came to a standstill with now sizeable RUF/SL units enclaved in the bush.

The forest is rich in diamonds and there are always dealers willing to supply fresh arms and other necessities. The RUF/SL forest enclaves thus remain indefinitely viable, and not even the relatively well-trained Nigerian troops of the West African peace-keeping force (ECOMOG) can dislodge them.

The NPRC regime was replaced by the democratically elected government of Ahmad Tejan-Kabbah in early 1996, but despite a fine-sounding peace agreement signed between Kabbah and the RUF/SL on 30 November 1996 the war on the ground never halted. For its own political reasons the Kabbah government used the ceasefire and peace agreement to stand down an army dominated by officers and other ranks thought to be loyal to older political patrons (in the APC and NPRC), and chose instead to weld various local civil defence militias into a single national Civil Defence Force (CDF) to continue to carry the attack against the RUF/SL.

The policy failed. Army officers mutinied in May 1997 in protest at the army's marginalization from the peace process and its rumoured punitive dismemberment by demobilization and, in a risky move perhaps indicative of some desperation on the part of the mutineers, invited the RUF/SL to abandon its bush positions to join a government of national unity. After a period of near anarchy under this unstable junta the RUF/SL, together with some of its new-found army friends, retreated into the forest in the face of concerted action by ECOMOG and CDF mercenary-supported forces to recover Freetown and restore the Kabbah regime to power (February 1998 onwards).

The RUF/SL has always seen its natural constituency as dispossessed youth. Its values are dominated by egalitarian attitudes, some of which reflect the simple meritocratic calculus of primary-school life. It eschews tribalism and sectarianism, and imposes Krio, the lingua franca of the younger generation. Its revolutionary talk derives more from Reggae than Marx. Sankoh, like Pol Pot (the Khmer Rouge leader Saloth Sar), was trained as a radio technician, and young RUF cadres are proud of their ability to use solar-powered field radios to sustain communications in the bush (RUF/SL 1995). This enthusiasm for communications technology first became evident when RUF/SL commanders burst in on various mission and development project shortwave frequencies in March and April 1991. Since then radio communications equipment has been high on the list of items targeted in RUF attacks.

From the outset the movement craved media access; many Sierra Leoneans laughed at Sankoh's first stumbling BBC broadcasts, in which the leader breathlessly repeated his demand 'I must have an international press conference'. British diplomats later vetoed a plan to supply the RUF/SL with satellite telecommunications to negotiate an end to a hostage crisis centred on two VSO volunteers captured (probably without prior intention) in a raid on Kabala in November 1994. But until it gained international television coverage in 1995 in return for releasing the British and other hostages the movement became ever more introverted, and with this introversion went rising levels of terror violence aimed at dirt-poor rural civilians, seen in some way as the irritating symptom of an utterly corrupted society tolerant of internationally scandalous rural poverty in the midst of untold diamond wealth. Unable to reach the levers of patrimonial power responsible for this distressing inequality, the RUF/SL chose instead to tear the supine civil body politic limb from limb. Driven back into the forest during the fighting to restore the Kabbah government, the RUF/SL is now thought to be stronger than ever. Communicating through looted cell phones – and recently resupplied with weapons, probably from diamond networks in Guinea and Liberia – the movement has also resumed its horrendous atrocities against civilians.

Since 1996 the RUF/SL has attempted to justify these actions as vengeance for systematic ceasefire violations by the CDF and, as yet unsubstantiated, mercenary atrocities. Few RUF/SL prisoners have been taken since the major push by mercenary-assisted CDF that led to the routing of the main forest bases of the RUF/SL in eastern Sierra Leone in September–October 1996. CDF leaders say RUF/SL combatants are 'shy' to come to town. South African mercenaries have, allegedly, been dumping RUF/SL captives from helicopters overflying the Gola Forest.

A combination of the initial unprovoked violence against civilians by the RUF/SL, RUF/SL ruthlessness in making escape impossible, army and mercenary extra-judicial killing of prisoners and civilian revenge, has driven a wedge between civil society and the RUF/SL enclaves in the bush. Elsewhere, I have argued that this has accelerated a tendency towards a secular sectarianism (Richards 1998). RUF/SL values reflect a complete distrust of the values of patrimonial hierarchy in the wider society. Violent egalitarianism takes its place.

Unable to relate to the abhorrent values of an egalitarian enclave culture, or understand under what conditions of violent dislocation they have been instituted, the rest of Sierra Leone and the outside world makes the mistake of thinking that abhorrent values are no values at all. Opponents thus regularly underestimate the strength and determination of the movement.

British involvement in the restoration of the Kabbah government, a laudable project, has been marred by the tendency to assume that a show of force would quickly end a 'rebellion without cause'. This is to act in ignorance of the anthropological insight that values and institutions develop together. However misbegotten, RUF/SL violence against civilians is not simply random or meaningless violence. It is indeed calculated to express a point of view.

Nothing could be clearer from the pattern of atrocities against villagers in the north of the country following the ECOMOG action to restore Kabbah. By June 1998 reports were emerging of villagers being subjected to the RUF/SL 'lottery of life' in which villagers were forced to draw lots to determine who would live, who would die, who would lose what limb or what body part.

Anthropological theorists of enclave culture have pointed out that the lottery is often taken as a regulatory device where hierarchical selection procedures are deemed to have failed (see Douglas 1992, 1993). Time and again, RUF/SL cadres complain that their educational life chances were ruined through no fault of their own (by corrupt political allocation of educational opportunity or through loss of sponsorship). Having been ploughed under – by what they see as a politically corrupt educational lottery – they believe they are rising to avenge themselves upon normal society. Through this exemplary violence they randomize life itself. The international community vacuously deplores this meaningless atrocity. It might do better to deplore it from the standpoint of having understood what it was intended to signify.

Voices in the wilderness?

The picture painted is of two alien life worlds, and the great difficulty of forging shared understandings across a hazardous gap. The enclaves cannot be finished by force. But civilian groups in no-man's-land are sitting targets.

In 1996 some women in Kenema decided that the only way to make peace was to meet rebels face to face and treat them as fellow humans, not monsters; but the meeting ended in disaster, with several of the women gunned down. Was this sabotage by government elements unwilling for the war to end, or a step too far too quickly for a group of rebels paranoid about being sucked into an ambush?

Social theory of the enclave predicts that boundary crossing between life-worlds and value systems will always be hazardous for individuals. The first thing to be said about radio broadcasting is that it carries human messages across the gap without immediately incurring dangers. In exploring this point it will then become apparent that more is required than simply carrying a voice across a gap, bringing us to a discussion of local radio in social interaction and value formation.

We know already that the RUF/SL is very broadcasting-centred. The beginning of the peace process was when the International Red Cross and the conciliation agency International Alert reached RUF/SL camps to negotiate hostage release, and the Ghanaian journalist (and public relations spokesman for Charles Taylor) Akyaba Addai-Seiboh, on contract to International Alert, filmed television footage of RUF/SL camp life and the hostage release. Addai-Seiboh's actions in making this film were highly controversial, but it seems that it was a major factor, from the RUF/SL side, in allowing the hostage negotiations to proceed and, with the confidence thus established, for International Alert to arrange the process leading to the Abidjan peace accords.

This material was extracted and shown internationally. In the UK it appeared on Channel 4 News. Typical of the bad luck dogging peace efforts in Sierra Leone, the first planned screening was knocked off the schedules by the 'resignation' of then British prime minister, John Major, a peculiar non-event intended to instill discipline in his divided party. When eventually shown, the footage was effective in establishing that Sankoh really existed (a fact contested by the NPRC) and that the RUF was a considerably well-organized bush insurgency of children and youth.

Radios were a priority item for cadres in the bush. In the early days of the ceasefire (around February 1996) villagers in Bo North reported that groups had stopped killing civilians. If they apprehended someone by the way a first concern was to acquire torch batteries for use in radio sets.

The movement in the bush monitored any scrap of information it could glean about Sierra Leone from the radio, and when it could, tried to get its own point of view across via spokespersons phoning the BBC Africa Service in London from Abidjan or Accra.

It is against this background that we turn now to consider the specific uses being made of local radio broadcasting by civilians and rebels, apparently conscious that their life-worlds had radically diverged, with disastrous consequences, but still imbued with the faint hope that one day the talking would have to resume.

Kiss 104 FM and the battle for Bo

The main targets of the initial RUF/SL campaign in 1991 were the two provincial capitals of eastern and southern Sierra Leone, Bo and Kenema. Bo was principal target for the group attacking from across the south-east of the country. Both army and police Special Security Division forces (SSDs) had withdrawn from the territory; chiefs received letters predicting the dates on which their settlements would be attacked and the consequences of resistance, and the RUF entered towns and villages largely unopposed. The Liberian irregulars never hesitated to make good these predictions; captured chiefs, traders and minor government officials were brutally murdered in public beheadings, village youngsters often being forced to take part. Teachers and health workers were given the option of being killed or joining the RUF/SL.

A picture of the movement and its aims was beginning to build up in Bo during the first two weeks of April 1991 from accounts of people fleeing the RUF/SL advance across Pujehun District. The atmosphere of incipient panic was heightened by expatriate aid and humanitarian agency evacuations triggered by rumours of imminent attack. The second of these evacuations followed a report that the Bo authorities had received a letter announcing the RUF/SL would attack the town on 26 April.

President Momoh in Freetown dithered, fearing that the rebellion was indeed a rising of the Mende people orchestrated by the renascent SLPP. On 24–5 April thousands of Guineans and northerners involved in the diamond trade, deciding no reinforcements were forthcoming, evacuated the town, chartering every available truck and taxi to take them to the northern provincial headquarters, Makeni, and to Pamelap on the Guinean border.

The BBC Africa Service 'Focus on Africa' programme on the evening of 25 April carried an item by a BBC Freetown-based stringer who had interviewed a truck driver fleeing Bo, who assured him that 'Bo town was empty'. The item was greeted with derision by the 40,000 or so citizens of Bo who had nowhere else to hide.

The evening and night were busy with preparations by a variety of youth leaders and Poro Society officers to mobilize a makeshift defence. This was among the first stirrings of a commitment to civil defence that has become such an important feature of the war in Sierra Leone. The view of these organizers was that the RUF/SL was tiny, and Bo a large and complex town; the RUF/SL's Liberian mercenaries might rule villages by terror, but they would be unable to control Bo so long as the citizens were determined to resist.

If the letter was sent the attack never came. The RUF/SL knew it could only attempt to take over the town if it first temporarily scattered its panic-stricken and demoralized citizenry in the bush.

The 'Focus on Africa' broadcast was something of a turning point. People began openly to question the capacity of broadcasters, located in a studio in central London, to cross-check facts relating to events in central Sierra Leone when they had no better link than a stringer retailing truck-driver tittle-tattle in Freetown. Radio interviews with Charles Taylor and Foday Sankoh were regarded with heightened scepticism, and civilians became more alert to the potential uses of rumour (in Krio, *den se*) as a weapon of war. Bo was not attacked again until 27 December 1994.

Further RUF/SL advance through Sierra Leone during 1991 was checked, mainly by Liberian 'special forces' opposed to Charles Taylor and government army units reinforced with local irregulars, and the rebel movement became enclaved in forest fastnesses mainly in the eastern part of the country.

NPRC military rule replaced Momoh's one-party APC regime in April 1992. Good satellite telephone communications came to Bo and Kenema; and the BBC Africa Service recruited stringers in both places to report developments in the war more directly. The locally-owned Kiss FM 104 went on air in 1994, broadcasting from Kandi Mountain, site of a presidential lodge constructed for Siaka Stevens on the north-western outskirts of Bo.

Bo was supplied with reliable 24-hour electricity from a Chinese-built hydro-electric plant at Dodo and a Danish-built back-up heavy-fuel electricity-generating plant, and FM broadcasting quickly gathered a large and loyal local audience untroubled by high battery costs. The station's official range is about 35 kilometres, but in fact it could be regularly heard in Kenema in the east and the important Sierra Rutile mining complex in the south.

The NPRC had originally offered the RUF/SL an amnesty in 1992 but ceasefire offers came to nothing. By the end of 1993 regular army (RSLMF) units and the 'border guard' irregulars were poised to drive its leadership back into Liberia. But the NPRC was itself divided. Soldiers were making money from the war and some were keen to see conflict continue. This provided the RUF/SL with a chance to rebuild, by mining in the forest and exchanging rough diamonds for army weapons supplied by corrupt army officers, sometimes using the ruse of a prearranged bogus ambush.

The RUF/SL had meanwhile trained and thoroughly indoctrinated some 5,000 or so young people from the border regions to fight under the movement's surviving hard-core 'commando' leadership. The RUF/SL resumed its pattern of terror attacks on soft civilian targets, but now stretching the army by ranging these attacks as widely as possible across the country from a new series of forward bases. These included the Kangari Hills north of Bo, overlooking the main road to the Kono diamond fields, and the Malal Hills, a steep and wooded inselberg site well placed for strikes on the main roads from Makeni and Bo into Freetown. The forest camps were surrounded by so-called ideology zones where the RUF/SL kept the local population cowed and in a state of continuous terror through atrocity and systematic hostage-taking. On the threat that a family member held hostage would be killed if they did not return with the required items, civilians would be sent down to Bo and Kenema to shop for the rebel leadership.

Civilians in ideology zones were forced to grow food or to work in diamond pits in conditions of *de facto* slavery. Having entered into corrupt deals with some army officers, the RUF/SL also knew how to turn the growing disenchantment of civilians with the soldiery to its own advantage: capturing or requesting latest army-pattern fatigues for its own combatants, and carrying out raids dressed as government soldiers, so feeding the local notion of the 'sobel' (soldier by day, rebel by night).

It was such a raid that brought Bo under attack for a second time, beginning on 27 December 1994. In civilian dress, an RUF/SL unit of about 100 fighters (including some female combatants) first infiltrated the large refugee camp at Gondama south of Bo while the defending Nigerian soldiers, and many of the camp inmates, were at a Christmas carnival in Bo. The infiltrators claimed to be young people from Pujehun visiting their relatives for the holiday. They then donned RSLMF battle fatigues and unpacked weapons, putting the camp population to flight, before setting off to approach Bo in a semi-circle from the west, and mounting a dawn raid on Bo from the old railway line village of Mattru-on-the-Rails at dawn on 27 December. Determined to preach their cause to early morning crowds of civilians, RUF/SL cadres were confronted by rapidly organized civil defence opposition and put to flight. Several RUF/SL fighters were beaten to death by enraged and increasingly self-confident civilians, before army reinforcements engaged and drove off the remnant during a mid-morning bombardment. The only time Kiss FM 104 fell silent was for several hours on the morning of the attack, Kandi Mountain being not far from the army line of fire.

As the rebels advanced in the days preceding the attack, disc jockeys ingeniously combined their regular output of requests with messages counselling peace, followed by 'bottom-drawer' reggae songs with appropriate lyrics. These items, not normally part of the station's play list, were clearly aimed at the advancing rebel forces, reflecting a shrewd understanding of the revolutionary consciousness of a cadre formed more by street life and the lyrics of Bob Marley than by the writings of Karl Marx (see below).

A three-way stand-off then ensued, with rebel forces regrouping to attack softer targets in the Bo environs, the CDF imposing its own curfew on the army for several nights in Bo township (at least one looting soldier was lynched), and an army struggling to reassert its authority from brigade headquarters on the outskirts of Bo.

Liaison across the lines

The 1994 battle for Bo was the context in which agents for army–civilian liaison in Bo began actively to exploit the potential of radio: to mend fences between the RSLMF and Bo citizenry, and to open up lines of contact with the ever more violently unstable and destructive RUF/SL.

Central to the idea of liaison, with all its inherent ambiguity, and of the use of local radio as a tool of liaison, was the judgement on the part of some elements within both army and the Bo town civilian population that the war was a product of a diamond political economy no longer readily controllable through traditional resources, the ethnic politics of chiefs and 'strangers' so well described for the Kono diamond districts in a book by William Reno (1995). Not only were the combatant forces made up of deracinated, detribalized youths, many well below the age for official military service, but the battle for Bo town was also a struggle for the loyalty of young people from all parts of the country attracted to the town by the diamond trade or educational opportunity.

The RUF/SL got into difficulties on the outskirts of Bo on 27 December 1994 because it was so convinced that, as a radicalized movement of socially excluded youth, it only had to preach its message to the many similarly deracinated and much put-upon young people of Bo town for them to rally to the cause. But others, having long realized that in Bo any civil defence strategy had to be based on youth rather than ethnic mobilization, had got there before them. Rural districts had already mobilized young people into traditionally oriented hunter militia (a mobilization taken forward on a much larger scale by the Kabbah government's deputy minister of defence, Sandhurst-trained Capt (ret'd) Samuel Hinga Norman, regent chief of Telu Bongor south of Bo). The civil defence movement within Bo itself involved many young people born outside Mende country, and was centred on pursuits such as soccer and other sports activities, and membership of trans-ethnic carnival societies such as the Paddle Masquerade. Some of the active workers in this field were also well known on the street drug scene. Others had links with army intelligence and with traders' and transporters' groups operating across check-points into the rebel-held enclave areas. There was an active interest in deflating the conflict by furthering common youth enthusiasms crossing the divide between town and rebel enclave. And for this radio was an excellent medium given that direct contact was dangerous.

The Mende singer Steady Bongo (Lansana Sheriff) had the hit of the moment coinciding with the RUF/SL attack in December 1994. The radio played the singer repeatedly, and householders signalled their defiance of the RUF/SL by dancing Christmas and New Year away to the beat of 'Eh-Eh-Eehel'. But at the same time as the RUF/SL cadres were expressing utter disdain for all traditional values, burning every village they entered, this song was common property through which they proclaimed some kind of continuing commitment to the idea of Sierra Leone. It is said that when the RUF/SL units regrouped and turned their attention to halting bauxite and rutile mining operations south of the Bo, the main sources of revenue for the NPRC regime, they wound up the rutile mine's canteen amplifiers so that Steady Bongo's song could be heard for miles around.

Where other norms fail

In 1995–6 the idea of a single national heritage within which there was space for rebel and orthodox civil society hung by a thread.

In Freetown the NPRC were busy denying the existence of Foday Sankoh and any such movement as the RUF/SL. The RUF/SL stepped up its campaign of hostage-taking and destruction, laying waste to large swathes of rural Sierra Leone, but not yet willing to come out of the bush and declare a stand, fearful that entry to any peace process would lead to it being rounded up and destroyed.

International media access, as described above, did facilitate the beginnings of a peace process. But this was significantly complicated by a democratic transition ousting the NPRC, and then by the new government's decision to try to reactivate the tradition of indirect rule inherited from the British: assisting the 'traditional' rural hunter militia forces with weapons and mercenary back-up in the hope of overwhelming the beleaguered RUF/SL during peace negotiations. This tipped the balance away from the tentative youth-to-youth strategies of conflict moderation, based on ambitious plans to provide access by competing parties to radio airtime, being proposed by street-level youth organizers in Bo (Richards 1996). But subsequent events suggest that because of demographic and social change within the country, neo-traditionalism is far from adequate to deal with the youth crisis that lies at the heart of the continued defiance of the RUF/SL.

The RUF/SL, driven back into the bush by Nigerian-led ECOMOG military action in February 1998, is re-emerging as a very serious military threat. RUF/SL cadres were strong enough to fight an eight-hour battle with Nigerian forces at the crucial Mile 47 road junction approaching Freetown on 16 June 1998; the Nigerians were forced to retreat. RUF/SL atrocity against rural civilians has reached new heights of brutality. The international community condemns this brutality but (as in Algeria) is incapable of understanding what has caused such an utter breakdown in values.

There is now no escape from the fact that RUF/SL rebels and the rest of Sierra Leonean society live in utterly distinct worlds dominated by completely different norms and standards. With the failure both of the peace process to bring in the RUF/SL from the bush, and also of the mercenary-backed traditional hunter militia strategy to wipe out the rebel enclaves where they stood, there is scope for a third approach based on the enclave social theory alluded to above.

As noted, this theory predicts that – where radical egalitarian enclaves have formed – re-establishing cooperative links with wider society is a matter of great difficulty. Individuals attempting to cross boundaries between enclave and wider society are branded defectors or infiltrators and their lives may be at risk, as seen in the case of the Kenema women's peace initiative already described.

Yet, as my analysis insists, RUF/SL enclave society has not been formed by choice but by circumstances and, since continued existence of the enclave threatens pathological violence, there is a strong case for seeking ways to let the enclavists off the hook.

Individualist theories of social agency offers little help. If any boundary-crossing contact is likely to prove highly dangerous for individual negotiators then resort to armed defence seems reasonable. But this triggers a vicious circle. The Kabbah government's strategy, of supporting hunter militia civil defence action to undermine the RUF/SL even while peace negotiations were taking place, first began to bite in mid-1996. The RUF/SL then carried out some particularly appalling massacres of defenceless civilians in the isolated northern Kamajei chiefdom. These massacres, they explained, were their way of revenging what they saw as unprovoked hunter militia attacks.

Yet just prior to these attacks some of the RUF/SL combatants in the area had waylaid an itinerant rice trader and sent him back to Bo with a radio request (reproduced as Appendix below), and insisted (a small but significant detail) on providing him with the Leones to pay for the dedication. In other words, they considered a radio request a legitimate transaction across the boundary between enclave and wider society demanding honest payment (this from young RUF/SL cadres equally capable of hacking off the legs of merchants they had apprehended). The trader was too scared to put in the request, and later nearly lost his house as an alleged rebel collaborator. But who knows what the effect might have been in averting the subsequent massacres had the perpetrators received back, via their pocket radios, this token that they were not alone in the world – that even enclavists remained included in the trivial, everyday, domestic Sierra Leonean routine of a dedication read out over the radio before the playing of one of the latest hits.

Conclusion

The young people of the RUF/SL are too strong and too desperate to be left in the bush. But it is equally apparent that the movement, however bizarre its values appear, cannot readily be divided by surrender inducements. However much the rest of the world may deplore their collective values, RUF/SL cadres are clear that defectors are guilty of betraying a collectivity. It is my prediction that, if violence is to be brought under control, a search for solutions based on an approach to the collectivity will have to be made. If picking off the movement's members one by one is not an option then re-convergence between the collective values of the enclave and of the wider society must be sought. There are precious few areas of shared social understanding upon which to try to build. Reliance by both enclave and civil society on listening to local radio, a shared enthusiasm for the popular culture it mediates, and the transactionalism of the broadcast dedication, are among the few resources with which local peace-makers might begin their work.

Appendix: RUF combatants' radio request

Text of a hand-written request for a hit record by South African musician Shaka Bundu to be played on Bo Radio Kiss 104 FM, for a group of RUF combatants operating in the northern half of Kamajei Chiefdom, Moyamba District, April 1996.

From [RUF] 6th Batt., Yeima.
South Africa New Relies [sic, i.e. release]
Revolutionary United Front of Sierra Leone

Subject – Request
From – The Northern Jungle
To – All RUF Freedom Fighters

NAMES (1) Rebel Marley – Commander (Patrick Samai)
              (2) RUF Cobra (Ambush Commander)
              (3) Braima S. Momoh (Arm [sic.] specialist)
              (4) Mohamed Musa
              (5) Sgt Tatika
              (6) Samuel Johnson
              (7) James Musa (Down the war)
              (8) Peleh Boy (Tee boy)
              (9) Justine Braima (the wanted man)
              (10) Sgt Kiloh

Meny [sic] greetings to all Brothers and Sisters
I am your Son Rebel Marley OK! [crossed out]

References

Amnesty International (1992) *The Extrajudicial Execution of Suspected Rebels and Collaborators*, London: Index AFR 51/02/92.

Douglas, Mary (1992) *Risk and Blame: Essays in Culture and Theory*, London and New York: Routledge.

—— (1993) *In the Wilderness: the Doctrine of Defilement in the Book of Numbers*, Sheffield: Journal for the Study of the Old Testament, Supplement Series no. 158, Sheffield Academic Press.

Reno, William (1995) *Corruption and State Politics in Sierra Leone*, Cambridge: Cambridge University Press.

Richards, Paul (1996) *Fighting for the Rainforest. War, Youth and Resources in Sierra Leone*. Oxford and Portsmouth, New Hampshire: International African Institute in association with James Currey and Heinemann.

—— (1997) 'Small wars and smart relief: radio and local conciliation in Sierra Leone', UCL/ Wageningen Joint War-Peace Research Programme.

—— (1998) 'Sur la nouvelle violence politique en Afrique: le sectarisme séculier au Sierra Leone', *Politique Africaine* (June) 70: 85–104.

RUF/SL 1995 *Footpaths to Democracy*, n.p.p.

Index

232   African Broadcast Cultures